AN INDEX OF LONDON SCHOOLS AND THEIR RECORDS

by Cliff Webb

Society of Genealogists
2000

First published by Society of Genealogists 1999

Second edition published by
Society of Genealogists Enterprises Limited
14 Charterhouse Buildings
Goswell Road
London EC1M 7BA

LND/SOCIAL

© Cliff Webb 2000

ISBN 1 903462 09 6

British Library Cataloguing in Publication Data
A CIP Catalogue record for this book is available from the British Library

Society of Genealogists Enterprises Limited is a wholly owned subsidiary of
Society of Genealogists, a registered charity, no. 233701

LIST OF CONTENTS

4

Introduction

The records of schools can be useful supplements and substitutes to others for the pursuit of genealogical research, and have considerable value for family history purposes in their own right.

This is a first and provisional attempt to list all schools within the area covered by the old London County Council (LCC), and any records of genealogical interest. Excluded, therefore has been such material as purely statistical records. Also excluded, unfortunately, because of difficulty of obtaining listings of surviving records are School Magazines. Omitted deliberately, have been some ephemeral private schools for which no record is known; the vast majority of children from the advent of state education went to state schools. Nursery schools have only been included when records are deposited. A note has been made of the more major private schools, and any where either records or histories are known. Also listed are any schools which were founded within the LCC area, even if they subsequently moved to a site outside that area, and a few approved schools, etc. which were operated by the LCC and thus contained London children, but which were physically sited outside the LCC area.

Schools were required to keep certain records under various school codes. For example the Elementary School Code, 1903 laid down that all schools should have (a) registers of admission, progress and withdrawal (b) attendance registers and (c) a register of summaries. Other ordinances laid down that each headmaster should keep a log book. It was specified that records were to be kept for not less than ten years after the last entry had been made in them. Unfortunately, many head teachers over the years have used this, salvage drives and general clear-outs as excuses for wholesale destruction of these invaluable sources, however, mercifully, a very large amount of material remains.

The information to be contained in the records was specified. Entries in admission registers were to be made for each child on entry to the school. Each entry had to contain an individual reference number, date of admission, full name, name and address of parent or guardian, whether exemption from religious education was claimed, date of birth, last school attended prior to this one, date of leaving school. Secondary school admission registers also usually give any educational attainments such as certificates, and brief details of immediate future career, be it higher education or a job. Most admission registers consist of long lists of entries (sometimes with integral indexes), each entry spreading over a wide double page. Some (especially later) ones, however, are much more lavish with space and have a page for each pupil.

For example, Robert William Cushion, pupil number 276 was admitted to a Fulham infants' school on the 20th March 1905. His father was Robert Cushion of 103 Clonmore Street; he was not exempted from religious instruction. He had been born 7th July 1899, had previously attended Holy Cross School, Fulham, was discharged 25 July 1906 on moving to the junior mixed school.

Admission and discharge registers are a very useful supplement to the Registrar General's records, helping to identify a correct individual from other known information. In an ideal case, it may be possible to trace an individual back from their first job, through a series of schools, and obtaining confirmation of father's name and various addresses which may enable other sources to be tapped.

Registers overlap and all should be searched for any individual. Often a register covering a period when a school is known by one name, has been deposited and allocated a reference denoting a different name. All names by which a given school was known **must** be researched therefore. although an attempt has been made to provide cross-referencing.

Log books were to be kept up daily with the 'briefest entry to specify the progress of the school or its teachers'. They are generally stout bound plain lined notebooks. Considerable details are given of the comings and goings, shortcomings and illnesses of staff. Rather less appears on individual pupils, though very informative items do occur. All manner of material may be found in log books. Surprising snippets of information appear 'it was very foggy this week, so many pupils absent'; 'Her Majesty Queen Victoria died today; God Save the King'; 'all the desks broken in to and Flower Festival money stolen'. Though not usually as directly genealogically useful as admission and discharge registers, they do give the flavour of the school which a person of interest attended.

5

Though for most schools, admission and discharge registers and log books are the only records to survive, a wide variety of miscellaneous records may be found more sporadically. The most common miscellaneous items are punishment books. Rather surprisingly, it seems there was no requirement to keep such books until after the Second World War, and even then, survival is poor. They list the name (and sometimes age) of the pupil, date of punishment and punishment given. In most schools, corporal punishment was the norm, though a few even at an early date had apparently abandoned its use, and detentions, and other non-physical punishments are recorded in the punishment book.

The vast majority of London school records are held at London Metropolitan Archives (LMA) (formerly known as the Greater London Record Office), where such records were deposited for schools closing before 1990. Most there, are in the official series of school records, though the records of some parish schools are to be found listed with the parish records. If a school was amalgamated with another school, the successor should have the records or know where they are.

Since 1990, however, Borough Archives are receiving new deposits of school records. The depth of coverage in this booklet of borough archives has depended to a large extent on the amount of information the archives in question have been able to supply. In some cases such as Hammersmith and Fulham, very full lists have been available; in others material has yet to be listed. In any case, Borough Archives should not be neglected, as they are likely to have material of interest to anyone researching a school within their area. Similarly, for the area where the *Victoria County History* has been published, much better and fuller details of school's histories have been included.

Private schools have generally retained their own records, though a number have deposited their older records at LMA or Borough Archives. Church of England schools records may also be found not only at LMA and the appropriate Borough Archives, but also at the Church of England Records Centre, Galleywall Road, Bermondsey.

All official school records containing personal information at LMA (with insignificant exceptions) are closed for a period of 65 years, **apart from** admission and discharge registers, which are closed for 30 years. This closure period dates from the last entry in the register in question which may, unfortunately, lengthen the period substantially. Consideration will not be given to breach this closure for genealogical research, though it may be possible for people who need access for legal reasons, such as those wishing to prove their own birth date for pension purposes and for whom other sources have failed. However, all admission and discharge registers at LMA have been filmed and so are readily available on open access there. Periods of closure in Borough Archives vary quite considerably, and must be investigated in each case individually.

The schools are listed in strict alphabetical order. In each entry, an attempt has been made to give: full name of school; address and postal area; date of foundation; any changes in name or premises; LMA call number for the school. There follows, generally, up to three sequences. Firstly, **A&D**, i.e. admission and discharge registers. Secondly, **LB** i.e. log books. Thirdly **Misc** covers the inevitable miscellany of records such as honour rolls, punishment books etc. Wherever a history of a school has come to the compiler's attention, it has been included, however, there has been no systematic search for such material.

This is, by necessity, a provisional list. To make for confusion, schools' addresses can appear as any of the streets on which their site borders. Those street names were subject to change, in any case. Also, the authorities seem to have taken delight in changing school names as often as possible - occasionally reverting to earlier names. A very large proportion of schools had their names changed around 1951, but there are a very large number of other name changes. With all this, there is every chance that on occasion two separate schools have had their entries combined, and equally that separate entries have been provided for the same school under different names. The editor would be most grateful if these and other errors and omissions could be drawn to my attention through the publisher, so that future editions can be more complete and correct.

I should like to acknowledge my grateful thanks to Jeremy Gibson for first suggesting this book, and to all the archivists and librarians who have helped in the compilation of this volume. Errors and omissions remain, of course, entirely my own responsibility.

Cliff Webb, March 1999.

NOTE TO SECOND EDITION

In this second edition, a list of schools arranged by area has been appended. There are also maps of London boroughs and a map showing London Postal Districts. I should like to thank my son, Mark Webb, for computer-enhancing the latter. Detailed maps - 'The School Board Map of London' - showing the position of schools at various times, are available for consultation at London Metropolitan Archives.

Cliff Webb, June 2000.

LIST OF ABBREVIATIONS

A&D = Admission and Discharge registers
LB = Log books
LMA = London Metropolitan Archives (formerly the Greater London Record Office)
Misc Miscellaneous items

LIST OF LONDON BOROUGHS

The records at London Metropolitan Archives are organised by London Borough. The records have been organised into nine groups, each Borough falling into one of these groups. In a few cases, there has been some confusion in the listing, so that a school's records are divided into two groups. However, it may be useful to have a list of the Boroughs and the group into which they fall.

	Greenwich 6	Poplar 5
Battersea 9	Hackney 4	St Marylebone 2
Bermondsey 8	Hammersmith 1	St Pancras 2
Bethnal Green 5	Hampstead 2	Shoreditch 4
Camberwell 7	Holborn 3	Southwark 8
Chelsea 1	Islington 3	Stepney 5
City 5	Kensington 1	Stoke Newington 4
Deptford 6	Lambeth 8	Wandsworth 9
Finsbury 3	Lewisham 7	Westminster 2
Fulham 1	Paddington 2	Woolwich 6

LONDON RECORD REPOSITORIES HOLDING SCHOOL RECORDS

Times of openings for all libraries and record offices are subject to change, and a telephone call in advance of a visit is always advisable and sometimes essential.

London Metropolitan Archives, 40 Northampton Road, London EC1R 0HB. 9.30 am to 7.30 pm Tuesday and Thursday (advance booking necessary for original documents), 9.30 am to 4.45 Monday, Wednesday, Friday Tel: 020-7332-3820.

Guildhall Library, Aldermanbury, London EC2P 2EJ. 9.30 am to 4.45 pm Monday to Saturday Tel: 020-7260-1683.

Chelsea Public Library, Local Studies Department, Old Town Hall, King's Road, London SW3 5EZ. Tel: 020-7361-4158.

City of Westminster Archives Centre, 10 St Ann's Street, London SW1P 2XR. Tel: 020-7798-2180. 9.30 am to 7 pm Monday to Friday, 9.30 am to 5 pm Saturday.

Corporation of London Record Office, PO Box 270, Guildhall, Aldermanbury, London EC2P 2EJ. 9.30 am to 5 pm Monday to Friday. Tel: 020-7332-1251.

Finsbury Local History Collection, Finsbury Library, 245 St John Street, London EC1V 4NB. Tel: 020-7619-6900.

Greenwich Local History Library, Woodlands, 90 Mycenae Road, Blackheath, London SE3 7SE 9 am to 5.30 pm Monday and Tuesday, 9 am to 8 pm Thursday, 9 am to 5 pm Saturday. Tel: 020-8858-4631

Hackney Archives Department, 43, De Beauvoir Road, London N1 5SQ. Tel: 020-7241-2886.

Hammersmith and Fulham Archives and Local History Centre, The Lilla Huset, 191 Talgarth Road, London W6 8BJ. 9.30 am to 8 pm Monday, 9.30 am to 1 pm Tuesday, Thursday and first Saturday in the month (advance booking essential for all visits) Tel: 020-8741-5159.

Holborn Local Studies Library, 32-38 Theobalds Road, London WC1X 8PA. Tel: 020-7413-6342.

Islington History Collection, Central Reference Library, 2 Fieldway Crescent, London N5 1PF. Tel: 020-7619-6900.

Lambeth Archives Department, Minet Library, 52 Knatchbull Road, London SE5 8QY. Tel: 020-7926-6076.

Lewisham Local History Library and Archives, 199 Lewisham High Street (corner of Limes Grove), London. 9.30 am to 1 pm, 2 pm to 5 pm Monday and Thursday, 9.30 am to 1 pm, 2 pm to 8 pm Tuesday Tel: 020-8297-0682.

Southwark Local Studies Library, 211 Borough High Street, Southwark, London SE1 1JA. Tel: 020-7403-3507.

Tower Hamlets Library and Archives, Bancroft Library, 277 Bancroft Road, London E1 4DQ. Tel: 020-8980-4366 X 129.

Wandsworth Local History Library, Battersea Library, 265 Lavender Hill, London SW11 1JB. Tel: 020-8871-7467.

Abbey Wood Secondary School,
Eynsham Bridge, SE2. fl.1971.

Abbotshall Road School, SE6. (temporary).
Opened 1913; closed c1922
(LMA: EO/DIV 7/ABB)
A&D 1913-22 (infants); 1913-21 (mixed)
LB 1913-22 (infants); 1913-15 (mixed)

Acland Road School,
Lupton Street, St Pancras, NW5. Opened 1905; renamed Acland Central School 1911; merged with Burghley Road Secondary Mixed 1959 to form Burghley Comprehensive School. (LMA: EO/DIV 2/ACL)
A&D 1940-45 (boys)

Ackmar Road School, SW6. Opened 1885; school for deaf opened 1898; reopened 1942 as senior boys department; renamed Parsons Green Secondary School for Boys and Ackmar Primary School, 1951. (LMA: EO/DIV 1/ACK)
A&D 1899-1939 (mixed deaf); 1934-40 (infants)
LB 1884-1954 (boys); 1898-1981 (deaf centre); 1931-39 (girls); 1931-39 (infants)

Acorn Street School, Camberwell, SE5. Opened 1895; incorporated in Oliver Goldsmith School, 1931. (LMA: EO/DIV 7/ACO)
A&D 1895-1915 (girls)

Ada Street School, Hackney, E8. Opened 1840; renamed St Michael School, 1871; closed c1939.

Adamsrill Road School, SE26. Opened 1922.

Addey and Stanhope School, New Cross Road, SE14. (Independent) (mixed). Opened 1723.

Addington Street School, York Road, SE1. (LMA: EO/DIV 8/ADD)
A&D 1877-1926 (boys); 1877-1926 (girls); 1887-1938 (infants); 1926-38 (mixed)

Addison Gardens School, West Kensington, W14. Opened as Addison Gardens 1900; previously Brook Green Temporary School 1894-1900; renamed Addison Secondary School for Boys and Addison Primary School, 1951; senior school closed 1964. (LMA: EO/DIV 1/ADD)

Addison Gardens School [*continued*]
A&D 1918-1939 (boys); 1955-63 (senior boys); 1933-47 (junior girls); 1900-08 (mixed); 1941-55 (senior mixed and boys)
LB 1894-1900 (Brook Green Temporary School); 1913-64 (boys); 1932-47 (girls); 1900-13 (mixed)
Misc visitors 1909-36 (boys); 1948-62 (leavers: boys); punishment 1951-64 (boys)

Adys Road School, Peckham, SE15. Opened 1884; renamed Friern Square School, 1947; amalgamated with Honor Oak School, 1978 to form Waverly School. (LMA: EO/DIV 7/ADY)
A&D 1884-1936 (infants)
LB 1887-1916, 1936-39 (infants); 1892-1939 (evening); 1946-47 (senior mixed)

Akerman Road School, Brixton, SW9. (mentally defective). Closed 1927.
LB 1913-27 (mixed)

Albany Day School, Albany Place, N7. Opened 1848; closed early 1870s

Albany Road School, Camberwell, SE17. Opened 1877 as Boundary Lane School; renamed 1925; Silverthorne School, 1951; amalgamated with Peckham School, Peckham Manor School and Carlton School, 1983. (LMA: EO/DIV 7/ALB)
A&D 1895-1930 (girls); 1930-35 (senior boys)
Misc punishment 1948-52 (secondary girls)

Albemarle School, Prince's Way, SW19. fl.1971.

Albion Road East School, Dalling Road, W6. Opened 1879; renamed Brackenbury Road School 1886 (q.v.)

Albion Street School, Lower Road, Rotherhithe, SE16. Opened 1876; renamed Albion Primary School, 1951. (LMA: EO/DIV 7/ALN)
LB 1876-95 (infants)

Aldenham Street Roman Catholic School see **St Aloysius Roman Catholic School**

Aldenham Street School, Pancras Road, NW1. Opened 1874; renamed Edith Neville School, 1951. (LMA: EO/DIV 2/ALD)
A&D 1927-39 (infants); 1943-46 (mixed)
LB 1910-29 (infants)

Alderbrook School see **Oldridge Road School**

Aldersgate Ward and Packington School, Aldersgate Street, EC1.
A&D 1889-1908 (boys); 1908-40 (infants); 1911-28 (girls) (Guildhall Library)
LB 1863-1908 (boys); 1864-1908 (girls); 1875-1906 (infants); 1908-13 (mixed and infants); 1937-39 (general) (Guildhall Library)
Misc minute books 1748-97, 1812-1922; report books 1885-1911, 1917-38 (Guildhall Library)

Alderwood School, Rainham Close, Avery Hill, SE9. fl.1971.

Aldgate Ward School, Aldgate, EC3.
A&D 1800-68 (Guildhall Library)
Misc minute books 1770-1837, 1853-68, 1899-1907; administrative records 1723-1907 (Guildhall Library)

Alexander McLeod Primary School *see* **Bostall Lane School**

Alexandra Orphanage School, Maitland Park, Haverstock Hill, NW3.

Alexis Street School see **Alma Junior School**

Alfred Pritchard School, Islington, N7. Opened 1879 as Wellington Road later Westbourne Road; renamed 1951; closed by 1965. (LMA: EO/DIV 3/ALF)
A&D 1942-56 (boys); 1945-55 (junior girls)

Allen Edwards School, Studley Road, SW4.

Allen-Olney School, St John's Wood, NW8. Opened 1891; moved to Crossfield Road, NW3; closed by 1934.

Allen Street School, Islington, N1. Opened 1873; previously St Paul's National School; renamed Compton Street School, 1881.
LB 1873-81 (boys) (in LMA: EO/DIV 3/COM/LB/1)

Allen Street School, Kensington High Street, W8. Opened 1891. (LMA: EO/DIV 1/ALL)
LB 1929-33 (evening school)

Allenswood School, Albert Drive, SW19.

Alleyn's School, Townley Road, East Dulwich, SE22. (Independent) (boys). Opened 1619.

Allfarthing Lane School, St Anne's Crescent, SW18. Opened 1922.

All Hallows School. (LMA: EO/DIV 5/ALH)
LB 1883-1905 (girls)

All Saints' Church of England School, Francis Street, Paddington W2. Opened 1852; closed by 1903.

All Saints' Church of England School, Herbert Road, Plumstead, SE18.

All Saints' Church of England School, Margaret Street, W1. fl.1904/67.

All Saints Gordon Square School, St Pancras, WC1. Opened 1857.

All Saints National School, Bow Lane, Poplar, E3. Opened 1711. (LMA: EO/DIV 5/ALL 1)
LB 1863-92 (mixed); 1883-1905, 1910-14 (infants); 1890-1914 (boys); 1910-14 (girls)

All Saints Roman Catholic School, Tooley Street, SE1. Opened 1871.

All Saints' School, The Vale, Blackheath, SE3. Opened 1878.

All Saints School, Buxton Street, Mile End New Town, E1. Opened 1895. (LMA: EO/DIV 5/ALL 2)
LB 1928-38 (infants); 1928-46 (mixed)

All Saints School, East Street, Walworth, SE17. Opened 1873.

All Saints' School, Fulham High Street, SW6. founded in 16th or early 17th century; opened at Fulham High Street site 1862; moved to St Mark's School site 1996.

All Saints' School, Lower Common, Wandsworth, SW15. fl.1906/71.

All Saints School, Muriel Street, Wynford Road, N1. Opened 1842; closed 1947-51. (LMA: EO/DIV 3/ALL, EO/DIV 4/ALL and P83/ALL 1)
A&D 1909-39 (infants); 1913-38 (junior mixed)
LB 1882-1910 (boys); 1896-1909, 1911-12 (infants); 1911-13 (mixed); 1914-38 (junior mixed and infants)
Misc minute books 1902-15, 1919; visitors 1916-35, 1964-68

All Saints School, Newby Place, E14. fl.1905.

All Saints School, Putney Bridge Road, SW18. Founded *c*1858; opened 1894. (LMA: EO/DIV 9/ALL)
A&D 1908-29 (infants); 1943-47 (mixed)
Misc punishment 1931-46

All Saints School, Waterloo Road, SE1. Later St John with All Saints; opened 1900. (LMA: EO/DIV 8/ALL)
LB 1863-1900 (boys); 1863-1900 (girls)

All Souls School, Fairhazel Gardens, Finchley Road, Hampstead, NW6. Opened 1871; closed by 1951.

All Souls School, Foley Street, Westminster, W1. Founded 1825; opened 1860. (LMA: EO/DIV 2/ALS)
A&D 1930-39 (mixed)
LB 1913-39 (mixed and infants)

Alma Junior School, Alexis Street, SE16. Opened 1877.

Alma Senior School, Southwark Park Road, SE16. Opened 1885.

Alton Street School, Guildford Road, Poplar, E14. Opened 1883. (LMA: EO/DIV 5/ALT)
A&D 1887-1951. (infants); 1904-34 (boys); 1905-29 (girls)
LB 1906-34 (girls); 1913-34 (boys)

Alvering Secondary School. (LMA: EO/DIV 9/ALV)
A&D 1942-53, 1956-64 (mixed)

Alverton Street School, SE8. Opened 1875; renamed Duke Street School, 1919, renamed John Evelyn School, 1930; closed 1986 (LMA: EO/DIV 6/ALV)
A&D 1874-1935 (boys)

Amberley Primary School *see* Ancona Road

Amberley Road School, Harrow Road, Maida Hill, W9. Opened 1881; renamed Amberley Primary and Kemble Secondary, 1951; Amberley Primary closed 1954. The partially sighted school (opened 1919) renamed John Aird Secondary School, 1950. (LMA: EO/DIV 2/AMB)
A&D 1893-1914, 1945-54 (junior mixed); 1910-39 (girls); 1914-39 (boys); 1932-39 (infants); 1940-49 (mixed)

Amberley Road School [*continued*]
LB 1881-1913, 1945-56 (junior mixed); 1910-13, 1932-51 (infants); 1910-32 (girls); 1914-39 (boys); 1919-46 (mixed - myopic); 1932-39 (junior girls); 1951-54 (primary)
Misc visitors 1894-1938)

Ambler Road School, N4. *see* **Finsbury Park Junior and Secondary Schools**

Amherst School, Dalston Lane, E8. Opened as Sigdon Road School, 1898; renamed 1951.

Amicable Society School *see* **Peter Hills School**

Ancona Road School, Brewery Road, SE18. Opened 1893; renamed Waverley Secondary School and Amberley Primary School, 1951; (Amberley closed 1950s). (LMA: EO/DIV 6/ANC)
A&D 1887-1931 (girls); 1887-1936 (infants); 1890-1948 (boys); 1940-43 (mixed)
LB 1882-1936 (evening); 1887-1931 (girls); 1887-1936 (infants); 1890-1913, 1931-48 (boys); 1901-26 (manual training centre)

Angel Court Ragged School, Rufford's Buildings, Islington, N1. Opened 1848; still in being 1871.

Anglers Gardens School, Essex Road. N1. Opened 1875; renamed Popham Road, 1895; Charles Lamb School, 1951. (LMA: EO/DIV 3/ANG)
A&D 1875-99 (boys); 1875-1916 (girls)
LB 1875-87 (boys); 1875-93 (girls); 1875-99 (infants)

Annandale Primary School *see* **Calvert Road**

Approach Road School, Bethnal Green, E2. (Wesleyan). Opened 1869. (LMA: EO/DIV 5/APP)
A&D 1890-1927 (infants); 1906-27 (mixed)
LB 1869-1927 (mixed); 1869-1927 (infants)

Archbishop Sumner's School, Reedworth Street, Kennington Road, SE11. Opened 1871. (LMA: EO/DIV 8/ARC)
LB 1913-39 (girls); 1935-38 (infants)
see also St Philip's School

Archbishop Tait's School, Lambeth Road. SE1. Opened 1875 as Lambeth St Mary's Infants School.

Archbishop Tait's School [*continued*]
A&D 1890-95, 1905-74 (Lambeth Archives)
LB 1879-1967 (Lambeth Archives)
Misc minute books 1913-47 (LMA: A/LPI
and A/LPS); punishment 1906-53 (Lambeth
Archives)

Archbishop Temple Central School, Lambeth
Road, SE1. Opened 1902; renamed
Archbishop Michael Ramsay School, 1972
on union with St Michael and All Angels
School, Farmers Road, Camberwell, SE5.
(LMA: EO/DIV 8/ARC, A/LPB and
A/LPS)
A&D 1817-1946
LB 1862-1961
Misc minute books 1780-1947; schoolkeepers
diaries 1972-75; visitors 1904-34; staff
1714-1960

Archbishop Tenison's Grammar School,
Kennington Oval, SE11. Founded 1697 in
Castle Street, St Martin in the Fields;
removed to Leicester Square 1872, and to
Kennington in 1928. (LMA: A/ATG,
A/LPS, ACC/2692)
LB 1865-1924
Misc minute books 1717-1947; visitors
1880-1939; punishment 1905-22 (LMA);
minute books 1825-62 (Lambeth Archives)

Archway Secondary School, Duncombe Road,
N19. Opened 1959; amalgamated 1981 to
help form George Orwell School.

Argyle School, Whichbourne Street, St Pancras,
WC1. Opened 1881 as Manchester Street
School; renamed 1937; Argyle Primary
School, 1951. (LMA: EO/DIV 2/ARG)
LB 1938-46 (senior mixed); 1943-55
(junior mixed)

Aristotle Road Secondary School, Clapham
High Street, SW4. Opened 1903 as
Clapham Secondary Central School;
renamed, 1951. (LMA: EO/DIV 9/ARI)
A&D 1947-65 (boys)
LB 1887-1913 (boys)

Arnold House School, Loudoun Road, St John's
Wood, NW8. Opened 1905.

Arthur Street School,
Old Kent Road, SE15. Opened c1888 as
Asylum Road School; renamed 1893 Bird
in Bush School, 1894 Arthur Street School;
renamed Camelot Street School, 1938.
(LMA: EO/DIV 7/ART)

Arthur Street School [*continued*]
A&D 1903-21, 1926-29 (boys); 1909-38 (girls);
1917-39 (infants)

Arundell House School, Highbury New Park,
N5. Opened 1903; closed by 1934.

Ashburnham School, Upcerne Road,
Kings Road, SW10. Opened 1885; renamed
Ashburnham Primary School, Blantyre
Street, 1951. (LMA: EO/DIV 1/ASH)
A&D 1925-37 (infants)
LB 1912-13 (infants)

Ashby Mill School, Prague Place, Brixton,
SW2.
Misc 1878-1993 (Lambeth Archives; not yet
listed)

Ashington Road Roman Catholic School,
Ashington Road, New Kings Road, SW6.
Opened 1884; renamed Holy Cross Roman
Catholic School 1951.

Ashmole School, Kennington, SW8. Opened
1879 as Church Street School; renamed
1935.

Ashmount School, Ashmount Road, N19.
Opened 1957.

Aske's *see* **Haberdashers'**

Aspen House School, Christchurch Road, SW2.
(Delicate children).
A&D 1949-95 (Lambeth Archives)
LB 1944-57 (Lambeth Archives)
Misc punishment 1949-68; Staff 1963-74
(Lambeth Archives)

Asylum Road School, Peckham, SE15. Opened
c1888; renamed Bird in Bush School, 1893,
Arthur School, 1894, Camelot Street
School, 1938. (LMA: EO/DIV 7/ASY)
A&D 1888-1903 (boys)

Athelney Street School,
Bellingham Estate, Catford, SE6. Opened
1922; renamed Athelney Primary School.
(LMA: EO/DIV 7/ATH)
A&D 1934-39 (senior girls); 1942-58
(senior mixed)
LB 1934-39 (junior boys); 1934-39 (senior
girls); 1938-39 (infants); 1942-54 (junior
mixed and infants)
Misc staff 1952-58

Atley Road School,
Old Ford Road, E3. Opened 1873; renamed
George Lansbury Primary School, 1951.
(LMA: EO/DIV 5/ATL)
A&D 1872-82, 1888-1939 (boys); 1872-1945
(girls); 1874-1946 (infants); 1940 (mixed)
LB 1873-1919, 1922-37 (infants); 1889-1906,
1913-27, 1937-41 (boys); 1889-1928
(girls); 1908-13 (mixed); 1929-32 (junior
boys)

Auxiliary National School, Wandsworth.
Opened 1812.

Avenue Secondary School, Bethwin Road,
Walworth, SE5. Opened 1878 as Beresford
Street School; renamed John Ruskin School
1929; renamed 1936; closed 1964.
(LMA: EO/DIV 8/AVE)
A&D 1939-46 (boys); 1939-45 (girls); 1945-47
(senior girls); 1946-64 (senior boys)
LB 1938-39, 1947-62 (boys)
Misc punishment 1947-52

Avery Hill Training College, Eltham, SE9.

Avigdor High School, Lordship Road, N16.
Opened 1947; closed 1961.

Avigdor Primary School, Lordship Road, N16.
Opened 1948.

Avondale Park School, Sirdar Road, Notting
Hill, W11. Opened 1880 as St Clements
Road School; renamed Sirdar Road School
and St Clements, Notting Hill, 1904; closed
1961. (LMA: EO/DIV 1/AVO)
A&D 1941-45 (mixed); 1945-61 (girls)
LB 1936-48 (senior boys); 1936-61
(senior girls)

Avonmore School, Avonmore Road, W14.
Previously primary part of William Street
School; renamed 1936; destroyed 1944 but
rebuilt 1949.

Aylwin School, The, Southwark Park Road,
Bermondsey, SE16. Opened 1906.

Babington House School, North Park, SE9.

Bacon's Free School, Grange Road, SE1.
Founded 1718; opened 1890.
(LMA: A/BFS)
LB 1863-1913
Misc minute books 1785-1888

Baden-Powell School, Ferron Road, E5.
Opened 1970.

Baileys Lane School. (LMA: EO/DIV 4/BAI)
LB 1898-1909 (evening)

Baker Street School, E1. Opened 1876; closed
1927 (LMA: EO/DIV 5/BAK)
A&D 1872-87 (mixed); 1878-1927 (infants);
1884-1926 (boys); 1891-1926 (girls)

Baldwin's Gardens National School, St Andrew
Holborn, EC1. There appear to be no
surviving pupil records, but estate records
1843-48 are at Guildhall Library

Balham and Tooting College of Commerce,
Tooting Broadway, SW17.

Balham Central School later **Balham School,**
Hearnville Road, SW12. Opened 1905.

Balham Grammar School, Balham High Road,
SW17. (Independent) In existence 1909/45.

Balham High School, Bedford Hill, SW12.

**Balham St Mary's Church of England Primary
School,** Balham High Road, SW12. Opened
1858.
A&D c1868, 1871-86, 1903-25 (boys); 1869-98
(infants); 1904-14 (girls); 1942-68 (junior
mixed and infants) (Church of England
Records Centre)
LB 1863-1905 (boys); 1865-1905 (girls);
1872-1939 (infants); 1906-37 (junior
mixed); 1938-68 (junior mixed and infants)
(Church of England Records Centre)
Misc minute books 1905-38, 1947-79
(Church of England Records Centre)

Ballamore Road School, Downham Estate,
Lewisham. Opened 1929; renamed
Ballamore School, 1951; closed 1970s.
(LMA: EO/DIV 7/BAL)
A&D 1927-39 (junior mixed); 1929-44 (mixed);
1939-44 (infants)
LB 1929-39 (junior boys); 1929-39
(junior girls); 1929-52 (infants); 1945-51
(junior mixed)

Ball's Pond Road Mission School, Ball's Pond
Road, N1. Opened 1866; closed by 1893.

Baltic Street School, EC1. Opened 1889.
(LMA: EO/DIV 3/BAL)
LB 1900-39 (boys); 1914-20 (infants); 1914-20
(mentally defective)

Bancroft's School, Mile End (Independent).
Opened 1737, moved to Woodford, Essex
1889.
see A History of Bancroft's School 1737-1987
(K.R. Wing)

Bankside School, SE1. Opened 1878.

Bannockburn Primary School
see **High Street School, Plumstead**

Bantry Road School, SE5.

Baptist Women's Training College, Carlton
Drive, SW15.

Barclay Hall School, Effie Road, SW6 (also
known as Walham Green School). Opened
by 1882, closed 1906.

Baring Road School, Lewisham, SE12.
Opened 1883.

Barlby Road School, Ladbroke Grove, W10.
Opened 1880. (LMA: EO/DIV 1/BAR)
A&D 1895-1928 (mixed); 1918-44 (infants)
LB 1927-39 (infants)

Barnado's School, Doctor.
(LMA: EO/DIV 5/BAR)
see also Copperfield Road School
A&D 1886-97 (mixed)

Barnsbury Central School, Hope Street,
Islington, N7. Opened 1904 (girls) as
Offord Road School; opened 1931 (boys)
see Barnsbury Secondary School; renamed
1951 as Barnsbury School for Girls. (LMA:
EO/DIV 3/BAR 1)
A&D 1932-39 (boys)
LB 1913-32 (senior mixed)

Barnsbury Park School, N1. Opened 1910.
closed by 1951.

Barnsbury Secondary School, Barnsbury Park,
Liverpool Road, N1. Opened 1931 as
Barnsbury Boys' Central School; closed
1967. (LMA: EO/DIV 3/BAR 2)
Misc Exam and athletic results 1948-55 (boys)

Barrett Street School, Duke Street, Oxford
Street, W1. Closed 1914. (LMA:
EO/DIV 2/BAR)
LB 1873-1914 (girls); 1873-1914 (infants);
1892-1914 (boys)

Barrow Hill Road School, St Marylebone,
NW8. Opened 1879.

Bartram's Roman Catholic School,
Haverstock Hill, NW3. Opened *c*1867;
renamed Rosary Roman Catholic School
after World War II.

Basnett Road School, Lavender Hill, SW11.
Opened 1884; renamed John Burns School,
1951. (LMA: EO/DIV 9/BAS)
A&D 1883-88, 1901-12 (infants)

Bassein Park Road School, Starch Green, W12.
Opened 1892; renamed Cobbold Road
School 1901; Wendell Park School. 1925.
(LMA: EO/DIV 1/BAS)
LB 1892-94 (mixed)

Bath Street School, City Road, EC1. Opened
1881; renamed Moorfields Primary School,
1951. (LMA: EO/DIV 3/BAT)
A&D 1892-1901, 1916-39 (girls);
1921-39 (boys)
LB 1918-39 (boys)

Battersea Central School, Bridge Lane, SW11.
Opened 1885.

Battersea Grammar School, St John's Hill,
SW11 or Abbotswood Road. (Independent)
(boys). Opened 1700.

Battersea Park Road School, SW11. Opened
1874; renamed Chesterton Primary School,
1951. (LMA: EO/DIV 9/BAT)
A&D 1875-1939 (boys); 1899-1939 (infants);
1900-39 (girls)
LB 1882-1913 (boys); 1894-1939 (manual
training centre); 1897-1939 (girls);
1899-1939 (infants); 1934-39 (junior boys)

Battersea Polytechnic Secondary School *see*
Henry Thornton School

Battersea St Mary's Parochial School, Vicarage
Crescent, SW11. Opened 1850; closed
1985.
A&D 1850-57, 1874-1939, 1941-50 (infants);
1878-1939 (girls); 1905-39 (boys) (Church
of England Records Centre)
LB 1913-85 (Church of England
Records Centre)
Misc punishment 1934-72 (boys)
(Church of England Records Centre)

Bay Street School, Dalston, E8. (temporary)
Opened 1906; closed 1923.
(LMA: EO/DIV 4/BAY)
A&D 1883-90 (boys); 1908-20 (mixed);
1911-23 (infants)
LB 1896-1904 (girls); 1906-23 (mixed);
1906-23 (infants)

Bayswater Jewish School, Lancaster Road,
W11. Opened 1867; moved and became
Kensington Bayswater Jewish School,
Lancaster Road, 1930; later Solomon
Wolfson School.

Bayswater National School see
St Matthew School, Queensway

Bayswater Ragged School, Poplar Place,
Moscow Road, W2. fl.1873 later part of St
Mathew School.

Beatrix Potter School *see* **Magdalen Road
School**

Beaufort House School, Lillie Road, SW6.
Opened 1903 (ESN school opened 1904).
(LMA: EO/DIV 1/BEA)
A&D 1904-39 (boys)
LB 1904-38 (boys); 1904-31 (girls); 1911-13
(evening); 1913-39 (infants)

Beaufoy School *see* **Borough Beaufoy School**

Beavers' Holt School, Stag Lane, SW15.
fl.1971.

Bec School, Beachcroft Road, Tooting, SW17.
Opened 1926. (LMA: EO/DIV 9/BEC)
A&D 1926-41 (boys)

Beckford School, Dornfell Street, Hampstead,
NW6. Opened 1886.

Bedford Park High School, Priory Road, W4.

Beethoven Street School, Queens Park,
Paddington, W10. Opened 1881; renamed
Beethoven School, 1950; closed 1961.
(LMA: EO/DIV 2/BEE)
A&D 1880-81 (junior boys); 1881-1961
(mixed); 1914-30 (infants)
LB 1880-1960 (mixed); 1913-15, 1931-39
(evening)
Misc punishment 1941-61

Bellenden Road School, Camberwell, SE15.
Opened 1877; renamed Bellenden School,
1951. (LMA: EO/DIV 7/BEL)

Bellenden Road School [*continued*]
LB 1902-03, 1913-38 (boys); 1904-39 (girls);
1905-39 (infants)

Belleville Road School, Clapham, SW11.
Opened 1877. (LMA: EO/DIV 9/BEL)
A&D 1877-1939 (boys); 1889-1951. (girls);
1939-51 (junior mixed)

Bell Green Church of England School (later
St Michael and All Angels School),
Champion Road, SE26. Opened 1871.

Bell Street School, NW1. previously
Bell Street Ragged School to 1874;
renamed Bellfield Secondary School, 1951.
(LMA: EO/DIV 2/BELL)
A&D 1872-86, 1900-39 (girls); 1874-1932
(infants); 1891-1910 (boys); 1932-45 (boys
secondary); 1945-60 (mixed secondary)
LB 1872-1946 (girls); 1874-1922, 1946-53
(infants); 1925-39 (senior girls)

Bellfields Secondary School, NW1. formerly
Bell Street School. (LMA: EO/DIV 2/BEF)
LB 1954-60 (mixed)
Misc punishment 1960

Belsize School, Buckland Crescent, NW3.
Opened 1889; later Hall School, Crossfield
Road, NW3.

Benevolent Society of St Patrick School,
Stamford Street, SE1. Opened 1820; closed
1921.

Ben Jonson School, Harford Street, Stepney,
E1. Opened 1873. (LMA: EO/DIV 5/BEN)
A&D 1918-38 (boys); 1932-39 (junior girls);
1938-39 (junior boys)
LB 1878-1939 (infants); 1932-39 (junior boys);
1933-38 (junior girls)

Bennett's Grove School see **Waller Road School**

Benthal Road School, N16. Opened 1876 as
Rendlesham Road School; renamed 1903.

Bentworth Road School, W12. Opened 1929.
renamed Bentworth School, 1951.

Beresford Street School, Walworth, SE18.
Opened 1878; renamed John Ruskin School
1929; Avenue Secondary School 1936;
closed 1964.
A&D 1925-39 (boys)
LB 1892-1903, 1926-38 (boys)

Berger Road School, Wick Road, Homerton, E9. Opened 1879; renamed Berger School, 1951. (LMA: EO/DIV 4/BEG)
A&D 1889-1900 (girls); 1899-1930 (mixed); 1906-33 (boys)
LB 1882-1913 (evening); 1888-1913 (mixed); 1920-31 (girls); 1926-33 (boys); 1932-33 (junior girls)
Misc visitors 1922-26

Berkshire Road School, Wallis Road, Hackney, E9. Opened 1899 as Windsor Road; renamed 1906; renamed Lea Marsh Secondary School, 1951; partially sighted school (opened 1930) renamed Ryder School (Primary and Secondary), 1951; closed by 1966. (LMA: EO/DIV 4/BER)
A&D 1896-1924 (mixed)
LB 1896-1915 (girls); 1906-12 (boys); 1915-24 (junior mixed); 1939-48 (senior mixed)
Misc punishment 1932-63

Bermondsey Board of Guardians see **South Metropolitan School District**

Bermondsey Central School, Monnow Road, Southwark Park Road, SE1. Opened 1874 as Monnow Road School; renamed 1915. (LMA: EO/DIV7/BER and EO/DIV 8/BER)
A&D 1916-28, 1931-39 (boys); 1930-39 (girls)
LB 1929-43 (boys); 1940 (mixed)

Bermondsey County Secondary School, SE1. Opened 1907. (LMA: EO/DIV 8/BES)
A&D 1906-48 (senior girls)

Bermondsey United Charity Schools. (LMA: P71/MMG)
Misc minute books 1753-84, 1807-65, 1953-68; infant school accounts 1951-57

Berner Street School, St George in the East, E1. Opened 1872; closed 1927; physically handicapped removed and renamed Garrett School, 1950. (LMA: EO/DIV 5/BER)
A&D 1872-1927 (boys); 1874-1928 (infants); 1879-1930 (girls)
LB 1899-1921 (evening)

Bessemer Grange Primary School, Dylways, SE5. Opened 1905 as Denmark Hill School; renamed 1951.

Betts Street School, Cable Street, Stepney, E1. Opened 1884. (LMA: EO/DIV 5/BET)
A&D 1884-1934 (infants); 1889-92 (girls); 1899-1930 (boys); 1930-33 (junior mixed)

Beverley School see **Randall Place School**

Bevington Road School, Kensington, W10. Opened 1930.

Billingsgate and Tower Wards School Billingsgate opened early 18th century; united to Tower Wards School, 1874; merged with Bridge, Candlewick and Dowgate Wards School, 1891 and St Botolph Parochial School, 1905.
A&D 1771-1905 (boys); 1889-1905 (infants) (Guildhall Library)
LB 1873-1905 (Guildhall Library)
Misc minute books 1718-24, 1743-1885 (Guildhall Library)

Bird in Bush Road School, Peckham, SE15 see **Arthur Street School**

Biscay Road School, Biscay Road, SW6. Opened 1885; became part of St Dunstan's Road School c1889.

Bishop Challoner Secondary School, E1. Opened 1905 as Johnson Street Roman Catholic School; renamed 1951. (LMA: EO/DIV 5/BIS)
A&D 1957-64 (boys)
LB 1958-64 (boys)

Bishop Gifford Roman Catholic Secondary School, N1. Opened 1961 in former Gifford Street School; closed 1967. (LMA: EO/DIV 3/BIS)
LB 1946-67 (senior mixed)

Bishopsgate Ward School, Peter Street. Opened 1821.
A&D 1863-91 (girls); 1867-89 (boys) (Tower Hamlets Library)
LB 1868-82 (girls); 1868-89 (boys) (Tower Hamlets Library)
Misc apprenticeship register 1810-19 (Tower Hamlets Library)

Bishop's Park Secondary School, Finlay Street, SW6. Opened 1921 as Fulham Central School; renamed 1951; became part of Gilliatt School, 1961.

Bishop Thomas Grant Roman Catholic School, Belltrees Grove, SW16.

Blackfriars School, Gray Street, Southwark, SE1. Opened 1875; formerly Marlborough Street. (LMA: EO/DIV 8/BLA)

Blackfriars School [*continued*]
LB 1936-39 (boys); 1936-39 (girls); 1936-39
(infants)

**Blackheath and Kidbrooke Bluecoat Church of
England School**, Old Dover Road, SE3.
Founded 1700; closed 1958.
(LMA: EO/DIV 6/BLU)
A&D 1942-58
LB 1949-52 (girls)

Blackheath High School, Vanbrugh Park, SE3.
(Independent) (girls). Opened 1880.
see The Book of the Blackheath High School
(includes lists of Old Girls 1890-1925)
(M.C. Malim and H.C. Escreet, 1927)

Blackheath Proprietory School, Blackheath,
SE3. (Independent). Opened 1830.
A&D 1831-91 (Lewisham Local History Lib)
Misc minute books 1832-1906; shareholders
1832-1902; visitors 1835-98; letter book
1830-34 (Lewisham Local History Lib)
see A History of Blackheath Proprietory School
(J.W. Kirby, 1933)

Blackheath Road School, SE10.

Blackheath St John's School,
Blackheath Road, SE10. Opened 1854;
renamed Brookmell Primary School, 1951.
(LMA: EO/DIV 6/BLA)
A&D 1902-07 (boys)
LB 1904-39 (manual training centre)

Blackstock Road School, Highbury, N4. *see*
Finsbury Park School

Blackwall Lane School *see* Dreadnought School

Blakesley Street School, Sutton Street,
St George in the East, E1. Opened 1905.
(LMA: EO/DIV 5/BLA)
A&D 1891-99 (boys)
LB 1913-26 (boys); 1913-24 (girls);
1913-24 (infants)

Blandford Square Roman Catholic School (later
St Edward), Marylebone Road, NW1.
Opened 1851.

Blenheim House School, Oxgate Gardens,
NW2.

**Blessed Sacrament Roman Catholic Primary
School**, Boadicea Street, N1. Opened
*c*1965.

Bloomfield Road School,
Sandy Hill Road, SE18. Opened 1877;
renamed Bloomfield Primary School, 1951.
(LMA: EO/DIV 6/BLO)
A&D 1877-1944, 1958-73 (boys);
1888-1958 (girls)
LB 1877-1928 (boys); 1877-1939 (girls);
1900-09 (manual training centre); 1912-13,
1931-39 (junior girls); 1935-38 (infants)

Bloomsbury School, WC1. Opened 1844.
(LMA: EO/DIV 3/BLO)
LB 1913-35 (infants)

Bluecoat School, Westminster
Misc 1698-1761 (Westminster Archives)

Blundell Street School, Caledonian Road, N7.
Opened 1873; renamed Robert Blair
School, 1936. (LMA: EO/DIV 3/BLU)
LB 1872-90, 1900-13 (boys); 1905-13 (infants)

Bolingbroke Road School, Battersea, SW11.
Opened 1873; renamed Bolingbroke
School, 1937. (LMA: EO/DIV 9/BOL)
LB 1873-87 (boys); 1873-90 (infants);
1874-98 (girls)

Bonner Street School, Bethnal Green, E2.
Opened 1876.
A&D 1876-1939 (infants); 1930-39 (junior
girls); 1941-63 (boys) (Tower Hamlets
Library)
LB 1878-80 (boys) (LMA: EO/DIV 5/BON);
1898-1913, 1939-42 (infants) (Tower
Hamlets Library)
Misc roll of service 1914-18; punishment
1933-69 (Tower Hamlets Library)
see Bonner Schools 1876-1976 (W.Wilford)

Bonneville Road School,
Cavendish Road, Clapham, SW4. Opened
1905; renamed Bonneville School,1938.
(LMA: EO/DIV 9/BON)
LB 1933-39 (girls)

Boone Street British School, Lewisham, SE13.
fl1905.

Borough Beaufoy School, Black Prince Road,
SE11; Founded as Lambeth Ragged School
1851; renamed 1946; renamed Beaufoy
School, Lollard Street, SE11, 1964.
(LMA: EO/DIV 8/BOB)
A&D 1905-64 (boys)

Borough Paragon Secondary School, Searles Road, SE1. Opened 1900 as Paragon School; renamed 1951; closed 1960. (LMA: EO/DIV 8/BOP)
A&D 1953-60 (senior girls)

Borough Polytechnic Technical Day School, Borough Road, SE1.

Borough Road School, Southwark, SE1. (LMA: EO/DIV 6/BOR)
LB 1863-73 (girls)

Bostall Lane, Abbey Wood, SE2. Opened 1903; renamed Alexander McLeod Primary School, 1951. (LMA: EO/DIV 6/BOS)
A&D 1929-41 (infants)
LB 1913-39 (infants boys); 1933-39 (infants)

Botolph Road School, E3. Opened 1932.

Boundary Lane School, Camberwell, SE17. Opened 1877; renamed Albany Road School, 1925; Silverthorne School, 1951; amalgamated with Peckham School, Peckham Manor School and Carlton School, 1983. (LMA: EO/DIV 7/BOU)
A&D 1886-1920 (girls); 1897-1930 (boys)
LB 1899-1926 (girls)
Misc visitors 1924-42 (infants)

Boutcher School, Grange Road, Bermondsey, SE1. Opened 1870.

Bowbrook School, Cranbrook Terrace, E2. Opened 1881; renamed Cranbrook Terrace School, 1938; Cranbrook School, 1951; Bowbrook School, 1957.
A&D 1946-60 (senior girls) (LMA: EO/DIV 5/BBK); 1960-75 (Tower Hamlets Library)
LB 1956-75 (girls) (LMA: EO/DIV 5/BBK)

Bow Central School. Opened 1912.

Bow Chapel School (Wesleyan) (LMA: EO/DIV 5/BOW 2)
LB 1872-89 (mixed)

Bow Creek School, E14. Opened 1896; closed 1936. (LMA: EO/DIV 5/BOW 1)
LB 1913-36 (mixed); 1913-36 (infants); 1908-31 (manual training centre)

Bow Road Open Air School, E3. Opened 1922. (LMA: EO/DIV 5/BOW 4)
LB 1922-39 (mixed)

Bow Secondary School for Girls, Fairfield Road, E3. (LMA: EO/DIV 5/BOW 3)
LB 1945-54 (senior girls)

Boxgrove School, Boxgrove Road, Abbey Wood, SE2. fl.1971.

Brackenbury Road School, Goldhawk Road, W6. Opened 1879 as Albion Road East School, renamed 1886; renamed Brackenbury School, 1951; the ESN school opened 1902, was renamed Elizabeth Burgwin School in 1950 and moved to Cambridge Road, 1965. (LMA: EO/DIV 1/BRA)
LB 1934-52 (girls)

Bradmede School, Wandsworth Road, SW8. Opened 1874 as New Road School; renamed 1951.

Brandlehow School, Putney Bridge Road, SW15. Formerly Deodar Road School; opened 1901. (LMA: EO/DIV 9/BRA)
A&D 1897-1944 (boys); 1897-1913 (junior girls); 1905-44 (infants); 1916-44 (girls); 1951-58 (junior mixed and infants)
LB 1912-29 (girls); 1913-22 (boys); 1913-44 (infants); 1932-39 (mixed)

Branston Street School, W10. (LMA: EO/DIV 1/BRN)
LB 1918-34 (mixed)

Bravington Road Special School, Paddington, W9. Opened 1913; formerly Harrow Road School; renamed Maryfields Primary School, 1950. (LMA: EO/DIV 2/BRA)
A&D 1896-1951. (mixed)
LB 1913-56 (mixed)
Misc punishment 1913-56

Brecknock School, York Road, Camden Town, NW1. Opened 1881 as Gloucester Grove School, renamed 1945; closed 1961. (LMA: EO/DIV 2/BRE)
A&D 1881-1948 (girls); 1901-29 (infants); 1931-38 (senior boys)
LB 1881-1913 (infants); 1901-13, 1930-38, 1945-47 (girls); 1913-31 (boys); 1931-60 (senior mixed)

Brent Knoll School, Mayow Road, SE23. fl.1971.

Brentwood School District. Constututed by Hackney and Shoreditch Boards of Guardians. (LMA: BSD)

Brentwood School District [*continued*]
A&D 1877-86
LB 1877-86
Misc staff 1877-86

Brewhouse Lane School, Wapping High Street,
E1. Opened 1874. (LMA: EO/DIV 5/BRE)
A&D 1913-39 (girls); 1932-39 (infants)
LB 1932-38 (girls); 1932-38 (infants)

Brightlands Preparatory School,
Dulwich Common, SE21. (Independent)
(boys)

Briset Secondary School see **Eltham Hill School**

Bristol Street Temporary School see
Janet Street School

Britannia Row School, Essex Road, N1.
(LMA: EO/DIV 3/BRI)
A&D 1874 (girls)
LB 1872-83 (boys); 1872-74 (infants)

Brixton Central School, Durand Gardens,
Kennington, SW9. Opened 1913.

Brixton Hill Industrial School. (girls)
(LMA: LCC/EO/SS/7)
A&D 1910-19

Brixton Parish Church School, Water Lane,
SW2. (LMA: P85/MTWW 1)
Misc minute books 1919-40

Broad Street School, E1. see
Nicholas Gibson School

Broad Street Ward School, Leg and Ball Alley,
London Wall, EC2. Opened 1713;
amalgamated with Sir John Cass School,
1907.
A&D 1793-1898 (girls); 1816-59 (boys);
attendance registers 1897-1907 (boys)
(Guildhall Library)
Misc minute books 1713-1907 (Guildhall
Library)

Broadwater School, Gatton Road, Upper
Tooting Road, SW17. Opened 1904;
Broadwater Road School to 1930; later
Gatton School. (LMA: EO/DIV 9/BRO)
A&D 1901-34, 1940-45 (infants)
LB 1913-32 (girls); 1922-49 (mixed)

Brockley Central School, Wallbutton Road,
Vesta Road, SE4. Opened 1874 as Mantle
Road School; renamed 1914; closed 1940s.
(LMA: EO/DIV 6/BRO 1)
A&D 1910-39 (boys); 1910-43 (girls)
LB 1928-45 (boys); 1928-42 (girls)

Brockley County School, Hillyfields, SE4.
Opened 1880.

Brockley Road School, Brockley, SE4. Opened
1894; renamed Brockley Primary School,
1951. (LMA: EO/DIV 6/BRO 2)
A&D 1934-39 (infants)
LB 1893-1913 (mixed); 1913-32 (infants);
1935-39 (junior mixed)

Brockley Roman Catholic School (later St Mary
Magdalen School), Howson Road, SE4.
Opened 1895.

Brockwell School, Tulse Hill, SW2.

Bromley Hall Road School, Poplar, E14.
Opened 1882.

Bromley National School, Bromley St Leonard.
(LMA: P88/MRY 2)
Misc minute books 1901-06

Brompton National School, Churchyard and
Montpelier Street, SW7. Opened 1871;
later renamed Brompton School.
(LMA: EO/DIV 1/BRM and P84/TRI 2)
A&D 1901-38 (junior mixed); 1906-38
(infants); 1927-38 (girls)
LB 1899-1906 (boys)
Misc minute books 1904-39

**Brondesbury and Kilburn High School for
Girls**, Salusbury Road, NW6.

Brooke House Secondary School, Kenninghall
Road, E5. Opened 1960; merged with
Upton House School to form Homerton
House School, 1982.

Brookfield Secondary School, NW5. Burghley
Road 1924-48; renamed Burghley Central
School, 1948; Brookfield Secondary
School, 1951. (LMA: EO/DIV 2/BRO)
A&D 1952-63 (senior girls)
LB 1945-61 (senior girls)

Brook Green School, W6. Opened 1902, closed
1956. (LMA: EO/DIV 1/BRO)
A&D 1894-1900 (mixed)
LB 1902-47 (mixed)

Brooklands School, Medebourne Close, Casterbridge Road, SE3. fl.1971.

Broomwood Hall School, Nightingale Lane, SW12. Opened 1984.

Brownhill Road School,
Rushey Green, SE6. Opened 1905; renamed Brownhill School, 1951; closed c1957. (LMA: EO/DIV 7/BRO)
A&D 1903-11 (junior mixed and infants); 1905-28 (senior mixed); 1907-29 (junior mixed); 1911-39 (infants); 1929-39 (senior boys); 1953-57 (primary)
LB 1903-25 (mixed); 1913-39 (junior mixed and infants); 1913-29 (senior mixed); 1925-39 (boys); 1929-39 (senior boys); 1945-57 (infants)
Misc honours 1932-38

Bruce Road School, E3.
(LMA: EO/DIV 5/BRU)
LB 1879-80 (girls)

Brunel Secondary School, Kensal Road, W10. Opened 1878 as Middle Row School; renamed Brunel Secondary School, 1951. (LMA: EO/DIV 1/BRU)
Misc punishment 1952-57

Brunswick Park School, Camberwell, SE5. Opened 1915.

Brunswick Street Special School, Shoreditch, E2. Opened 1881. (LMA: EO/DIV 4/BRU)
A&D 1894-1940 (mixed); 1909-31 (infant girls)
LB 1918-24 (junior mixed); 1925-39 (senior boys)

Buckingham Gate Central School,
Wilfred Street, SW1. Opened 1882; formerly James Street School. (LMA: EO/DIV 2/BUC)
A&D 1917-45 (mixed)
LB 1863-84, 1913-14 (infants); 1900-50 (mixed - manual training centre); 1905-13 (boys); 1905-13 (girls); 1913-45 (mixed); 1917-21 (mixed - myopic)
Misc 1933-51 (school leavers)

Buckingham Street School, Boadicea Street, Edward Square, N1. Opened 1887; renamed Copenhagen School, 1937. (LMA: EO/DIV 3/BUC)
A&D 1887-1918 (infants); 1918-31 (girls)
LB 1887-1906, 1913-31 (girls); 1913-32 (infants)

Buckingham Terrace School, Lonsdale Road, Portobello Road, W11. Opened 1879; renamed Colville School, 1939. (LMA: EO/DIV 1/BUC)
A&D 1895-1910 (mixed); 1911-33 (girls); 1916-26, 1936-46 (infants)
LB 1932-50 (infants)

Buckle Street Jews' School, Leman Street, Whitechapel, E1. Opened 1898.

Burbage Primary School, N1. Opened 1907 as Hoxton House School; renamed 1951. (LMA: EO/DIV 4/BUR)
A&D 1954-63 (mixed); 1955-64 (infants)

Burdett Coutts and Townsend Foundation, Rochester Street, SW19. Founded 1849; opened 1903. (LMA: EO/DIV 2/BUR)
LB 1936-39 (infants)

Burdett Road School, E3. Opened 1901; closed 1922. (LMA: EO/DIV 5/BUR)
A&D 1901-22 (infants)
LB 1901-22 (mentally defective)

Burgess Hill School, Hampstead. Opened 1936; closed c1960.

Burghley Road and Burghley Central Schools, Highgate Road, St Pancras, NW5. Opened 1884; Central School opened 1911; formerly Fortress Road; renamed Brookfield Secondary School, 1947. (LMA: EO/DIV 2/BGH)
A&D 1884-1956 (infants); 1893-1936 (boys); 1895-1924, 1932-52 (girls)
LB 1884-1933 (girls); 1884-1930, 1933-44 (infants); 1889-1913 (evening)

Burlington Danes School, Wood Lane, W12. founded 1699 in Old Burlington Street, W1; moved to Hammersmith 1936.

Burne-Jones ESN Secondary School,
Hugon Road, SW6. Formerly known as Hurlingham ESN School, renamed 1950; closed 1965 and amalgamated with Elizabeth Burgwin School

Burns Road School, Battersea, SW11.

Burnt Ash Hill School, SE12.
Opened 1914; closed 1936. (LMA: EO/DIV 6/BUN)
A&D 1914-36 (infants)
LB 1914-36 (mixed); 1914-36 (infants)

Burrage Grove School, SE18. Opened 1874; Burrage Road to 1917; Burrage Secondary School for Girls 1951; closed 1960s. (LMA: EO/DIV 6/BUR)
A&D 1914-32 (boys); 1932-54 (mixed); 1955-59 (infants); 1955-62 (attendance)
LB 1882-1914 (evening)
Misc honours 1932-43 (boys)

Bute House Preparatory School for Girls, Luxemburg Gardens, W6. Opened 1958.

Buxton Street School, E1. Opened 1910.

Cable Street School, E1. Opened 1899; renamed St George in the East Central School, 1925. (LMA: EO/DIV 5/CAB)
A&D 1899-1928 (mixed)

Cadogan Terrace Temporary School, Hackney, E9. Opened 1879; closed 1883.

Caldecot Road School, Bessemer Road, Denmark Hill, SE5. Opened 1914; renamed Caldecot School, 1951; later Willowfield School. (LMA: EO/DIV 8/CAD); some unlisted records at Lambeth Archives.
A&D 1935-48 (senior mixed)
LB 1935-45 (senior mixed)

Caldwell Primary School, Caldwell Street, SW9. (LMA: EO/DIV 8/CAL)
A&D 1950-51, 1958-59 (mixed)

Caledonian Road School, N1. Opened 1872; closed 1931. (LMA: EO/DIV 3/CAL)
A&D 1917-31 (infants)

Calvert Road School, Woolwich Road, SE10. Opened 1879; renamed Annandale Primary School, 1951. (LMA: EO/DIV 6/CAL)
A&D 1883-1929 (boys); 1922-47 (infants)
LB 1899-1929 (boys); 1902-13 (girls); 1929-39 (junior mixed)

Camberwell Board of Guardians see **South Metropolitan School District**

Camberwell Open Air School. Opened 1917. (LMA: EO/DIV 7/COA)
A&D 1917-29 (senior mixed)

Camberwell Parochial School (Sir John Kirk Mission), Toulon Street, SE5. Founded c1841. (LMA: EO/DIV 7/CAB)
A&D 1917-29 (senior mixed)

Camden Church of England School, Sumner Road, SE15. Opened 1847.

Camden School for Girls, Sandall Road, NW5. Opened 1871 as North London Collegiate.

Camden Secondary School (Independent). Opened 1907.

Camden Street School, Camden Town, NW1. Opened 1874; renamed King Street School, 1919; Richard Cobden School, 1937. (LMA: EO/DIV 2/CAM)
A&D 1882-1935 (infants); 1892-1931 (boys); 1893-1933 (girls)
LB 1872-1939 (infants); 1874-1931 (boys); 1874-1913 (girls)

Camden Town All Saints' Parish Church of England School, Camden Street, NW1. Opened 1847.

Camelot Street School, Peckham, SE15. Opened c1888 as Asylum Road School; renamed Bird in Bush School, 1893, Arthur Street School, 1894, Camelot Street School, 1938. (LMA: EO/DIV 7/CAM)
A&D 1938-40 (junior mixed)
LB 1929-40 (infants); 1938-40 (junior mixed)

Cameron House, The Vale, Chelsea, SW3. Opened 1980.

Campbell Street School, Cuthbert Street, Maida Vale, Paddington, W2. Opened 1881; renamed Campbell School, 1951; Paddington Green Primary School, 1962. (LMA: EO/DIV 2/CAB)
A&D 1881-1951. (infants)
LB 1890-1910 (evening); 1913-27, 1937-39 (infants)

Campden Hill School, St George's, Edge Street, W8. Opened 1845 as St George's School. (LMA: EO/DIV 1/CAM)
A&D 1944-63 (junior mixed)
Misc 1944-63 (infants)

Campden Institute of Home Training, Lancaster Road, W11. (LMA: EO/DIV 1/CAM 1)
LB 1936-51

Canal Road School, Hoxton, N1. Opened 1877; renamed Edmond Halley School, 1936. (LMA: EO/DIV 4/CAN)
A&D 1924-37 (infants)
LB 1882-1909 (evening)

Canberra School, Australia Road, W12. Opened 1951.

Canon Barnett School, Gunthorpe Street, E1. fl.1971.

Canonbury Road School, N1. Opened 1877 (but originated in Union Chapel British Schools 1807); renamed Canonbury School, 1951. (LMA: EO/DIV 3/CAN)
LB 1877-95 (boys)

Canterbury Road School, Old Kent Road, SE15. Opened 1874; renamed Canterbury School, 1936; closed 1940s. (LMA: EO/DIV 6/CAN; EO/DIV 7/CAN)
A&D 1874-82, 1930-37 (boys); 1885-95, 1905-37 (infants); 1886-1939 (girls); 1894-1930 (junior mixed)
LB 1874-1939 (infants); 1930-37 (boys); 1937-39 (girls)

Cantlowe Secondary School, NW1. Royal College Street School until 1951. (LMA: EO/DIV 2/CAN)
A&D 1952-57 (mixed)
Misc punishment 1952-57

Capland Street Primary School, Lisson Grove, NW8. Opened 1876; renamed Gateforth Street School, 1914. (LMA: EO/DIV 2/CAP)
A&D 1896-1916, 1927-39 (infants); 1913-39 (senior mixed); 1916-32 (junior mixed)
LB 1899-1928 (junior mixed and infants); 1912-32 (mixed - Central)

Capland Street Secondary School, Grove Road. Opened 1887; became Central School, 1912; renamed Regents Park Central School, 1928. *see above*

Captain Marryat Infant School, St Dunstan's Road, W6. Opened 1886 as St Dunstan's Road School; renamed 1951; closed 1977. (LMA: EO/DIV 1/CAP)
A&D 1885-1940 (boys); 1886-1937 (infants); 1896-1939 (girls); 1947-77 (mixed)
LB 1886-1939 (girls); 1896-1927 (evening); 1913-39 (boys); 1935-38, 1947-77 (infants)

Cardinal Griffin Roman Catholic School, Canton Street, E14. fl.1960/71.

Cardinal Manning Roman Catholic School, Kensington. fl.1963.

Cardinal Pole Roman Catholic Secondary School, Kenworthy Road, E9. Opened 1959 in Wenlock Road, N1; moved 1964.

Cardinal Vaughan Memorial School, Addison Road, Kensington, W14. Opened 1914.

Carlton School *see* **Grafton Road School**

Carlyle Girls School, Hortensia Road, SW10. Opened 1908 as Chelsea County School; renamed 1914; closed 1970 and amalgamated with Buckingham Gate School, Ebury School and Sloane School to form Pimlico Comprehensive. (LMA: EO/DIV 1/CAR)
A&D 1906-56 (girls)
LB 1914-45 (girls)
Misc staff 1908-37

Carpenters' Company Technical School, Stratford le Bow. Opened 1891.
see The Story of the Carpenters' Company Technical School 1891-1905 (1964)

Cassland Road School, Well Street, Mare Street, E9. Opened 1913. (LMA: EO/DIV 4/CAS)
A&D 1913-26 (junior mixed and infants)
LB 1902-08 (junior mixed); 1902-40 (evening)

Castle Baynard Ward School, City.
Misc minute books 1753-1835 (Guildhall Library)

Catford Central School, Brownhill Road, SE6 (boys); Hither Green, SE6 (girls). Opened 1904. (LMA: EO/DIV 6/CAF)
A&D 1940-45 (boys)
LB 1940-45 (boys)

Catherine House School, Greenwich. Opened 1904; closed 1930. (LMA: EO/DIV 6/CAT)
A&D 1925-30 (mixed)
LB 1904-30 (mixed)

Catherine Street School, Hoxton, N1. Opened 1887; renamed Laysterne School, 1932. (LMA: EO/DIV 4/CAT)
A&D 1909-19 (mixed)
LB 1887-1913 (girls)

Cator Street School, Peckham, SE15. Opened 1881; closed 1930s. (LMA: EO/DIV 7/CAT)
A&D 1881-1936 (girls); 1890-1933 (infants); 1895-1936 (boys)

Cavendish Road School,
Hydethorpe Road, Clapham, SW12. Opened 1899, deaf school until 1907; renamed Henry Cavendish Primary School, 1951. (LMA: EO/DIV 9/CAV)
A&D 1907-38 (mixed); 1923-37 (girls); 1936-39 (infants)
LB 1899-1906 (deaf)

Cavendish School, Arlington Road, NW1. Opened 1875.

Cayley Street School, E14. Opened 1875.

Central Church of England School, High Street, Marylebone, W1. renamed St Marylebone Church of England School, 1951; closed 1957. (LMA: EO/DIV 2/CEN)
A&D 1883-1906 (mixed and infants); 1890-1900 (girls); 1906-57 (infants); 1945-57 (junior mixed)
Misc 1792-1833, 1858-71 (Westminster Archives)

Central Foundation School for Boys,
Cowper Street, EC2. (Independent). Opened 1726.
A&D 1888-1907, 1932-45 (Church of England Records Centre)
Misc calendars 1898-1953; staff records 1882-1968 (Church of England Records Centre)

Central Foundation School for Girls,
Spital Square, E1. (Independent). Opened 1892; merged with Bowbrook Secondary Girls' School in 1970s.

Central London School District (Boards of Guardians of City, St Saviour Southwark, and from 1853-68 St Martin in the Fields) (LMA: CLSD)
A&D 1852-1933
LB 1849-1930
Misc staff 1866-1930

Central School of Arts and Crafts, Southampton Row, WC1.

Central School of Speech Training and Dramatic Art, Kensington Gore, SW7.

Central Street School, Old Street, EC1. Opened 1874. (LMA: EO/DIV 3/CEN)
A&D 1911-39 (boys); 1938-39 (infants)
LB 1874-1933 (boys); 1874-1918, 1928-39 (infants); 1913-32 (girls)

Cephas Street Secondary School, Mile End, E1. Opened 1928 renamed Cephas School, 1951. (LMA: EO/DIV 5/CEP)
A&D 1942-45 (boys); 1945-63 (mixed)
LB 1930 (evening); 1942-43 (senior boys); 1945-63 (secondary); 1945-75 (infants)
Misc punishment 1939-52 (mixed); 1941-56 (senior boys); 1959-63 (secondary)

Chailey Industrial School see
Mile Oak Approved School

Chalcot School *see* **Harmood Street School**

Channing School, Highgate, N6. Opened 1885.

Chapel Street School *see* Waterloo Street School

Chapman School, Bigland Street, E1. Opened 1874.

Charing Cross Road School, WC2. Opened 1877. (LMA: EO/DIV 2/CHA)
LB 1877-1911 (girls); 1899-1913 (infants); 1900-08 (boys); 1911-13 (evening)

Charles Dickens School, Lant Street, Borough High Street, SE1. Opened 1877 as Lant Street School; renamed 1909. (LMA: EO/DIV 8/CHA)
A&D 1903-40 (girls); 1910-22 (mixed); 1937-40 (boys)
LB 1913-24 (girls); 1913-39 (infants)

Charles Edward Brooke School for Girls,
Halsmere Road, Camberwell, SE5 and Langton Road, SW9. Founded 1879 as Kennington Pupil Teachers Centre; renamed 1926.

Charles Lamb Primary School, Popham Road, N1. Opened 1875 as Anglers Gardens (q.v.); renamed Popham Road (q.v.) 1903; renamed Charles Lamb 1951.

Charlotte Sharman School, West Square, SE11. fl.1971.

Charlton Central School, Sherington Road, SE7. Opened 1907; renamed Sherrington Road School, 1911; then reorganised as a Central School; later Charlton Secondary School. (LMA: EO/DIV 6/CHA)
A&D 1911-39 (boys)
LB 1911-17 (boys); 1913 (manual training centre); 1934-49 (girls)

Charlton Manor School, Hornfair Road, SE7.
Opened 1931; closed 1980s.
(LMA: EO/DIV 6/CHM)
A&D 1931-39 (junior mixed)

Charlton National School, Woolwich Road,
SE7. Opened 1861; closed c1907-10.
(LMA: EO/DIV 6/CHN)
A&D 1873-1906 (infants); 1874-89, 1905-06
(boys); 1878-1906 (girls)
LB 1882-1906 (girls)

Charlton Park Open Air School,
Charlton Park Road, SE7. Opened 1929;
later renamed Charlton Park School.
(LMA: EO/DIV 6/CHP)
A&D 1949-62 (mixed)
LB 1949-62 (mixed)

Charlton School, Woolwich Road, SE7.
Closed 1980s. (LMA: EO/DIV 6/CHS)
A&D 1942-45 (mixed); 1945-51, 1955-78
(senior boys)

Charterhouse School also known as **Sutton's
Hospital**, Smithfield (Independent) (boys).
Opened 1614; moved to Godalming, Surrey
1872.
A&D 1616-1893 (LMA: ACC/1876)
Registers Alumni Carthusiani: a Record of the
Foundation Scholars of Charterhouse
1614-1872 (B. Marsh and F.A. Crisp,
1913); Charterhouse Register 1769-1872,
with appendix of non-Foundationers
1614-1769 (R.L. Arrowsmith, 1872);
Charterhouse Register 1872-1931 (anon,
1932); Charterhouse Register 1925-75
(anon, 1980); List of Carthusians 1800-79
(W.D. Parish, nd)

Chartfield School, St Margaret's Crescent,
SW15. fl.1971.

Chatham Gardens School, Provost Street, City
Road, N1. Opened 1875. (LMA:
EO/DIV 4/CHT)
A&D 1875-83, 1891-1927 (boys); 1877-85,
1893-1913 (girls)
LB 1875-96 (girls); 1931-35 (junior mixed)

Chatham Place School, Hackney, E9.

Chatsworth Road Temporary School, E5.
Opened 1901; closed 1908.

Chaucer School. Opened 1877.

Chelmer Road School, Homerton, E9.

Chelsea Board of Guardians see **Kensington and
Chelsea School District; North Surrey
School District**.

Chelsea Central Secondary School, Upcerne
Road, SW10. Opened 1904; moved to into
Townmead Road School (SW6) buildings
1947; closed 1968 and moved to Glebe
Place, SW3.

Chelsea Parochial School
School reports 1869-1902 (Chelsea Lib)

Chelsea Polytechnic, Manresa Road, SW3.

Chelsea Post Office Messenger Classes
(LMA: EO/DIV 1/CHM)
LB 1911-13

Chelsea Pupil Teachers, William Street,
Hammersmith Road, W4. Opened 1887.
(LMA: EO/DIV 1/CHP)
LB 1901-08

Chelsea Secondary School, Bagleys Lane,
New Kings Road, SW6. Opened 1911;
merged into Hurlingham Chelsea School,
1982. (LMA: EO/DIV 1/CHS)
A&D 1924-68 (mixed)
LB 1962-68 (mixed)
Misc punishment 1962-68

Chequer Street School, Bunhill Row,
Old Street, EC1. Opened 1877; renamed
Northampton Secondary School, 1951.
(LMA: EO/DIV 3/CHE)
A&D 1897-1915 (girls); 1912-25 (infants)
LB 1899-1928 (mixed)

Cherry Orchard School, Rectory Field
Crescent, SE7. fl.1971.

Chester Road School, NW1. Opened 1914;
after 1931 premises used by Burghley Road
Central School. (LMA: EO/DIV 2/CHE)
A&D 1914-32 (infants)

Chesterton Primary School,
Battersea, SW11. Opened 1874 as Battersea
Park Road School; renamed 1951.
(LMA: EO/DIV 9/CHE)
A&D 1945-55 (infants)
LB 1955-63 (junior mixed and infants)

Chicksand Street School, E1. Opened 1875;
closed 1924. (LMA: EO/DIV 5/CHI)
A&D 1885-1924 (boys); 1889-1925 (infants);
1896-1924 (girls)

Childeric Road School,
Clifton Rise, New Cross, SE14. Opened 1893; renamed Childeric School, 1951. (LMA: EO/DIV 6/CHL)
A&D 1893-1939 (infants); 1913-26 (mixed); 1919-39 (girls); 1926-40 (boys); 1938-45 (handicraft)
LB 1893-1939 (infants); 1915-19 (evening); 1919-26 (mixed); 1926-40 (boys); 1928-39 (junior girls)

Childerley Street School, Childerley Street, SW6. Opened 1904; became part of Fulham Central School, 1920 and of Henry Compton School, 1951.

Chisenhale Road School, Bethnal Green, E3. Opened 1893.

Choumert Road School, Peckham, SE15. Opened 1894; closed c1932. (LMA: EO/DIV 7/CHO)
A&D 1888-1925 (girls); 1888-96, 1907-22 (junior mixed); 1899-1925 (boys); 1903-32 (infants); 1925-27 (senior mixed)

Chrisp Street School, E14. transferred to Culloden Street, 1899; closed 1929. (LMA: EO/DIV 5/CHP)
A&D 1896-1929 (special) (junior mixed)

Christ Chapel School. (LMA: EO/DIV 2/CHR)
LB 1874-1903 (infants)

Christ Church Albany Street School, St Pancras, NW1. Opened 1837. (LMA: EO/DIV 2/CHC 2)
LB 1913-32 (mixed); 1913-32 (infants); 1935-39 (junior mixed and infants)

Christ Church Cosway Street School, Marylebone, NW1. Opened 1852. (LMA: EO/DIV 2/CHC)
A&D 1913-29, 1943-49 (infants); 1926-39 (boys)
LB 1862-1936, 1943-49 (infants); 1914-31 (girls); 1937-39 (boys)

Christ Church National School, Poplar. Founded 1862; transferred to LCC, 1876.

Christchurch School, Bear Lane, Southwark, SE1. Opened 1713. (LMA: EO/DIV 8/CHC 2 and A/CCP)
A&D 1936-67 (mixed)
LB 1874-1950
Misc minute books 1746-1965

Christ Church School, Brick Lane, Spitalfields, E1. Founded c1708.

Christ Church School, Cancell Road, Brixton, SW9. Opened 1860. (LMA: EO/DIV 8/CHC 1 and P85/CTC 2)
A&D 1885-1936 (boys); 1907-36 (girls)
LB 1863-1936 (boys); 1876-1936 (girls)
Misc punishment 1936-64; minute books 1871-1929; Sunday School minute books 1885-1907, 1929, 1955-71

Christ Church School, Christchurch Road, Streatham Hill, SW2. Opened 1856.
Misc minute book 1844-87 (LMA: P95/CTC 1)

Christ Church School, Christchurch Street, SE10. Opened 1870 now Blackwell Lane, East Greenwich, SE10. (LMA: these records cannot currently be traced)
LB 1871-1913 (infants); 1870-1913 (girls); 1871-1913 (boys)

Christ Church School, Este Road, Battersea, SW11. Opened 1865.

Christ Church School, Forest Hill, SE23. Opened 1858. (LMA: EO/DIV 6/CHC)
A&D 1905-24 (girls); 1912-35 (infants)
LB 1896-1926, 1931-39 (boys); 1896-1924 (girls); 1915-34 (infants); 1929-39 (junior boys)
Misc minute books 1893-1969 (Church of England Records Centre)

Christ Church School, Hampstead Square, NW3. Opened 1855.

Christ Church School, Palmer Street, SW1. fl.1907/12.

Christ Church School, Shooter's Hill, SE18. Opened 1857. Known from 1906 as Shooter's Hill Church of England School (q.v.); Shooter's Hill School for Senior Boys opened in 1930s, and Junior Mixed and Infants Schools became Christ Church Primary School, 1951.

Christchurch School, Herbrand Street, Holborn, EC1. Opened 1872 as Christ Church National School; renamed 1907. (LMA: EO/DIV 3/CHC)
A&D 1917-35 (boys); 1932-39 (infants); 1935-39 (junior girls)
LB 1928-35 (boys)

Christ Church School, Jamaica Road, Rotherhithe, SE16. Opened 1840.

Christ Church School, Royal Hospital Road, Chelsea, SW3. Opened 1841.

Christ Church School, Somers Town, NW1. Opened 1869.

Christ Church School, Union Grove, Clapham, SW8. Opened 1902.

Christian Street School, Commercial Road, E1. Opened 1901; renamed John Rennie School, 1951. (LMA: EO/DIV 5/CHR)
A&D 1901-55 (boys); 1901-39 (girls); 1901-39, 1944-45 (infants)
LB 1901-34 (girls); 1901-50 (infants); 1912-39 (boys); 1934-39 (junior girls); 1950-54 (junior mixed and infants)
Misc visitors 1886-1906; punishment 1926-59

Christopher Hatton School, EC1. formerly Laystall School (1876-1899) and Rosebery Avenue School (1899-1951); closed 1968. (LMA: EO/DIV 3/CHH)
A&D 1941-69 (junior mixed and infants)
LB 1936-55 (mixed); 1953-66 (junior mixed and infants)
Misc punishment 1945-67

Christopher Marlowe School, Angus Street and Monson Road, SE14. fl.1971.

Christopher Wren School, Bloemfontein Road, W12. Renamed 1951, previously Hammersmith Secondary Technical School for Boys; amalgamated with North Hammersmith Secondary Boys School, 1956.

Christ's College, Blackheath, SE10. Opened 1823 (private)
see A View of Christ's College, Blackheath (A.E.O. Crombie, 1980)

Christ's Hospital, Great Tower Street, EC3. (Independent) (boys). Opened 1552; moved to Horsham, Sussex, 1902.

Christ's Hospital [*continued*]
A&D 1563-1911 (Guildhall Library)
Misc apprentice bindings 1675-1711; minute books 1556-1948 (Guildhall Library)
Registers Christ's Hospital admissions 1554-99 (anon, 1937); University Exhibitioners 1556-1885 (A.W. Lockhart, 1886); University Scholars Supplementary List 1886-1899 (A.W. Lockhart, 1900); Christ's Hospital Exhibitioners to the Universities of Oxford and Cambridge 1566-1923 (G.A.T. Allan, 1924)

Christ the King Roman Catholic Primary School, Tollington Park, N4. Opened 1961.

Churchdown School. Opened 1929.

Churchill Gardens School, Ranelagh Road, SW1. fl.1971.

Church Manor Way School, SE2. Opened 1903; renamed Manorway Primary School and Church Manorway Secondary School, 1951; closed 1960s. (LMA: EO/DIV 6/CHU)
A&D 1903-31 (senior mixed); 1903-31 (junior mixed); 1946-56 (infants)
LB 1903-26 (senior mixed); 1903-26 (junior mixed); 1926-31 (boys); 1926-31 (girls)

Church Street School, Clapham Road, SW8. Opened 1879; renamed Ashmole School, 1935. (LMA: EO/DIV 8/CHU)
A&D 1872-92, 1906-21 (infants); 1893-1934 (boys); 1903-25 (girls); 1929-38 (junior mixed)
LB 1879-1933 (boys); 1879-1933 (infants); 1913-20 (girls)

Church Street School, Stoke Newington, N16. Opened 1892; renamed William Patten School, 1951. (LMA: EO/DIV 4/CHU 1-2)
A&D 1879-94 (boys); 1880-1905 (girls); 1891-1912, 1925-34, 1943-50 (infants); 1931-39 (junior girls); 1945-54 (junior mixed)
LB 1889-1913 (boys); 1889-1934 (infants); 1889-1913 (girls); 1921-32 (evening); 1931-39 (junior girls)
Misc visitors 1892-1954

Cirencester Street Roman Catholic School, W2. fl.1905.

City and Guilds of London Institute, Exhibition Road, SW7. Opened 1881.
A&D 1882-1943 (Guildhall Library)

City Board of Guardians see **Central London School District**

City of London Freemen's School, Ferndale Road, Brixton, SW4. Opened 1854 as City of London Freemen's Orphans School; moved to Ashtead, Surrey c1926.
A&D Registers 1853-1955; apprenticeships 1876-1918 (Corporation of London Record Office)
Misc Staff records 1853-1914 (Corporation of London Record Office)
see Centenary 1854-1954 (anon, 1955)

City of London School, Victoria Embankment, EC4 (Independent) (boys). Opened 1442, Honey Lane Market, reconstituted 1834; moved 1882.
List Pupils 1837-1900 (typescript at Corporation of London Records Office, which also has Honours lists 1914-37)
see also The City of London School (A.E. Douglas-Smith, 1937); City of London School, Past and Present (anon, 1965); Carpenter's Children (T. Hinde, 1995)

City of London School for Girls, Barbican, EC2. Opened 1894 Carmelite Street, EC4; moved 1969.
see Daughters of the City (J. Carden, 1996)

City of London School of Instruction and Industry, St James Duke's Place, EC3.
A&D 1807-41; attendance 1811-45 (Guildhall Library)

Clapham Central School, Aristotle Road, SW4. Opened 1903.

Clapham Church Girls School, Rectory Grove, SW4. (LMA: P95/TRI 1)
LB 1898-1913 (girls); 1913-45 (girls and infants)

Clapham College, Nightingale Lane, SW11. (Independent) (boys). Opened 1897.

Clapham County School, Broomwood Road, SW11. Opened 1909.
Registers 1909-59 (E. Freeth, 1960)

Clapham High School (girls). Opened 1875.

Clapham Manor School, Stonhouse Street, SW4. Opened 1881; renamed Stonhouse Street School, 1951. (LMA: EO/DIV 9/CLM)
LB 1946-56 (junior mixed and infants)

Clapham Park School, King's Avenue, SW4. (Partially sighted).

Clapham Parochial School, Macaulay Road, SW4. Opened 1648. Also known as Macaulay School. (LMA: P95/TRI 1)
A&D applications for admission to Macaulay School 1973-80
LB 1896-1910 (infants); 1914-33 (boys)
Misc minute books 1905-35

Clapham School (private) (boys). Opened 1884.

Clapham School of Art, Edgley Road, SW4.

Clapham Trade School, Clapham Road, SW9.

Clapton Park Secondary School, Laura Place, Lower Clapton Road, E5. Opened 1906; renamed John Howard Secondary School, 1949; merged into Clapton Comprehensive School, 1977.
A&D 1929-69 (Hackney Archives)
LB 1906-52 (Hackney Archives)
Misc punishment 1948-53 (LMA: EO/DIV 4/CLA); staff records 1906-22 (Hackney Archives)

Clapton Roman Catholic School, Kenninghall Road, Upper Clapton, E5. Opened 1868; renamed St Scholastica School, c1972.

Clarence Street School, Rotherhithe, SE16. Opened 1844; renamed Green School, 1929. (LMA: EO/DIV 6/CLA and EO/DIV 8/CLA)
A&D 1905-39 (infants); 1910-33 (girls)
LB 1909-32 (infants); 1913-31 (girls)

Clarendon Square Roman Catholic School *see* **St Aloysius School**

Clark's College, Upper Richmond Road, SW15.

Claylands Road School, SW8. (LMA: EO/DIV 3/CLA)
LB 1872-79 (infants)

Clerkenwell Parochial School, Amwell Street, EC1. Opened 1700.
Records 18th-20th century (Finsbury Local History Collections)

Clifton Hill School, New Cross, SE14. Opened 1873; renamed Clifton Rise School, 1937; Marlowe Primary School and Christopher Marlowe Secondary School, 1951; closed 1958. (LMA: EO/DIV 6/CLI)
A&D 1873-74, 1885-1936 (boys); 1874, 1924-39 (infants); 1928-41 (senior girls); 1939-45 (mixed); 1939-40 (attendance)

Clipstone School, St Marylebone, W1. Opened 1914 as Upper Marylebone School; renamed 1936. (LMA: EO/DIV 2/CLI)
A&D 1914-39 (infants)

Clissold Park School, Clissold Road, N16. Opened 1967; merged 1982 in Stoke Newington Comprehensive School

Clissold Secondary School, N16. Opened 1927 as Stoke Newington Central School; renamed 1951.

Cloudesley School, Dowrey Street, N1 (handicapped). Opened 1909; closed 1972,

Clyde Street School, Wotton Road, Deptford, SE8. Opened 1886; renamed Grinling Gibbons School, 1951. (LMA: EO/DIV 6/CLY)
LB 1907-08 (pupil teachers); 1930-39 (junior girls)

Cobbold Road School, Askew Road, W12. Opened 1896 as Bassein Park Road School; renamed Cobbold Road School, 1901; Wendell Park School, 1925. (LMA: EO/DIV 1/COB)
LB 1896-1913 (mixed)

Coborn School for Girls, Bow Road, E3.

Cobourg Road School, Old Kent Road, SE5. Opened 1887; renamed Cobourg School, 1951. (LMA: EO/DIV 7/COB)
A&D 1921-29 (girls); 1933-39 (infants)
LB 1884-1901 (boys); 1913-39 (infants)

Cold Blow Lane School, New Cross, SE14. Opened 1879; renamed Monson Road School, 1895; Monson School, 1951. (LMA: EO/DIV 6/COL)
A&D 1879-83 (mixed); 1883-95 (boys)

Colebrooke School, Colebrooke Row, N1. Opened 1914.

Coleman Street Ward School, London Wall, City, EC2. Opened 1717 (early administrative and estate records at Guildhall Library).
A&D 1871-1905 (boys); 1898-1917 (girls); 1895-1908 (infants) (Guildhall Library); 1905-62 (boys); 1908-26 (infants); 1918-62 (girls) (LMA: EO/DIV 5/COE)
LB 1878-1913 (boys); 1879-1913 (girls); 1895-1906 (infants) (Guildhall Library); 1913-26 (boys); 1913-35, 1946-62 (infants); 1913-26 (girls); 1926-62 (mixed) (LMA: EO/DIV 5/COE)

Colet Court, Hammersmith Road, W6. Opened 1883 in Edith Road; moved 1890; renamed St Paul's Junior School, 1949 but retained name; moved to Barnes, 1968.

Colet Girls' School, Brook Green, W6. Opened 1932; renamed St Paul's Girls' Preparatory School 1944.

Colfe's Grammar School, Horn Park Lane, Lewisham, SE12 or Granville Park, SE13. (Independent) (boys). Opened 1652.

College Lane Deaf School. Opened 1903; closed c1940. (LMA: EO/DIV 4/COL)
LB 1900-15 (evening)

College of Physical Education, Paddington Street, W1.

College Park Secondary School, Monmouth Road, W2. fl.1971.

College Park Secondary School, Valliere Road, NW10. Opened 1880 as Kenmont Gardens School; renamed 1950.

Colls Road School, Peckham, SE15.
see also Woods Road School. Opened 1885; renamed Collingwood School, 1951; merged with Samuel Pepys School, 1982 to form Hatcham Wood School. (LMA: EO/DIV 7/COL)
A&D 1883-85, 1894-1939 (boys); 1883-85 (mixed); 1885-1928 (girls); 1885-1932 (infants); 1929-38 (senior boys)
LB 1883-1935 (boys); 1900-26 (manual training centre)

Columbia Road School, Hackney Road, E2. Opened 1875; renamed Columbia School, 1951. (LMA: EO/DIV 5/COL)
A&D 1905-30 (boys)
LB 1896-1923 (evening); 1913-31 (boys)

Colverstone School, Colverstone Crescent, E8. Opened 1949.

Colville School, Kensington, SW7.
Opened 1879 as Buckingham Terrace School; renamed 1939.

Comber Grove School, Camberwell New Road, SE5. Opened 1877 as Leipsic Road School; renamed 1921; closed 1950s. (LMA: EO/DIV 7/COM)
A&D 1877-1939 (boys); 1877-1900, 1912-39 (infants); 1907-39 (girls)

Commercial School, Regent Street (Independent) (boys). In existence 1909.

Commercial Street School, Whitechapel High Street, E1. Opened 1901; renamed Canon Barnett School, 1951. (LMA: EO/DIV 5/COM)
A&D 1911-35 (girls); 1913-39 (infants); 1916-35 (boys); 1940 (mixed)
LB 1913-36 (boys); 1936-39 (mixed); 1936-39 (infants)

Compton House School for Boys, Sutton Court Road, W4.

Compton Primary School, Compton Street, Clerkenwell, EC1. St Paul's Allen Street to 1873; Allen Street School 1873-81; Compton Street School 1881-1951; renamed Compton Primary School, 1951. (LMA: EO/DIV 3/COM)
A&D 1957-76 (infants)
LB 1871-1940 (boys); 1877-1922, 1928-39 (infants); 1902-39 (girls); 1945-59 (junior mixed and infants)

Convent of Mercy School, Hazlewood Crescent, W10.

Conway Road School, Lakedale Road, SE18. Opened 1897; renamed Conway School, 1951. (LMA: EO/DIV 6/CON)
A&D 1881-93 (infants)
LB 1894-1913 (boys); 1897-1913 (infants); 1907-20 (manual training centre)

Cook's Ground School, Glebe Place, Kings Road, SW3. Opened 1874; Cook's Ground School and Park Walk School amalgamated 1905 and renamed Park Walk School; renamed Kingsley Secondary School, 1951. (LMA: EO/DIV 1/COO)
A&D 1930-48 (senior girls); 1940-42 (mixed)
LB 1885-1924 (evening)

Coopers' Company's School, Tredegar Square, Bow, E3. (Independent) (boys). Opened 1538.
Misc estate records 1520-1607; administrative records 1823-89 (Guildhall Library)

Cooper's Lane School, Grove Park, SE12. Opened 1936; renamed Grove Park Secondary School, 1951; closed 1960s. (LMA: EO/DIV 7/COO)
A&D 1936-39 (infants); 1936-56 (mixed); 1940-45 (boys); 1940-45 (girls)
LB 1941-45 (mixed)

Copenhagen School, Boadicea Street, N1. Opened 1887 see Buckingham Street School

Copenhagen Street Ragged School, N1. Opened c1852; closed by 1878.

Copperfield Road School, E3. Opened 1867. Ragged school founded by Dr Barnardo; now Ragged School Museum; closed 1908. (LMA: EO/DIV 5/COP) *see also* Barnardo's
A&D 1897-1904 (boys); 1906-08 (infants)

Coram Fields School, Guilford Street, WC1. (open air). (LMA: EO/DIV 2/COR)
A&D 1949-63 (junior mixed and infants)
Misc punishment 1949-60

Cordwainer and Bread Street Wards Charity School, City.
Misc administrative records 1715-27 (Guildhall Library)

Cork Street School, SE5. Opened 1915; renamed Oliver Goldsmith School 1931; Brunswick Park School, 1938. (LMA: EO/DIV 7/COR)
A&D 1915-31 (boys); 1915-31, 1936-39 (girls); 1915-36 (infants); 1932-36 (mixed)
LB 1913-36 (infants)

Cormont Road School, Myatts Fields, Flodden Road, SE5. Opened 1898; renamed Cormont School, 1951; closed 1960. (LMA: EO/DIV8/COR)
A&D 1898-1937 (girls); 1903-14, 1920-27, 1930-39 (boys); 1937-48 (senior mixed); 1948-60 (mixed)
LB 1898-1936 (girls); 1936-39 (senior girls); 1936-47 (senior boys)
Misc punishment 1945-51, 1957-60

Cornhill, Lime Street and Langbourn Wards School, City. Cornhill and Lime Street Wards School opened 1711; amalgamated with Langbourn Ward School, 1874.
A&D 1738-1903 (Guildhall Library)
LB 1875-1902 (Guildhall Library)
Misc minute books 1709-1903 (Guildhall Library)

Corpus Christi Roman Catholic School, Trent Road, Brixton Hill, SW2. Opened 1903.

Cosway Street School, St Marylebone, NW1. Opened 1874 as Stephen Street School; renamed 1911; renamed Cosway School, 1951. (LMA: EO/DIV 2/COS)
A&D 1909-33 (boys); 1929-63 (infants); 1940-53 (mixed); 1953-63 (junior mixed)
LB 1913-57 (infants); 1943-63 (mixed)
Misc punishment 1911-61

Cotswold School, Franciscan Road, SW17. Formerly Franciscan Road School.

Cottenham Road School, Marlborough Road, N19. Opened 1873; renamed Hanley School, Sussex Way, 1938; Hanleigh Primary and Archway County Secondary School, 1951. (LMA: EO/DIV 3/COT)
A&D 1875-1939 (boys); 1885-1939 (girls); 1903-39 (infants)
LB 1872-1937 (girls); 1882-1913 (evening); 1891-1931 (infants)

Cotton Street School, E14. (LMA: EO/DIV 5/COT)
A&D 1903-06 (infants); 1905-06 (girls)

County Secondary School, The, Brownswood Road, Clapham, SW11. Opened 1909.

Coverdale Road School, Uxbridge Road, Shepherds Bush, W12. Opened 1916 as Thornfield Road School; renamed 1917; renamed Coverdale School, 1951; Miles Coverdale School, 1960. (LMA: EO/DIV 1/COV)
A&D 1916-36 (boys); 1916-33 (girls); 1916-30 (infant girls); 1916-68 (junior mixed); 1932-69 (infants)
LB 1916-39, 1042-78 (infants); 1933-39 (junior mixed)
Misc punishment 1943-57 (infants)

Cowley School, Cowley Road, Kennington, SW9. Opened 1936. (LMA: EO/DIV 8/COW)
LB 1936-39 (junior boys)

Crampton Street School, Newington Butts, SE17. Opened 1883; renamed Crampton School, 1951. (LMA: EO/DIV 8/CRA)
A&D 1928-39 (infants)
LB 1883-1905 (girls); 1931-36 (handicrafts centre)

Cranbrook Road School, Green Street, E2. Opened 1881; renamed Cranbrook Terrace School, 1938; Cranbrook School, 1951; Bowbrook School, 1957. (LMA: EO/DIV 5/CRA 1)
A&D 1877-1937 (boys); 1895-1939 (girls); 1909-24 (infants)
LB 1881-1923, 1926-39, 1945-51 (boys); 1881-1939, 1943-47 (girls); 1881-1913 (infants); 1920-24 (myopic)

Cranbrook Terrace School, Bethnal Green, E2. *see* Cranbrook Road School. (LMA: EO/DIV 5/CRA 2)
A&D 1942-68 (senior girls); 1942-51 (senior boys)

Craven Hill Congregational Church School. Opened 1862; closed c1874.

Craven Park School, Castlewood Road, Stamford Hill, N16. Opened 1896. (LMA: EO/DIV 4/CRA)
A&D 1931-39 (junior mixed); 1931-35 (infants)
LB 1935-39 (junior mixed)

Crawford Street School, Camberwell, SE5. Opened 1884; renamed Crawford School, 1936. (LMA: EO/DIV 7/CRA)
A&D 1937-39 (infants)
LB 1882-1910 (mixed); 1890-1955 (evening); 1897-1939 (manual training centre); 1913-40 (infants)

Credon Road School, Rotherhithe New Road, SE16. Opened 1882; renamed Credon School, 1951; closed 1960s. (LMA: EO/DIV 7/CRE)
A&D 1882-92, 1909-40 (boys); 1902-11, 1917-33 (infants); 1930-57 (senior girls); 1939-45 (mixed)
LB 1893-1939 (boys); 1908-58 (girls)
Misc punishment 1933-54

Creek Road School, SE8. Opened 1873; renamed Creek Manor School, 1951; closed 1960s. (LMA: EO/DIV 6/CRE)
A&D 1873-1938 (boys); 1897-1904, 1942-44 (junior mixed); 1899-1956 (infants); 1902-54 (girls); 1938-55 (senior boys); 1954-62 (senior mixed)

LONDON SCHOOL RECORDS

Creek Road School [*continued*]
LB 1872-1939 (infants); 1902-46 (girls);
1930-38 (boys); 1942-44 (junior mixed)
Misc honours 1927-44 (girls)

Cripplegate Within Ward School, EC1.
A&D attendance 1823-33 (Guildhall Library)
LB 1863-92 (boys and girls) (Guildhall Library)
Misc minute books 1712-92, 1819-92
(Guildhall Library)

Crofton Park Central School, SE4.
Opened 1901.

Cromer Street School, Gray Inn Road, WC1.
Founded c1841 as St Peter Regent Square
School in Dutton Street; LCC 1884;
renamed Cromer Street British School,
1891. (LMA: EO/DIV 2/CRO)
LB 1866-78 (girls)

Cromwell High School, Putney Bridge Road,
Putney (Independent) (boys). Opened 1888.

Crondall Street School, Hoxton Street, N1.
Opened 1927; renamed Crondall School,
1951; merged into Haggerston School,
1959. (LMA: EO/DIV 4/CRO)
A&D 1931-59 (girls)
LB 1931, 1945-59 (girls)
Misc punishment 1948-59

Crown Lane School, Crown Lane, SW16.

Crown Woods School, Riefield Road, SE9.
fl.1971.

Crusoe House School, Clissold Road, N16.
Opened 1972; moved to Nile Street,
Hoxton, 1982.

Cubitt Town School, Poplar, E14. Opened
1891. (LMA: EO/DIV 5/CUB)
A&D 1871-86, 1891-1935 (infants); 1876-95,
1918-35 (girls); 1877-93 (boys); 1905-22,
1943-70 (infants)
LB 1889-95, 1918-35 (boys); 1891-95, 1918-35
(girls); 1891-1931 (infants); 1895-1918,
1942-50 (mixed); 1910-35 (handicrafts
centre)

Culloden Street School, Brunswick Road,
Poplar, E14. Opened 1899; Brunswick
Road School; later Culloden Street School;
renamed Culloden School, 1951.
(LMA: EO/DIV 5/CUL)
LB 1896-1929 (mentally defective)

**Cumberlow Lodge Approved School and
Remand Home**, South Norwood.
(LMA: LCC/CH/D/CUM)
A&D 1922-48
LB 1936-61
Misc punishment 1936-61

Curtain Road School, Old Street, EC2. Opened
1878. (LMA: EO/DIV 4/CUR)
A&D 1886-1932 (girls); 1891-1938 (infants);
1899-1913 (junior boys); 1907-32 (boys)
LB 1875-1928 (boys); 1903-28 (infants);
1905-28 (girls); 1928-32 (senior mixed);
1928-38 (junior mixed and infants)
Misc honours 1911-18

Curzon Street School, W1. Opened 1860.
(LMA: EO/DIV 2/CUR)
LB 1886-1915 (infants); 1913-15 (mixed)

Cyril Jackson School, Northey Street,
Three Colt Street, E14. Opened 1874 as
Northey Street School; renamed 1925.
(LMA: EO/DIV 5/CYR)
A&D 1924-39 (infants); 1947-50
(physically handicapped)
LB 1936-39 (infants); 1947-50
(physically defective)

Dalgleish Street School,
Salmon Lane, E14. Opened 1880; renamed
Sir William Burrough School, 1951.
(LMA: EO/DIV 5/DAL)
A&D 1880-1932 (boys); 1880-1932 (girls);
1880-86, 1892-1939 (infants); 1932-39
(senior mixed)
LB 1880-1934 (boys); 1880-1931 (girls);
1880-1939 (infants); 1931-38
(senior mixed)
Misc visitors 1886-1906

Dalling Road School, Dalling Road, W6.
Opened 1877; closed 1887 when Flora
Gardens School opened.

Dalmain Road School,
Brockley Rise, Forest Hill, SE23. Opened
1874; renamed Dalmain School, 1951.
(LMA: EO/DIV 7/DAL)
A&D 1894-1904 (infants)
LB 1874-1939 (junior mixed and infants)
Misc punishment 1916-23

Dalston Central School, Lansdowne Drive, E8.
Opened 1913; merged into Hackney Downs
and Kingsland Secondary Schools after
1947. (LMA: EO/DIV 4/DAL 1)
A&D 1913-33 (mixed)

Dalston County Secondary School, Shacklewell Lane, E8. Opened 1848 (council 1905); formerly Kingsland Birkbeck School. (LMA: EO/DIV 4/DAL 2)
A&D 1905-36 (girls)

Dalston Wesleyan School, Mayfield Terrace, E8. Opened 1866 as Mayfield Terrace Wesleyan School; renamed 1904. (LMA: EO/DIV 4/DAL 3)
A&D 1903-08 (mixed)
LB 1871-1909 (infants); 1871-96 (mixed)

Dame Alice Owen School, Goswell Road, Islington, N1. Opened 1613.
A&D 1842-50, 1879-1914 (Guildhall Library)
Misc estate records 1845-1918; administrative records 1600-1928 (Guildhall Library)

Dame Anne Packington School, St Botolph Aldersgate, EC1.
A&D 1829-67 (Guildhall Library)
Misc administrative records 1829-75 (Guildhall Library)

Danebury School, Danebury Avenue, SW15. fl.1971.

Daneford School, Gosset Street, E2. fl.1971.

Daniel Defoe School, Ayrsome Road, N16. formerly Oldfield Road School. (LMA: EO/DIV 4/DAN)
LB 1947-65 (mixed)
Misc punishment 1963-65

Daniel Street School, Gossett Street, Bethnal Green Road, E2. Opened 1900 (partially sighted opened 1929); renamed Daniel School 1951; closed 1959. (LMA: EO/DIV 5/DAN 1)
A&D 1900-30, 1945-59 (boys); 1900-39, 1945-54 (girls); 1940 (mixed)
LB 1900-39, 1945-59 (boys); 1900-13 (girls); 1900-13, 1925-39 (infants); 1913-29 (mentally defective); 1923-32 (evening); 1931-39, 1945-54 (senior girls)
Misc punishment 1951-59

Dartmouth Road School, SE26. Opened 1905; renamed Sydenham County School, 1938. (LMA: EO/DIV 7/DAR)
A&D 1923-32 (boys)

Daubeney Road School, Ashenden Road, Clapton, E5. Opened 1886; renamed Daubeney School, 1951; (LMA:EO/DIV 4/DAU)

Daubeney Road School [*continued*]
A&D 1911-39 (girls)
LB 1886-1931 (girls)

Davenant School, St Mary Street, Whitechapel Road, E1. Founded 1686 as Whitechapel Foundation School; renamed 1888; Elementary School closed 1950; Secondary School moved to Loughton, Essex, 1965. (LMA: EO/DIV 5/DAV and A/DAV)
A&D 1906-39 (infants); 1915-39, 1945-56, 1958-64 (boys); 1858-1945
LB 1911-13 (infants)
Misc punishment 1946-64; minute books 1888-94, 1909-64
see History of Davenant Foundation Grammar School (R. Reynolds, 1966)

Deal Street School, Mile End, E1. Opened 1899 as Vallance Street School; renamed 1916; Robert Montefiore Primary School, 1951. (LMA: EO/DIV 5/DEA)
A&D 1896-1931 (boys); 1896-1939 (infants); 1897-1932 (special); 1913-31 (girls); 1945-50 (senior mixed)

Deansfield Road School, Rochester Way, SE9. Opened 1915; renamed Deansfield School, 1932. (LMA: EO/DIV 6/DEA)
A&D 1915-32 (infants); 1915-23 (junior mixed); 1924-33 (senior mixed); 1933-39 (junior boys); 1928-37 (emergency)
LB 1903-05 (infants); 1903-06 (mixed); 1915-33 (infants); 1915-33 (senior mixed); 1933-38 (junior boys)

De Beauvoir School, Tottenham Road, N1. Opened 1874 as Tottenham Road School; renamed 1951.

Defoe School, Broadwater Road, SW17. Opened 1908 as Fountain Road School; renamed 1928; Graveney Secondary School, 1951; closed 1959. (LMA: EO/DIV 9/DEF)
A&D 1932-39 (senior boys); 1940-42, 1945-47 (boys); 1940-42, 1945-59 (girls); 1940-51 (mixed)
LB 1929-39 (infants); 1932-39 (senior mixed)

De Lucy School, Cookhill Road, SE2. fl.1971.

Dempsey Street School, Jubilee Street, Mile End, E1. Opened 1882; partially sighted opened 1924; renamed Dempsey Secondary School, 1951. (LMA: EO/DIV 5/DEM)

Dempsey Street School [*continued*]
A&D 1882-1941 (boys); 1882-85, 1892-1923,
1940-41, 1944-45 (girls); 1898-1923,
1942-63 (mixed); 1900-23 (infants);
1924-39 (partially sighted)
LB 1882-1939 (boys); 1882-1934 (girls);
1934-35 (senior girls); 1945-62
(senior mixed)
Misc punishment 1953-63

Denmark Hill School, Grove Lane,
SE5. Opened 1905; renamed Bessemer
Grange Primary School, 1951.
(LMA: EO/DIV 7/DEN)
A&D 1923-32 (boys)

Denmark Terrace School, Blenheim Road,
Islington, N19. (LMA: EO/DIV 3/DEN)
LB 1885-91 (boys)

Deodar Road Temporary School, Putney,
SW15. Renamed Brandlehow School, 1901.
(LMA: EO/DIV 9/DEO)
LB 1897-1913 (boys); 1897-1913 (girls);
1897-1913 (infants)

Deptford Men's Institute, Queens Road, SE15.
Closed 1960s. (LMA: EO/DIV 6/DEP 1)
A&D 1920-25, 1937-39 (indexes of students)

Deptford Park School, Evelyn Street, SE8.
Opened 1876. (LMA: EO/DIV 6/DEP 2)
A&D 1934-39 (infants)
LB 1930-38 (boys)

Deptford Roman Catholic School. Deptford
High Street, SE8. Opened 1850; renamed
St Joseph Roman Catholic Primary School,
1951. (LMA: EO/DIV 6/DEP 1)
LB 1920-39 (mixed)

Deptford Pupil Teachers Institute
(LMA: EO/DIV 6/DPT)
LB 1899-1907

Derby Road School, E9. Opened 1892;
renamed Lauriston Road, 1927.
(LMA: EO/DIV 5/DER)
A&D 1918-39 (mixed)

Derinton Road School, Tooting, SW17. Opened
1916; later Hillbrook Road School.
(LMA: EO/DIV 9/DER)
LB 1913 (infants); 1913 (mixed)

Detmold Road School, Hackney, E5.
Opened 1886; renamed Southwold School,
1951.

Devonshire House Preparatory School,
Arkwright Road, NW3. Opened 1989.

Devons Road School, Campbell Road, E3.
Opened 1905; renamed Devons Primary
School, Knapp Road, Bow, E3, 1938.
(LMA: EO/DIV 5/DEV)
A&D 1905-28 (boys); 1905-21 (girls)
LB 1905-16 (girls); 1942-47 (junior mixed)

D'Eynsford Road School, SE5. Opened 1911;
closed 1915. (LMA: EO/DIV 7/DEY)
A&D 1911-15 (infants)
LB 1911-13 (infants)

Dick Sheppard School, Tulse Hill, SW2.
Unlisted records at Lambeth Archives.

Dingle Lane School, Poplar, E14.
Opened 1910.

Dissenters' Charity School,
Bartholomew Close, EC1.
A&D pupil lists 1807-18 (Guildhall Library)
Misc administrative records 1804-39
(Guildhall Library)

Dockhead Roman Catholic School *see*
St Michael's Roman Catholic School

Doctor Barnardo's School see **Copperfield Road
School**

Dog Kennel Hill School, Grovehill Road, SE5.
Opened *c*1938. (LMA: EO/DIV 7/DOG)
A&D 1938-53 (junior mixed)

Dovedale Manor School, SE5. Opened 1874 as
Southampton Street School; renamed
Dovedale Manor School then (1931) Oliver
Goldsmith School, then (1938)
Southampton Way School and Dovedale
Manor School again, 1951.
(LMA: EO/DIV 7/DOV)
A&D 1951-58 (boys)

Downderry Road School,
Downham Estate, Bromley. Opened 1927.
(LMA: EO/DIV 7/DOD)
A&D 1927-35 (junior mixed and infants);
1935-38, 1948-74 (infants)
LB 1927-50, 1954-74 (infants)

Downham Central School,
Goudhurst Road, Bromley. Opened 1926;
renamed Woodlands School, 1950; closed
1960s. (LMA: EO/DIV 7/DOW)

Downham Central School [*continued*]
A&D 1926-39 (senior girls); 1927-41 (junior boys); 1929-39, 1945-63 (senior boys)
LB 1927-38 (senior mixed); 1927-38 (senior girls); 1945-64 (senior boys)
Misc punishment 1949-57, 1963-64

Downs Side School, Rendlesham Road, E5. Opened 1969.

Draycott Avenue School, SW3. see **Marlborough School**

Drayton Park School, Holloway Road, N5. Opened 1860 as Highbury Wesleyan School; taken over by LCC 1908. (LMA: EO/DIV 3/DRA)
A&D 1905-27 (boys); 1927-69 (junior mixed); 1927-43 (senior mixed); 1931-57 (infants); 1940-43 (mixed) (emergency)
LB 1893-1927 (boys); 1906-27 (infants); 1909-27 (girls)
Misc visitors 1906-23

Dreadnought ESN School,
Tunnel Avenue, SE10. Opened 1893 as Blackwall Lane School; renamed 1918; Riverway Secondary School, 1950; closed 1970s. (LMA: EO/DIV 6/DRE)
A&D 1918-39 (junior mixed); 1927-64 (infants)
LB 1891-1933 (infants); 1927-64 (junior mixed)
Misc punishment 1922-62

Droop Street School, W10. Opened 1877; renamed Queen's Park Primary School, 1951.

Duke Street School see **Alverton Street School**

Dulwich Central School, Peckham Rye, SE22. Opened 1896.

Dulwich Church of England Infants School,
Turney Road, Dulwich Village, SE21. Founded 1833; opened 1864. (LMA: P73/BAN)
Misc minute books 1948-68; staff 1951-70

Dulwich College, College Road, SE21. (Independent) (boys). Opened 1619.
Registers College Register 1619-1926 (T.L. Ormiston, 1927); Dulwich College War Record 1914-19 (anon, 1923); Dulwich College War Record 1939-45 (anon, 1949)

Dulwich College Preparatory School,
Alleyn Park, SE21.

Dulwich Hamlet School, SE21. Opened 1887.

Dulwich Road Methodist Sunday School, SE21.
Misc minute books 1912-38 (Southwark Local Studies Lib)

Duncombe Road School,
Hornsey Rise, N19. Opened 1878; renamed Duncombe Primary School and Archway County Secondary School, 1951. (LMA: EO/DIV 3/DUN)
A&D 1888-1905, 1917-39 (boys); 1888-1900, 1905-39 (infants); 1890-1938 (girls); 1913-38 (junior mixed); 1940 (mixed)
LB 1878-86, 1899-1936 (boys); 1881-1928 (girls); 1898-1913 (evening); 1907-13 (junior boys); 1913-27 (junior mixed); 1931-39 (infants)

Dunraven School, Adare Walk, Streatham, SW16. Opened 1934.

Dunts Hill School, Earlsfield, SW18. Opened 1904; renamed Wandle School, 1906. (LMA: EO/DIV 9/DUN)
A&D 1904-17 (mixed)

Durand Primary School, Hackford Road, SW9.

Durham Hill School, Downham Estate. Opened 1928; closed 1958. (LMA: EO/DIV 7/DUR)
A&D 1928-39 (senior boys); 1928-39 (senior girls); 1939-46 (mixed)
LB 1928-51 (senior boys); 1928-51 (senior girls); 1956-58 (mixed)

Ealdham Square School, Ealdham Square, Eltham Green, SE9. Opened 1929; renamed Ealdham School, 1951.

Eardley Road School, Blegborough Road, Streatham, SW16. Opened 1894. (LMA: EO/DIV 9/EAR)
A&D 1886-1910 (boys); 1886-1932 (girls); 1886-1939 (infants); 1932-39 (junior boys); 1932-39 (junior girls)

Earl Rise School, Earl Rise, SE18. fl.1971.

Earlsfield School, Burntwood Lane, SW18. Opened 1903. (LMA: EO/DIV 9/EAF)
A&D 1916-44 (boys); 1960-63 (junior girls)

Earl Street School, Brewery Road, SE18. Opened 1875; later Earl Rise School, later South Rise Infant School. (LMA: EO/DIV 6/EAR)

Earl Street School [*continued*]
A&D 1875-1939 (boys); 1908-31 (girls)
LB 1874-1941, 1972-82 (infants); 1875-1931
(girls); 1890-1913 (evening); 1904-30
(boys); 1931-39 (junior mixed)

East Lane School, Bermondsey, SE16.
Renamed Riverside Senior School, 1931.
(LMA: EO/DIV 7/EAS)
LB 1913-14, 1921-28 (girls)
Misc diary 1905-18; roll of honour 1914-18
(Southwark Local Studies Lib)

Eastway School see **Gainsborough Road School**

Ebley House School, Manfred Road, SW15.

Ebury Secondary School, SW1. Westminster
Senior Technical School until 1951; closed
1970 amalgamated with Buckingham Gate
and Sloane Schools to form Pimlico
Comprehensive. (LMA: EO/DIV 2/EBU)
A&D 1961-70 (boys)
LB 1946-70 (boys)
Misc punishment 1969

Ecclesbourne Road School, New North
Road, N1. Opened 1886; renamed
Ecclesbourne Primary School, 1951.
(LMA: EO/DIV 3/ECC)
A&D 1938-54 (infants); 1940 (girls)
LB 1913-34 (evening)

Eden Road Methodist School, Chapel Road,
West Norwood, SE27. Opened 1893;
renamed John Wesley School; closed 1960.
Misc minute books 1945-49
(Lambeth Archives)

Edith Cavell School, Enfield Road, N1. Opened
as Enfield Road School, 1894; renamed
Kingsland Secondary School, 1951 and
Edith Cavell, 1963; closed 1992.
Misc punishment 1974-80 (Hackney Archives)

Edith Neville School see
Aldenham Street School

Edmund Halley School, Shoreditch, N1.
Opened 1877 as Canal Road School;
renamed 1936.

Edmund Waller Primary School see
Waller Road School

Edward Seguin School, Prah Road, N4. Opened
1963; renamed Jack Ashley School, 1975.

Edward Street School, SE8. Opened *c*1888;
closed 1930s. (LMA: EO/DIV 6/EDW)
A&D 1888-93 (boys); 1894-1920 (mixed)
LB 1889-93 (mixed); 1889-93 (infants)

Edward Wilson Primary School, Senior Street,
Harrow Road, W2. Opened as Senior Street
School 1915; renamed 1951.

Effra Parade School, Barnwell Road, Brixton,
SW2. Opened 1879; renamed Effra School,
1937. (LMA: EO/DIV 8/EFF)
A&D 1911-37, 1942-48 (boys); 1923-62
(infants); 1938-48 (junior mixed)
LB 1879-1939, 1943-49 (infants);
1903-13 (girls)
Misc punishment 1947-54

Eglington Road School, Herbert Road, SE18.
Opened 1886; renamed Eglington School,
1951. (LMA: EO/DIV 6/EGL)
A&D 1935-39 (junior mixed)
LB 1901-35 (boys); 1913-35 (girls);
1915-37 (evening)
Misc visitors 1886-1933

Eldon School, Wandsworth Road, SW8.
Opened 1829; closed 1891.

Eleanor Palmer School, Raveley Street, NW5.
fl.1971.

Eleanor Road School, Richmond Road,
Mare Street, E8. Opened 1898; closed by
1947. (LMA: EO/DIV 4/ELE)
A&D 1898-1931 (girls); 1899-1916 (infants)
LB 1898-1931 (girls)

Elementary School of the Assumption,
South End, W8.

Elfrida Primary School, Elfrida Crescent, SE6.
Opened 1924. (LMA: EO/DIV 6/ELF)
A&D 1925-39 (boys); 1934-39 (infants)
LB 1924-34 (boys); 1925-38 (infants)

Eliot Bank School, Thorpewood Avenue, SE26.
fl.1971.

Elizabethan Free School, Daisy Lane,
Broomhouse Lane, SW6. (special
tubercular school) founded 1855; taken
over by LCC 1904; renamed 1921; closed
1959. (LMA: EO/DIV 1/ELF)
A&D 1921-43 (mixed); 1951, 1959
(class registers)
LB 1921-37 (mixed); 1937-58 (open air)
Misc punishment 1944-45; staff 1953-59

Elizabeth Burgwin School,
Cambridge Grove, W6. Opened 1950;
previously in premises at Brackenbury
School; moved to Cambridge Grove 1965.
(LMA: EO/DIV 1/ELI)
A&D 1961-65 (class registers)

Elizabeth Garrett Anderson School, NW1.
(LMA: ACC/3774)
Misc minute books 1983-89

Elizabeth Newcomen School, Southwark.
Founded 1674; united to St Saviour
Southwark School early 19th century.
(LMA: A/NWC)
A&D 1835-57
Misc minute books 1706-1934

Elizabeth Street School, High Street, North
Woolwich, E16. Opened 1891 as Dock
Street School; renamed 1894; renamed
North Woolwich School, 1951.
(LMA: EO/DIV 6/ELI)
A&D 1891-1934 (boys); 1891-1912 (girls);
1891-1913, 1935-39 (mixed); 1934-39
(infants)
LB 1891-1913 (boys); 1891-1932 (girls);
1915-24, 1934-36 (evening); 1935-39,
1945-62 (mixed); 1945-62 (infants);
1946-61 (nursery)

Ellerslie Road School, Ellerslie Road, W12.
Opened 1894; renamed Ellerslie School,
1937; closed 1998.
A&D 1894-1991 (infants); 1894-1939 (girls);
1894-1939 (boys); 1941-85 (junior mixed)
(Hammersmith and Fulham Archives)
LB 1932-39 (infants) (Hammersmith and
Fulham Archives)

Elliott Central School, Merton Road, Putney,
SW18. Opened 1905 as Southfields School;
became Central School 1911.
LB 1913-25 (LMA: ACC/1886)

Elm Court School, SE27. (blind girls).
Opened 1902.

Elmfield School, Tooting, SW12. Opened 1915
as Ravenstone School; renamed Balham
High Road School 1926; Elmfield 1951.
A&D 1947-60 (LMA: EO/DIV 9/ELM)

Elm Wood Primary School, Carnac Street,
SE27.

Eltham Church of England School,
Roper Street, SE9. Founded 1813; opened
1851.

Eltham Central School Opened 1928;
renamed Briset Secondary School, 1951.
(LMA: EO/DIV 6/BRI)
LB 1946-58 (senior mixed)

Eltham College (The Royal Naval School),
SE9. (Independent) (boys). Opened 1842.

Eltham Green Comprehensive School,
Queenscroft Road, SE9. fl.1971.

Eltham Hill School, Eltham Hill, SE9. Opened
1906; Eltham Central School for Girls,
1928; renamed Briset Secondary School,
1951. (LMA: EO/DIV 6/ELT)
A&D 1906-50 (girls)

Elthorne Road School, N19. (special). Opened
1913. (LMA: EO/DIV 3/ELT)
A&D 1913-33 (mixed)

Eltringham Street School, York Road, SW18.
Opened 1886; renamed Eltringham School,
1951. (LMA: EO/DIV 9/ELT and
ILEA/DO10/02)
A&D 1891-1916, 1940 (girls); 1919-39,
1946-50 (boys); 1923-37, 1945-53
(infants); 1928-33 (mixed); 1937-85
(infants and junior)
LB 1913-29 (boys)

Elwell's Academy, Hammersmith
Misc List of pupils (*Genealogists' Magazine*
vol.14 pp.217-21 and letters pp.269-70,
304-05)

Emanuel School, Battersea Rise, Wandsworth
Common, SW11. (Independent) (boys).
Opened 1594 in Westminster, moved to
Wandsworth 1883.
see The History of Emanuel School
(C.W. Scott-Giles, 1937, 2nd ed. 1977)

Emmanuel School, Lyncroft Gardens,
Mill Lane, West Hampstead, NW6.
Opened 1846. (LMA: P81/EMM)
LB 1872-1913
Misc minute books 1894-1981

Emmanuel School, Northwick
Terrace, St John's Wood, NW8.
(LMA: EO/DIV 2/EMM and P89/EMM)

Emmanuel School [*continued*]
A&D 1884-1931 (girls); 1892-1937
(junior girls); 1892-1937 (boys)
LB 1862-1931 (girls); 1893-1907 (boys);
1903-37 (infants); Sunday School 1857-67
Misc minute books 1883-90

Enfield Road School, Kingsland Road, N1.
Opened 1894; part of Kingsland Secondary
School, 1951; renamed Edith Cavell
School, 1963; closed 1992.
(LMA: EO/DIV 4/ENF)
A&D 1894-1906 (boys); 1920-28 (mixed);
1935-39 (infants)
LB 1897-1913, 1934-40 (infants); 1899-1913,
1920-34 (junior mixed); 1909-13 (evening);
1912-16 (mixed); 1913-39 (boys)
Misc punishment 1900-15

English Martyrs Roman Catholic School,
Northampton Place, SE17. Opened 1903.
(LMA: EO/DIV 8/ENG)
A&D 1940-45 (boys); 1946-65 (girls)
LB 1913-39 (boys)

English Martyrs Roman Catholic School,
St Mark Street, E1. fl.1971.

Ennersdale School, The, Leahurst Road,
Lewisham, SE13. Opened 1898.
(LMA: EO/DIV 7/ENN)
A&D 1913-39 (girls); 1915-46 (infants)
LB 1895-1912 (mixed); 1899-1913 (boys);
1912-39 (girls)

Ensham Central School, Franciscan
Road, Tooting, SW17. Opened 1904.
(LMA: EO/DIV 9/ENS)
A&D 1900-32 (infants); 1900-38 (mixed);
1904-26 (girls)
LB 1900-13, 1932-50 (infants)

Erconwald Street School, Erconwald Street,
W12. Opened 1922, renamed Old Oak
School, 1932.

Essendine Road School, Paddington, W9.
Opened 1900; Essendine County Secondary
School closed 1962. (LMA:
EO/DIV 2/ESS)
LB 1901-13 (invalid); 1913-38
(physically defective)
see also Franklin Delano Roosevent School

Essex Street School, Globe Road, E2. Opened
1873; renamed John Scurr School, Wessex
Street, E2, 1938. (LMA: EO/DIV 5/ESS)

Essex Street School [*continued*]
A&D 1872-1920 (boys); 1880-1917 (girls);
1901-39 (infants); 1912-29, 1933-39 (junior
mixed)
LB 1921-28 (evening)

Estreham School, Streatham, SW16. Opened
1908 as Mitcham Lane School; renamed
1951. (LMA: EO/DIV 9/EST)
A&D 1954-60 (boys); 1954-60 (girls)

Ethelburga Street School, Battersea
Bridge Road, SW11. Opened 1896.
(LMA: EO/DIV 9/ETH)
A&D 1922-39 (infants)
LB 1936-39 (boys); 1936-39 (infants)
Misc memoir 1914-20 (LMA: ACC/4017)

Eveline Lowe School, Marlborough Grove,
SE1. fl.1971.

Everington Street School, SW6. Opened 1882;
renamed Everington Primary and
Secondary School, 1951; amalgamated with
Queens Court School to form Gilliatt
School, 1961. (LMA: EO/DIV 1/EVE)
A&D 1882-1930 (boys); 1906-39 (girls);
1919-59 (infants); 1940-61 (senior girls);
1940-58 (junior mixed)
LB 1882-1931 (boys); 1882-1939 (girls);
1930-39, 1947-59 (infants); 1945-61
(senior girls)

Exmouth Street School, Starcross Street, NW1.
Opened 1916. renamed Starcross School,
1937; including Medburn Emergency
School 1940. (LMA: EO/DIV 2/EXM and
ACC/3774/1-3)
A&D 1916-29 (girls); 1929-40 (senior boys)
LB 1928-29 (boys); 1929-38 (senior boys);
1931-62 (senior girls); 1975-84

Fairclough Street School, Back Church Lane,
Commercial Road, E1. Opened 1910;
renamed Harry Gosling Primary School,
1951. (LMA: EO/DIV 5/FAC)
A&D 1910-30 (boys); 1910-30 (girls); 1910-39
(infants); 1920-30 (mixed)
LB 1913-30 (girls); 1915-30 (boys)

Fairfield Road School, Bow Road, E3. Opened
1876; renamed Bow Secondary Boys
School, 1951.
A&D 1879-1929 (girls); 1929-46 (senior girls);
1930-46 (infants); 1940-46 (junior mixed
and infants) (LMA: EO/DIV 5/FAI)

Fairfield Road School [*continued*]
LB 1876-1935 (girls) (Tower Hamlets Lib);
1913-35 (boys); 1932-39 (infants); 1936-39
(senior mixed) (LMA: EO/DIV 5/FAI)

Fairlawn School, Honor Oak Road, SE23.
fl.1971.

Fair Street School, Horsleydown, SE1. Opened
1876; formerly Charles Street School;
renamed Tower Bridge Junior School,
1935. (LMA: EO/DIV 8/FAI)
A&D 1891-98 (infants); 1896-1934 (boys)
LB 1913-34 (boys)

Falconbrook School, SW11. Opened 1876 as
Mantua Street School; renamed 1951.
(LMA: EO/DIV 9/FAL)
A&D 1943-55 (junior mixed); 1945-64 (junior
girls); 1955-62 (junior boys)

Falkland Road Wesleyan School, St Pancras,
NW5. fl.1906.

Falkner House, Brechin Place, SW7.
Opened 1954.

Farncombe Street School, SE16. see
Riverside School

Faroe Road School, Faroe Road, W14
(physically disabled). Opened 1906; closed
1933.

Farrance Street School,
Burdett Road, E14. Opened 1882; renamed
Farrance Primary School and Sir
Humphrey Gilbert Secondary School, 1951.
(LMA: EO/DIV 5/FAR)
A&D 1931-39 (senior girls)
LB 1913-39 (infants); 1926-39 (boys);
1938-39 (girls)

Farringdon Within Ward Schools, City.
Misc administrative records 1756-1884
(Guildhall Library)

Faunce Street School,
Harmsworth Street, SE17. Opened 1891;
renamed Keyworth Primary School, 1951.
(LMA: EO/DIV 8/FAU)
LB 1891-1903 (girls); 1891-1903, 1910-39
(infants); 1933-39 (junior girls); 1941-45
(junior mixed)

Fellows Street School, Haggerston, N1.
(LMA: EO/DIV 4/FEL and N/M/22/1)
LB 1863-86; 1890-1908 (mixed)

Fenstanton School, Abbot's Park, Tulse Hill,
SW2.

Fieldgate Street School, E1. (temporary)
Opened   1913;   closed   1916
(LMA: EO/DIV 5/FIE)
A&D 1913-16 (infants)

Field Lane Foundation, Vine Street,
Clerkenwell, EC1. Opened 1841.
Misc (LMA: B98/98)

Field Road School, Field Road, W6.
Temporary School 1876-77.

Finch Street Special School, Stepney, E1.
Opened   1906;   closed   1909.
(LMA: EO/DIV 5/LUP)
A&D 1906-09

Finlay Street Reformatory School, Fulham,
SW6. (LMA: LCC/EO/SS/7)
A&D 1916-19

Finlay Street School,
Fulham Palace Road, SW6. Opened 1908;
renamed Finlay Primary School, 1951;
closed 1957. (LMA: EO/DIV 1/FIN)
A&D 1908-39 (infants)
LB 1908-53 (infants); 1908-42 (junior mixed);
1942-53 (mixed)
Misc 1908-57 (mixed)

Finsbury Park College, Green Lanes,
Stoke Newington (Independent) (boys).
Opened 1880.

Finsbury Park Junior School, N4. Opened
1898; Ambler Road 1933-51; renamed
Ambler   Primary   School   1951.
(LMA: EO/DIV 3/FIN 1)
A&D 1917-39, 1941-57 (infants); 1932-51
(junior girls)

Finsbury Park Secondary School, Blackstock
Road, N4. Opened 1888 as Ambler Road
School; renamed 1933; closed c1964.
(LMA: EO/DIV 3/FIN 2)
A&D 1942-64 (mixed)
LB 1914-32 (girls); 1921-55 (infants); 1932-35
(senior girls); 1932-39 (boys); 1932-54
(senior boys); 1941-42 (emergency);
1954-64 (mixed)
Misc punishment 1940-64

Finsbury Technical College, EC2.
Opened 1883.
A&D 1892-1926 (Guildhall Library)

Finton House School, Trinity Road, SW17. Opened 1987.

Fircroft Road School,
Glenburnie Road, Tooting, SW17. Opened 1896; renamed Fircroft School, 1951. (LMA: EO/DIV 9/FIR)
A&D 1894-1916 (infants); 1894-1933 (mixed)
LB 1894-96 (boys); 1896-1964 (mixed); 1896-1913 (girls); 1896-1935 (infants); 1898-1948 (evening); 1941-43 (emergency)

Fitzjohn's Primary School, Fitzjohn's Avenue, NW3. Opened 1954.

Fleet Central School, St Pancras. Opened 1901.

Fleet Road School, Hampstead, NW3. Opened 1879; later Fleet School.

Fleetwood School, Stoke Newington High Street, N16. Formerly Stoke Newington School; renamed 1951; closed by 1978.

Flint Street School, East Street, Walworth, SE17. Opened 1875. (LMA: EO/DIV 8/FLI)
A&D 1873-1939 (boys); 1886-1912, 1920-39 (infants); 1898-1909, 1913-39 (girls)
LB 1873-1915 (boys); 1875-1933 (infants); 1905-13, 1923-38 (girls); 1936-39 (junior boys)

Flora Gardens School, Ravenscourt Park, W6. Opened 1887; destroyed 1944, rebuilt 1950. (LMA: EO/DIV 1/FLO)
LB 1913-39 (girls); 1931-39 (infants)

Florence Gladstone Secondary School *see* Wornington Road School

Fordway School, Monier Road, E3. fl.1971.

Forest Gate School District. Constituted by Hackney Board of Guardians 1868-77; Poplar and Whitechapel Boards of Guardians 1868-97 (LMA: FGSD)
A&D 1854-1900
Misc minute books 1854-1907; staff 1868-97

Forest Hill Central School, Brockley Rise, SE23. Opened 1928; later Forest Hill School. (LMA: EO/DIV 7/FOR)
A&D 1946-55 (boys)
LB 1928-34 (girls)

Forest Hill House School (Independent) (boys). Opened 1886.

Forster Park School, Boundfield Road, SE6. fl.1971.

The Forster School, Hornsey Road, N17. started as Ragged School; became Holloway Free and Ragged School 1866-72; Hornsey Road School 1872-89; renamed The Forster School, 1889; William Forster School, c1955; closed 1961. (LMA: EO/DIV 3/FOR)
A&D 1933-39 (junior mixed)
LB 1929-33 (boys); 1949-61 (junior mixed and infants)

Fossdene Secondary School, Victoria Road, SE7. Opened 1896; previously Fossdene Road School. (LMA: EO/DIV 6/FOS)
A&D 1944-64 (senior boys)
LB 1932-64 (senior boys)
Misc punishment 1949-64

Foundation School, Whitechapel (Independent) (boys). Opened 1854. see **Davenant**

Foundling Hospital, Guilford Street, WC1. Also known as Coram's Hospital. Opened 1738; closed 1954. (LMA: A/FH)
Misc minute books 1739-1952

Fountain Road School, Garratt Lane, Wandsworth, SW18. Opened 1908; renamed Defoe School, 1928; Graveney Secondary School, 1951; closed 1959. (LMA: EO/DIV 9/FOU)
A&D 1905-36 (infants); 1905-23 (mixed); 1908-32 (girls)
LB 1905-29 (infants); 1905-13 (mixed); 1913-32 (boys)
Misc punishment 1906-47

Fountain Street School,
Wandsworth Road, Lambeth, SW8. Opened 1882; later Springfield School. (LMA: EO/DIV 8/FOU)
LB 1882-98 (girls); 1882-1902 (infants)

Fountayne School, Cazenove Road, N16. fl.1971.

Fox Hill School, Plumstead Common Road, SE18. Opened 1902.

Fox School, The, Edge Street, Church Street, Notting Hill Gate, W8. Opened 1880. (LMA: EO/DIV 1/FOX)
A&D 1876-1911 (boys); 1880-1911 (girls); 1880-98, 1911-39 (mixed); 1899-1932 (infants)

Fox School, The [*continued*]
LB 1880-1911 (girls); 1880-1951. (infants);
1882-1910 (boys); 1912-39 (mixed)

Franciscan Road School, Tooting, SW17.
Opened 1908; renamed Franciscan Primary
School, 1951; later Cotswold School.
(LMA: EO/DIV 9/FRA)
A&D 1907-23, 1937-39 (girls); 1907-31
(mixed); 1931-39 (boys)

Francis Holland School, Graham Terrace, SW1.
Opened 1881.

Francis Holland School, Clarence Gate, NW1.
Opened 1878.

Frank Barnes School, Central Street, EC1.
(deaf).

Frank Briant School, Kennington. Opened
1887.

Frankham Street School, Deptford High Street,
SE8. Opened 1876; was Regent Street
School; renamed Tidemill Primary School,
1951. (LMA: EO/DIV 6/FRA)
A&D 1876-1938 (girls); 1888-1938 (boys);
1893-1924 (junior mixed); 1922-39
(infants); 1938-39 (junior girls); 1938-39,
1945-57 (mixed)
LB 1885-1924 (junior mixed); 1892-1937
(girls); 1911-30 (boys); 1913-31 (infants);
1939-45 (mixed)

Franklin Delano Roosevelt School, Essendine
Road, W9. Opened 1901 as Essendine
Road School (Physically handicapped);
renamed 1950; moved to Avenue Road,
Hampstead, NW8, 1957.

Friar Street School, Blackfriars Road, SE1.
Opened 1885; renamed Pocock School,
1951. (LMA: EO/DIV 8/FRI)
A&D 1885-89, 1929-39 (infants) (1890-1913
under Pocock Street School; 1916-35
(girls); 1931-38 (boys)
LB 1913-37 (girls); 1930-47
(womens' evening institute)

Friern School, The, Peckham Rye, SE22.
Opened 1896; merged with Adys Road
School, 1947; merged with Honor Oak
School, 1978 to form Waverly School.
(LMA: EO/DIV 7/FRI)

Friern School, The [*continued*]
A&D 1905-19, 1933-50 (infants); 1906-24
(boys); 1911-30, 1942-45 (girls)
LB 1913-30 (boys); 1913-30, 1940-45 (girls);
1930-58 (infants); 1930-39 (junior mixed)

**Froebel Educational Institute Preparatory
School**, Colet Gardens, W14.

Frogmore School, Putney Bridge Road, SW18.
(LMA: EO/DIV 9/FRO)
A&D 1895-1909 (infants)

Frognal School, Fitzjohn's Avenue, NW3.
Opened before 1919; closed 1938.

Fulham Board of Guardians see
West London School District

Fulham Central School, Childerley Street,
SW6. Composed of Childerley Street
School, Finlay Street School and
Sherbrooke Road Central School; named
1921; Finlay Street part renamed Bishop's
Park Secondary School and Childerley
Street part renamed Henry Compton
Secondary School 1951.
(LMA: EO/DIV 1/FCE)
LB 1913-39 (boys)

Fulham County Secondary School,
Munster Road, SW6. Opened 1905; Star
Road School which opened 1880, renamed
Queens Court School; Queens Court
School, Bishops Park School and
Everington School amalgamated to become
Gilliat School 1954/5; 1973 Fulham County
and Gilliat School amalgamated to form
Fulham Gilliat School.
(LMA: EO/DIV 1/FCS)
A&D 1942-65 (girls, Fulham County); 1950-61
(girls, Star Road School and Queens Court
School); 1961-66 (girls, Gilliat School)

Fulham Day Sanatorium, New Kings Road,
SW6 (Tubercular). Opened 1917, closed
1921 and merged with Elizabethan Free
School.

Fulham Palace Road School, W6. Opened
1896; reorganised 1902 into separate
departments which merged again in 1932;
renamed Melcombe Primary School, 1951.
(LMA: EO/DIV 1/FRP)

Fulham Palace Road School [*continued*]
A&D 1896-1942 (infants); 1910-21 (senior boys); 1913-30 (girls); 1915-31 (boys)
LB 1896-1946 (infants); 1896-1902 (mixed); 1902-32 (boys); 1902-34 (girls); 1902-39 (manual training centre); 1927-39 (evening); 1932-37 (junior mixed)

Fulham Primary School. Formerly Halford School and Harwood School, which merged 1992.

Furrow Lane School, Homerton, E9.

Furzedown College, Welham Road, SW17.

Furzedown School, Welham Road, Mitcham, SW17. Opened 1928. (LMA: EO/DIV 9/MIT)
A&D 1913-39 (junior mixed and infants)
LB 1913-19, 1923-39 (mixed); 1913-19, 1923-39 (infants)

Gainsborough Road School, Eastway, Hackney Wick, E9. Opened 1875; renamed Gainsborough School, 1937; moved to Berkshire Road, c1964. (LMA: EO/DIV 4/GAI)
A&D 1899-1939 (boys); 1905-39 (girls); 1929-40 (infants)
LB 1875-1939 (girls); 1898-1940 (evening); 1933-40 (infants)

Gainsford School *see* Lucas Street School

Galley Wall Road School, Rotherhithe New Road, SE16. Opened 1876; renamed Galley Wall Primary School, 1951. (LMA: EO/DIV 8/GAL)
A&D 1876-1930 (infants)
LB 1876-1934 (infants)

Gallions Mount School, Plumstead High Street, SE18. Opened 1888 as Purrett Road School; renamed 1951. (LMA: EO/DIV 6/GAL)
A&D 1944-56 (infants)

Garden House School, Sloane Gardens, SW1. Opened 1951.

Garden Street School, Stepney, E1. (temporary) Opened 1910; closed 1915. (LMA: EO/DIV 5/GDN)
A&D 1910-15 (mixed)

Garford Street School, E14. closed 1886; pupils transferred to Gill Street School. (LMA: EO/DIV 5/GAR)
LB 1885-86 (mixed)

Garratt Green School, Burntwood Lane, SW17. fl.1971.

Garratt Lane School, near Swaffield Road, Wandsworth, SW18. Opened 1876; renamed Gertrude Sanson Primary School, 1951. (LMA: EO/DIV 9/GAR)
A&D 1876-1937 (boys); 1887-1939, 1942-56 (infants); 1902-22 (mixed); 1907-39 (girls)
LB 1867-1939, 1942-44 (infants); 1876-1949 (boys); 1876-1939 (girls); 1893-1925 (evening)
Misc visitors 1923-45; punishment 1945-50

Gateforth Street School, Church Street, St Marylebone, NW8. Opened 1876 as Capland Street School; renamed 1917; Gateforth Primary School, 1951; Gateway School, 1963. (LMA: EO/DIV 2/GAF)
A&D 1928-53 (junior mixed and infants); 1952-63 (infants); 1953-56 (class registers)
LB 1915-22 (infants); 1928-63 (junior mixed)
Misc punishment 1929-50

Gateway School, Church Street, NW8. Opened 1876 as Capland Street School; renamed Gateforth Street School, 1917; Gateforth Primary School, 1951; renamed Gateway School, 1963. (LMA: EO/DIV 2/GAT)
A&D 1963-70 (junior mixed); 1963-70 (infants)
LB 1963-80 (infants); 1963-80 (junior mixed)

Gayhurst Road School, London Fields, E8. Opened 1894; renamed Gayhurst Primary School, 1951. (LMA: EO/DIV 4/GAY)
A&D 1894-1931 (boys); 1894-1931 (girls); 1894-1939, 1942-63 (infants)
LB 1894-1931 (boys); 1894-1926 (girls); 1894-1973 (infants); 1931-39 (senior girls)
Misc visitors 1894-1939; punishment 1949-65

Geere House Open Air School, Mile End. Opened 1927. (LMA: EO/DIV 5/GEE)
A&D 1927-39, 1943-64 (mixed)
LB 1927-30, 1943-64 (mixed)
Misc punishment 1944-47

Geffrye School, Sarah Street, N1. fl.1971.

George Eliot School, Marlborough Hill, NW8. fl.1971.

George Green School, East India Rock Road, E14. Opened 1828; council 1883.
A&D 1884-1909 (boys); 1884-1910 (girls) (LMA: EO/DIV 5/GEO); 1898-1919, 1932-46 (girls); 1902-24, 1932-46 (boys); 1946-76 (mixed) (Tower Hamlets Library)
Misc staff 1908-28; testimonials 1886-1901
see A History of George Green's School 1828-1978 (E. Arnold, 1979)

George Lansbury School, Atley Road, E3. fl.1971.

George Orwell School, Turle Road, N4. Opened 1981.

George Street School, Camberwell Road, SE5. Opened 1878; reorganised to form Lomond Grove and Southampton Street Schools, 1931. (LMA: EO/DIV 7/GEO)
A&D 1901-16 (boys); 1906-31 (girls); 1906-16 (infants)

George Yard School, Whitechapel, E1. Opened 1898; closed 1906. (LMA: EO/DIV 5/GEY)
A&D 1887-1906 (infants); 1903-06 (mixed)

Gertrude Sanson Primary School, SW18. Opened Garratt Lane School, 1876; renamed 1951.

Gideon Road School, Battersea, SW11. renamed Gideon School, 1951. (LMA: EO/DIV 9/GID)
A&D 1888-1927, 1937-39 (senior boys); 1898-1931 (infants); 1906-27, 1942-56 (girls); 1931-35 (junior boys)

Gifford Street School, Caledonian Road, N1. Opened 1877; renamed Gifford School, 1951; closed 1960. (LMA: EO/DIV 3/GIF)
A&D 1886-1939, 1945-55 (girls); 1931-39, 1945-55 (boys); 1940-47, 1955-60 (mixed)
LB 1894-1939 (girls); 1930-39 (boys); 1940-60 (mixed)
Misc punishment 1956-60

Gillespie Road School, Blackstock Road, Highbury, N5. Opened 1879; renamed Gillespie Primary School, 1951. (LMA: EO/DIV 3/GIL)
A&D 1929-39 (infants)

Gilliatt School, Finlay Street, SW6. Consists of former Everington, Bishop's Park and Queen's Court Schools. Opened 1961.

Gill Street School, West India Dock Road, E14. Opened 1887. (LMA: EO/DIV 5/GIL)
A&D 1906-38 (boys); 1923-47 (infants); 1932-39 (senior girls)
LB 1929-39 (boys); 1929-35 (infants)

Gipsy Road School, West Norwood, SE27. Opened 1875; renamed Gipsy Hill Primary School, 1951. (LMA: EO/DIV 8/GIP)
A&D 1901-49 (boys); 1906-29 (infants); 1915-39, 1941-49 (girls); 1929-44 (junior mixed); 1937-48 (senior mixed)
LB 1868-1947 (girls); 1906-48 (mixed); 1927-33 (junior mixed); 1929-46 (boys)
Misc visitors 1909-22; punishment 1928-58 (boys)

Glenbrook School, Clarence Avenue, SW4. fl.1971.

Glendower Preparatory School, Queen's Gate, SW7. Opened 1895.

Glengall Road School, Manchester Road, Cubitt Town, E14. Opened 1876; renamed Glengall School, 1938. (LMA: EO/DIV 5/GLE 1)
A&D 1889-1922 (boys); 1902-39 (girls); 1922-39 (infants); 1939-68 (mixed); 1946 (senior girls)
LB 1876-1913 (boys); 1899-1939 (infants)
Misc visitors 1922-35

Glengall Secondary School, E14. (LMA: EO/DIV 5/GRE 2)
LB 1940-64 (mixed)

Glengyle School, Carlton Drive, SW15.

Glenister Road School, Blackwall Lane, SE10. Opened 1881 or 1888; renamed Glenister School, 1951; Vanburgh Primary School, 1960. (LMA: EO/DIV 6/GLE)
A&D 1903-29 (girls); 1938-39 (senior boys); 1939-46, 1948-57 (mixed); 1942-61 (boys)
LB 1910-28 (girls); 1936-39 (infants); 1942-61 (secondary boys)
Misc punishment 1952-61

Globe Terrace School, Bethnal Green, E2. Opened 1874; later Globe Road School; renamed Pilgrim School, 1951. (LMA: EO/DIV 5/GLO)
A&D 1874-1939 (infants); 1903-39 (boys); 1930-39 (junior boys)
LB 1874-1913 (boys); 1874-1930 (girls); 1874-1928 (infants); 1890-1913 (evening)

Gloucester Grove School, Clareville Street, SW7. Opened 1881; later Brecknock School. (LMA: EO/DIV 1/GLO)
LB 1913 (infants)

Gloucester Road School, Camberwell. Opened 1875; renamed Gloucester School, 1938. (LMA: EO/DIV 7/GLO)
A&D 1875-1931 (girls); 1900-30 (senior mixed)

Glyn Road School, Homerton High Street, E9. Opened 1892; renamed Glyn Secondary School and Elizabeth Carr Primary School, 1951.
A&D 1891-1955 (infants); 1931-38 (senior boys) (LMA: EO/DIV 4/GLY); 1892-1947 (girls); 1940-43 (emergency mixed) (Hackney Archives)
LB 1892-1955 (girls) (Hackney Archives); 1931-38 (senior mixed) (LMA: EO/DIV 4/GLY)

Goburne House Industrial School, Watford, Herts. (LMA: LCC/CH/D/GIS)
A&D 1912-56
LB 1912-59

Godolphin and Latymer Girls' School, Iffley Road, W6. Opened 1905.

Godolphin Boys' School, Iffley Road, W6. Opened 1856 in Great Church Lane, moved 1961, closed 1900.

Godolphin School, Hammersmith (Independent) (girls). Opened 1726.
see Godolphin School 1726-1926 (M.A. Douglas and G.R. Ash, 1927)

Goldie Leigh Hospital School, Abbey Wood, SE2; closed 1970s. (LMA: EO/DIV 6/GOL)
A&D 1950-75 (mixed)
LB 1924-75 (mixed)
Misc punishment 1934-60

Goodrich Road School, Lordship Lane, SE22. Opened 1886 (partially sighted opened 1928); renamed Goodrich Primary School and Thomas Carlton Secondary School, 1951. (LMA: EO/DIV 7/GOO)
A&D 1886-96, 1912-30 (boys); 1886-1908, 1928-30 (girls); 1900-28 (mixed)
LB 1886-1913 (boys); 1886-1913 (girls); 1886-98 (evening); 1900-13 (mixed)

Good Shepherd Roman Catholic School, Moorside Road, Bromley. fl.1955

Good Shepherd Roman Catholic School, Stepney Square, E1. Opened 1903.
A&D 1933-39 (Tower Hamlets Library)

Gopsall Street School, Haggerston, N1. Opened 1897; renamed The Whitmore School, 1931. (LMA: EO/DIV 4/GOP)
A&D 1904-30 (infants); 1911-38 (girls)
LB 1890-1930 (evening); 1897-1913 (girls); 1897-1913 (infants)

Gordonbrook Road School, Brockley, SE4. Opened 1905; renamed Gordonbrook Street, 1914; Gordonbrook School, 1951. (LMA: EO/DIV 7/GOR)
A&D 1902-34 (infants); 1902-14 (mixed); 1905-35 (girls); 1914-35 (boys)
LB 1902-52 (infants)
Misc visitors 1902-50; punishment 1904-39

Gordon School, Grange Hill Road, SE9. Opened 1904; Grange Hill Road School until 1904; previously Roper Street School. (LMA: EO/DIV 6/GOR)
A&D 1943-59 (boys); 1943-59 (girls); 1959-67 (mixed)
LB 1902-13 (infants); 1902-13, 1933-39, 1943-44 (boys); 1904-13 (girls); 1955-56 (mixed)

Gospel Oak School *see* **Mansfield Road School**

Grafton Road School, Seven Sisters Road, N7. Opened 1879 in Bowmas Place; Grafton Road School 1893-1938; renamed Grafton School, 1938; later Carlton School. (LMA: EO/DIV 3/GRA)
A&D 1879-1935 (boys); 1891-1939 (infants); 1916-36 (girls)
LB 1879-1936 (boys); 1913-35 (girls); 1913-35 (infants)

Granard School, Granard Avenue, SW15. fl.1971.

Grange Hill Road School see **Gordon School**

Granton Road School, Streatham Vale, SW16. Opened 1928.

Granville Sharp School, Fulham High Street, SW6. ESN School opened 1971.

Grasmere Primary School, Albion Road, N16. Opened 1965.

LONDON SCHOOL RECORDS

Gravel Lane School, Houndsditch, E1.
Opened 1885; closed 1931.
(LMA: EO/DIV 5/GRA)
A&D 1896-1931 (infants)

Graveney Secondary School, Gatton Road,
Tooting, SW17. Opened as Fountain Road
School, 1908; renamed Defoe School,
1928; renamed 1951; closed 1959.
(LMA: EO/DIV 9/GRA)
A&D 1945-59 (boys); 1951-58 (mixed)
LB 1953-57 (mixed)

Grays Yard School, W1.
(LMA: EO/DIV 2/GRA)
LB 1873-92 (boys)

Grazebrook Primary School, Lordship Road,
N16. Opened 1970.

Great College Street School, Kentish Town
Road, NW1. Opened 1874; renamed
Robert Louis Stevenson Primary School
and Cantlow Secondary School, 1951.
(LMA: EO/DIV 2/GRE)
A&D 1876-1931 (girls); 1889-1927 (boys);
1897-1931 (infants); 1927-52 (senior
mixed)
LB 1874-1930 (boys); 1874-1924 (infants);
1890-1938 (girls); 1931-38 (senior boys);
1938-57 (senior mixed)
Misc visitors 1889-1939

Greenacres School, Witherston Way, SE9.
fl.1971.

Green Coat Church of England School,
Camberwell Green, SE5. Opened 1872.

Greencoat Hospital School, Westminster
Misc 1641-1873 (Westminster Archives)

Greening Road School, SE2.
Opened c1902. (LMA: EO/DIV 6/GRE)
A&D 1902-03 (infants); 1902-03 (mixed)
LB 1902-03 (infants); 1902-03 (mixed);
1903-30 (manual training centre)

Greenmead Primary School, Littleton Street,
SW18. Formerly Littleton Street School.

Green School, Canon Beck Road,
Brunel Road, Rotherhithe, SE16. Opened
1844 as Clarence Street School; renamed
1929. (LMA: EO/DIV 7/GRE)
LB 1931-39 (junior mixed and infants)

Greenwich Board of Guardians see
South Metropolitan School District

Greenwich Central School, Catherine Grove,
SE10. Opened 1904 as Greenwich School;
renamed 1911; renamed Greenwich Park
Secondary School, 1940s; closed 1980s
(boys). (LMA: EO/DIV 6/GRE 1)
A&D 1919-39 (boys)
LB 1913-26, 1931-38 (boys)

Greenwich Park Central School, King George
Street, SE10. Opened 1914 (girls).

Greenwich Road Temporary School, SE10.
Opened 1905. (LMA: EO/DIV 6/GRE 2)
LB 1905-14 (boys)

Grenfell School *see* **Myrdle Street School**

Gresham College, Basinghall Street and
Gresham Street, EC2.

Grey Coat Hospital Girls' Day School,
Grey Coat Place, Westminster, SW1.
Misc 1698-c1950 (Westminster Archives)

Griffin Manor School, Plumstead High Street,
SE18. Opened 1893 as Plumstead School;
renamed 1951. (LMA: EO/DIV 6/GRI)
A&D 1943-66 (mixed)
LB 1943-66 (mixed)

Grinling Gibbons School *see*
Clyde Street School

Grove House School, Elmcourt Road, SE27.
(Independent) (boys). Opened 1825.

Grove Park Secondary School, Coopers Lane,
Lewisham, SE12. Opened 1936 as Coopers
Lane Secretarial School; renamed 1951;
closed 1960s. (LMA: EO/DIV 7/GRO)
A&D 1951-62 (mixed)
LB 1952-61 (mixed)
Misc punishment 1936-62

Grove Road School, E3. Opened 1872.
(LMA: EO/DIV 5/GRO)
A&D 1876-1918 (girls); 1877-1919 (boys)
LB 1872-92 (boys); 1873-1913 (mixed)

Grove Street School, Evelyn Street, SE8.
Opened 1893. (LMA: EO/DIV 6/GRO)
A&D 1893-1938 (boys); 1893-1930 (girls);
1893-1935 (infants)
LB 1893-1930 (girls); 1893-1935 (infants);
1908-39 (boys)

Grove Vale School, East Dulwich, SE22.
Opened 1900.

Guardian Angels Roman Catholic School,
Whitman Road, E3. Opened by 1874.
A&D 1925-39 (girls); 1946-55 (infants)
(Tower Hamlets Library)
LB 1874-1939 (girls and infants); 1874-1944
(boys); 1944-59, 1992 (mixed) (Tower
Hamlets Library)

Guildhall School of Music and Drama,
Barbican, EC2. Opened 1880 in
Aldermanbury; moved to John Carpenter
Street, EC4, 1886, to Barbican 1977.
A&D c1880-1968 (Corporation of London
Record Office)
Misc Exam registers 1910-1986 (Corporation of
London Record Office)

Haarlem Road Pupil Teachers School,
Brook Green, W6.
(LMA: EO/DIV 1/HAA)
LB 1885-1900

Haberdashers' Aske's Boys' School later
Haberdashers' Aske's Hatcham College,
Pepys Road, New Cross, SE14.
(Independent, later State). Opened in New
Cross, 1875.
A&D 1875-1919 (Guildhall Library, also
Lewisham Local History Lib)
Misc minute books, etc. 1689-1979
(Guildhall Library); records 1875-1991
(Lewisham Local History Lib)

Haberdashers' Aske's Girls' School,
Jerningham Road, SE14. Opened 1876.
A&D 1875-1919 (Lewisham Local History Lib)

Haberdashers' Aske's School, Westbere Road,
Cricklewood, NW2. (Independent) (boys).
Opened 1690 at Hoxton; moved 1898;
moved to Aldenham, Herts, 1961.

Hackford Road School, Russell Street, SW9.
Opened 1887; renamed Durand School,
1951. (LMA: EO/DIV 8/HAC)
A&D 1931-39 (infants)
LB 1899-1939 (boys); 1926-39 (infants)

Hackney Board of Guardians see
Brentwood School District; **Forest Gate
School District**

Hackney Central School *see* **Lauriston
Road Central School**
LB 1913-18 (LMA: ACC/3454/2)

Hackney Day Nursery. Opened 1934.
A&D 1934-35, 1941-42 (Hackney Archives
Department)

Hackney Downs School, Downs Park Road,
E5. Formerly The Grocers Company
School; opened 1876; renamed 1905.
A&D scholarships 1885-95 (Guildhall Library);
1910-37 (boys) (LMA: EO/DIV 4/HAC 1);
1876-1923, 1945-47 (Hackney Archives)
Misc minute books 1873-1906
(Guildhall Library); diaries 1908-33,
1941-59; miscellaneous 1876-1959
(Hackney Archives)
see Hackney Downs School (formerly the
Grocers' Company School) 1876-1926
(J.E. Medcalf, 1926)

Hackney Free and Parochial School, Isabella
Road and Paragon Road, Homerton, E9.
Founded 1714. (LMA: EO/DIV 4/HAC 2
and P79/JN 1)
A&D 1898-1906 (girls)
LB 1883-1913 (boys)
Misc minute books 1817-1935; accounts
1813-1926

Hackney Pupil Teachers Training Centre,
Tottenham Road. Opened 1887.
(LMA: EO/DIV 4/HAP)
LB 1895-1910

Hackney Unitarian School, Paradise Fields later
Chatham Place, E9. Opened 1790; closed
1884.

Haggerston Road School, N1. Opened 1879;
closed 1933. (LMA: EO/DIV 4/HAG)
A&D 1892-1903 (girls) (under Sidney Road
School); 1895-1931 (boys); 1899-1906
(infants); 1903-20 (girls)
LB 1879-1932 (girls); 1890-1908 (evening)

Hague Street School, Bethnal Green Road, E2.
Opened 1883; renamed Hague School,
1951. (LMA: EO/DIV 5/HAG)
A&D 1883-1939 (boys); 1883-1939 (infants)
LB 1883-1913 (girls); 1883-1936 (infants);
1883-97 (mixed); 1910-45 (boys)

Haimo Road School, Westhorne Avenue, SE9.
Opened 1925; renamed Haimo Primary
School, 1951. (LMA: EO/DIV 6/HAI)
A&D 1925-39 (junior mixed and infants);
1926-31 (mixed); 1927-31 (girls); 1931-39
(junior girls); 1931-39 (junior boys)
LB 1925-39 (junior mixed and infants);
1927-31 (girls); 1931-36 (junior girls)

Halford Road School, North End Road, SW6.
Opened 1890; renamed Halford School,
1938; renamed Fulham Primary School,
1992. (LMA: EO/DIV 1/HAL)
A&D 1885-1939 (boys); 1890-1945 (girls);
1931-39 (infants); 1942-45 (mixed)
LB 1890-1913 (girls); 1902-31 (boys); 1931-39
(junior boys); 1931-45 (junior girls);
1931-39 (infants); 1944-73 (junior)

Halley Street School, E14. Opened as St John
the Evangelist School; renamed Halley
Street School, 1874; Halley Primary School
and Martin Frobisher Secondary School,
1951. (LMA: EO/DIV 5/HAL)
A&D 1875-1936 (infants); 1899-1932 (girls);
1902-32 (boys)

Hallfield Primary School, Porchester Gardens,
W2. Opened 1953.

Hall School, Crossfield Road, Hampstead,
NW3. Opened 1889 as Belsize School,
Buckland Crescent, NW3.

Hall School, The, Sydenham (Independent
Preparatory School) (boys). Opened 1857.

Hall Street Wesleyan School, EC1. fl.1905/6.

Halstow Road School, Woolwich Road,
Westcombe Park, SE10. Opened 1893;
renamed Halstow School, 1951.
(LMA: EO/DIV 6/HAL)
A&D 1893-1929 (junior mixed)
LB 1893-1913, 1916-32 (junior mixed)

Hamlet of Ratcliff Church of England School,
White Horse Street later Road, E1.
Founded 1710.
LB 1877-99 (boys and girls); 1881-1924
(infants); 1899-1939 (mixed) (Tower
Hamlets Library)
Misc punishment 1900-14; list of subscribers
1710-1859; minute books 1710-1850,
1867-1942 (Tower Hamlets Library)
see A Short History of the Hamlet of Ratcliff
School (J.V. Pixell, 1910)

Hammersmith Board of Guardians see
West London School District

**Hammersmith, Chiswick and Turnham Green
British Schools**, Chiswick. Opened 1839,
closed 1860.

Hammersmith County School, The Curve,
W12. Previously North Hammersmith
Secondary School for Girls; opened 1957.

Hammersmith Literary Institute,
Brook Green, W6. Opened 1929.
(LMA: EO/DIV 1/HAM)
LB 1929-36 (evening)

Hammersmith Road School, Hammersmith
Road, W6. Temporary school fl 1873-76.

Hammersmith Roman Catholic School for Girls,
Hammersmith Road, W6. Opened 1893;
renamed Sacred Heart High School for
Girls by 1903.

**Hammersmith Secondary Technical College for
Boys**. Opened 1950 in Kensington;
renamed Christopher Wren School, 1951
and moved to Hammersmith 1956.

**Hammersmith Secondary Technical School for
Girls**, Lime Grove, W12. Opened 1909;
renamed Mary Boon School, 1951.

Hammond Square School, Hoxton Street, N1.
Opened 1873; renamed Burbage Primary
School, 1951. (LMA: EO/DIV 4/HAM)
A&D 1874-78, 1882-1939 (infants); 1890-1931
(girls); 1931-39 (junior boys); 1931-39
(junior girls)
LB 1873-90, 1913-38 (girls); 1897-1913,
1930-39 (infants); 1915-39 (boys)

**Hampden Gurney with St Luke's Church of
England School**, Nutford Place, W1.
Opened 1904.

Hampshire School, The, Ennismore Gardens,
SW7. Opened 1928.

Hampstead Parochial School, Holly Bush Vale,
NW3. Founded 1788 as Holly Bush Vale
School. (LMA: EO/DIV 2/HAD)
A&D 1897-1932 (girls); 1901-32 (boys);
1903-39 (infants)

Hampstead Preparatory School, Shepherd's
Walk, Hampstead (Independent) (boys).

Hampstead School, Westbere Road, NW2.
Opened 1961.

Hanbury Street School, Whitechapel, E1.
Opened 1872; closed 1915.
(LMA: EO/DIV 5/HAN)
A&D 1891-1903 (boys); 1892-1902 (infants)

Hanley School, Islington, N4. Opened 1873.

Hanover Street School, St Peter Street, N1.
Opened 1877; renamed Hanover School,
1938. (LMA: EO/DIV 3/HAN)
A&D 1877-1932 (girls); 1917-23 (mixed and
infants); 1928-40 (junior boys); 1928-39
(junior girls); 1932-39 (infants); 1941-44
(mixed; emergency)
LB 1904-13, 1948-65 (infants); 1913-32 (boys);
1913-34 (girls); 1933-39 (junior boys);
1934-39 (junior girls); 1940-45
(emergency)

Harben Secondary School, Kelson Street,
Netherwood Street, Hampstead NW6.
Opened 1881 as Netherwood Street School;
renamed 1931; closed 1961.
(LMA: EO/DIV 2/HAB)
A&D 1939-61 (mixed)
LB 1931-48 (boys); 1950-61 (mixed)
Misc punishment 1953-61

Harbinger School, Cahir Street, E14.
Opened 1873.

Harborough School,
Elthorne Road, N19. Opened 1885;
Laycock Partially Sighted School
1913-1950. (LMA: EO/DIV 3/HAB)
A&D 1917-57 (mixed)
LB 1944-67 (mixed)
Misc 1944-56 (correspondence)

Hargrave Park School, Junction Road, Upper
Holloway, N19. Opened 1877.
(LMA: EO/DIV 3/HAG)
A&D 1896-1931 (girls); 1913-31 (boys);
1931-33 (junior boys); 1931-47 (junior
girls)
LB 1877-1930 (boys); 1877-1937 (girls);
1878-1929 (infants); 1931-37 (junior boys)

Harmood Street Special School, Chalk Farm
Road, NW1. Opened 1910; renamed
Harmood Secondary School, 1950; later
Chalcot School. (LMA: EO/DIV 2/HAM)
LB 1923-39 (junior mixed); 1943-61 (mixed)

Harper Street School, New Kent Road, SE1.
Opened 1874; renamed Joseph Lancaster
School, 1933. (LMA: EO/DIV 8/HAR)
A&D 1872-1932 (girls); 1882-97, 1907-16,
1929-40 (infants)
LB 1872-1910, 1913-39 (infants); 1913-46
(girls); 1926-39 (boys); 1940 (senior boys)

Harrington Hill Primary School, E5. Opened
1972.

Harrow Road School, W9. Opened 1884;
renamed Bravington Road Special School
and Moberley School, 1913.
(LMA: EO/DIV 2/HAR)
A&D 1884-95 (boys); 1884-92 (girls);
1894-99 (infants)
LB 1907-15 (infants); 1913-20 (boys)

Harry Gosling School, Henriques Street, E1.
fl.1971.

Harry Roberts Nursery School, Harford Street,
E1. Opened 1971.
A&D 1971-96 (Tower Hamlets Library)
LB 1971-87 (Tower Hamlets Library)

Harvist Road School, N7. Opened 1901; closed
1910. (LMA: EO/DIV 3/HAV)
A&D 1891-1910 (infants); 1901-10 (girls)

Harwood Road School, Brittania Road, SW6.
Opened 1873; renamed Harwood School,
1928; closed 1992 and merged in Fulham
Primary School.
LB 1873-1933 (boys); 1873-1928 (girls);
1873-1939 (infants); 1933-48 (junior
mixed) (Hammersmith & Fulham Archives)

Haselrigge Road School, Clapham, SW4.
Opened 1887. (LMA: EO/DIV 9/HAS)
LB 1889-1952, 1977-81 (infants); 1893-1913
(evening); 1905-29 (senior mixed);
1913-52, 1965-81 (junior mixed); 1951-65
(junior boys); 1952-65 (girls)
Misc 1904-16 (statistics - infants)

Haseltine Road School, Bell Green,
Lower Sydenham, SE26. Opened 1885;
renamed Haseltine School, 1951.
(LMA: EO/DIV 7/HAS)
A&D 1882-1938 (boys); 1935-45 (girls);
1938-53 (senior mixed)
LB 1882-1930, 1934-38 (boys); 1882-1913
(girls); 1889-1922 (evening); 1900-10
(manual training centre)

Hatcham Church of England School see
St James School, Hatcham

Hatcham School, Old Kent Road, SE15.

Hatfield Street School, Stamford Street.
renamed John Rennie School, 1937.
(LMA: EO/DIV 8/HAT)
A&D 1900-26 (infants)

Hatton Garden Charity School, St Andrew Holborn, EC1.
Misc estates records 1761-1800
(Guildhall Library)

Haverstock Hill School and Haverstock Central School, NW3. Opened 1874; Central School opened 1911. (LMA: EO/DIV 2/HAV)
A&D 1888-1939 (mixed); 1919-39 (boys); 1928-37 (aftercare)
LB 1874-1948 (infants); 1874-1916 (mixed); 1900-14 (manual training centre); 1911-34 (boys - Central); 1911-38 (girls - Central); 1916-30 (boys); 1921-39 (handicraft centre); 1931-49 (senior boys); 1935-39 (physically defective)

Haverstock School, Crogsland Road, NW1. fl.1971.

Hawley Crescent School, Buck Street and Kentish Town Road, NW1. Opened 1874; renamed Hawley Primary School, 1951. (LMA: EO/DIV 2/HAW)
A&D 1882-94, 1929-32 (boys); 1900-25 (infants)

Hawthorn Cottage School, Welton Road, SE18. fl.1971.

Hay Currie School, Poplar, E14. Opened 1878.

Hazelbank Road School, SE6.
Opened 1901; closed before 1910 (LMA: EO/DIV 7/HAZ)
A&D 1901-06 (infants)

Hearnville Road School, Chestnut Grove, Balham, SW12. Opened 1905; renamed Hearnville School, 1951. (LMA: EO/DIV 9/HEA)
A&D 1905-17 (boys); 1905-24 (senior girls); 1917-27 (senior mixed)
LB 1928-39 (deaf - mixed)

Heathbrook School, St Rule Street, Clapham, SW8. Opened 1886.

Heathfield School. (LMA: EO/DIV 9/HEF)
A&D 1888-93 (infants)

Heathmere School, Alton Road, SW15. fl.1971.

Heath Mount Preparatory School, Hampstead (Independent) (boys). Opened 1896.

Heath Street British School, Heath Street, NW3. Opened 1862; closed 1906.

Heathview School
A&D 1971-85 (LMA Modern Records Section)

Heber Road School, Lordship Lane, SE22. Opened 1883; renamed Heber School, 1951. (LMA: EO/DIV 7/HEB)
A&D 1883-1930 (boys); 1883-1939 (girls); 1930-39 (junior boys) (for records during World War II evacuation to Ashtead *see* Surrey History Centre, Woking)
LB 1883-1930 (girls); 1911-30 (boys)
Misc visitors 1909-30

Heckford Street School, Brook Street, Ratcliff, E1. Opened 1879; renamed Christian Scott School, 1951. (LMA: EO/DIV 5/HEC)
LB 1931-38 (junior girls); 1938-39, 1945-56 (infants)

Hellenic College of London, Pont Street, SW1. Opened 1980.

Hemp Row Temporary School, SE17. Opened 1896; closed 1900, children going to Paragon School, New Kent Road. (LMA: EO/DIV 8/HEM)
LB 1896-1900 (girls)

Henley House School, Mortimer Road (later Crescent), NW6. Founded *c*1878; closed *c*1910.

Henrietta Barnett School, NW11. Opened 1911.

Henry Cavendish Primary School, Hydethorpe Road, Balham, SW12.

Henry Compton School, Kingswood Road, SW6. Part of Fulham Central School; renamed 1951.

Henry Fawcett School, Clayton Street, Kennington, SE11. Opened 1937. (LMA: EO/DIV 9/HEN)
A&D 1896-1928, 1942-56 (infants)

Henry Street School
A&D 1866 (Southwark Local Studies Lib)

Henry Thornton School, South Side, Clapham Common, SW4. Opened 1894; formerly Battersea Polytechnic Secondary School. (LMA: EO/DIV 9/HET)
A&D 1907-48 (boys)

Henwick Road School,
Well Hall Road, SE9. Opened 1930; renamed Henwick Primary School, 1951; later Westhorne Manor School; closed 1962. (LMA: EO/DIV 6/HEN)
A&D 1930-39, 1942-46 (junior mixed and infants); 1946-53 (infants)
LB 1931-36 (boys); 1936-39 (junior mixed)

Herbrand Street School, WC1. *see* **Christchurch**, Holborn

Herewward House School, Strathray Gardens, NW3. Opened 1950.

Hermitage School, E1. Opened 1903.

Heygate Street (South London Jewish) School, Walworth Road, SE17. Opened 1867. (LMA: EO/DIV 8/HEY)
LB 1895-1939 (mixed); 1920-32 (infants)

Highbury and Islington High School, Canonbury Place, N1. Opened 1878; closed 1911.

Highbury County School,
Highbury Grove, N5. Opened 1901; formerly Northern Polytechnic Day School; renamed Highbury County School, 1951. (LMA: EO/DIV 3/HIG)
A&D 1905-43 (boys); 1905-23 (girls)

Highbury Hill High School, Highbury Hill, N5. Originally Highbury Fields School; opened 1844; council 1912. (LMA: ACC/3488)
A&D 1903-92
Misc staff 1904-80

Highbury Industrial School, N5. (LMA: LCC/EO/SS/7)
A&D 1909-22

Highbury Park School, Highbury Park (Independent) (boys).

Highbury Quadrant School, Highbury New Park, N5. fl.1971.

Highbury Vale School, Conewood Street, N5. Opened 1836.

Highbury Wesleyan School, N5. Opened 1867. (LMA: EO/DIV 3/HIW)
LB 1869-96 (infants)

Highfield School, Trinity Road, SW18. Opened 1888.

Highgate School, North Road, Highgate, N6. (Independent) (boys). Opened 1565.
Registers Highgate School: A Roll of the School (anon, 1913); School Register 1833-1988 (P. Hughes and I.F. Davies, 7th edition, 1989)

High School for Boys, Highbury Grange, Highbury (Independent) (boys). Opened 1897.

High School for Boys, Westbourne Park Villas (Independent) (boys). Opened 1894.

Highshore Secondary School *see* **Victoria Road Special School**

High Street Deptford Temporary School, SE8. closed 1875 and transferred to Creek Road School. (LMA: EO/DIV 6/HIG 1)
LB 1873-75 (girls)

High Street School, Bow, E3.
Opened 1875; closed 1932. (LMA: EO/DIV 5/HIG 1 and HIG 2)
A&D 1879-80, 1883-1932 (girls); 1886-1932 (boys); 1888-1932 (infants)
LB 1872-1932 (boys); 1875-1931 (girls); 1875-95, 1910-32 (infants)

High Street School, Plumstead
High Street, SE18. Opened 1893; renamed Plumstead High Street School, 1921; Bannockburn Primary School, 1951. (LMA: EO/DIV 6/HIG 2)
A&D 1893-1930 (boys); 1893-1931 (girls); 1919-40 (junior mixed); 1925-39 (infants)
LB 1893-1926 (boys); 1893-1926 (girls); 1900-26 (manual training centre); 1926-33 (senior mixed); 1931-38 (infants)

High Street School, Stoke Newington, N16. Opened 1876. (LMA: EO/DIV 4/HIG)
A&D 1891-1942 (boys); 1920-39 (infants); 1922-42 (girls)
LB 1871-1939 (girls); 1872-1940 (infants); 1891-1935 (boys); 1958-77 (mixed)
Misc visitors 1885-1928; punishment 1902-19, 1926-39

High View School, Plough Road, SW11.

Highway School, The, St George Street, E1. Opened 1887. (LMA: EO/DIV 5/HWY)
A&D 1882-1900, 1906-12, 1917-39 (infants); 1902-30 (boys), 1908-31 (girls); 1928-39 (junior girls); 1931-39 (junior boys)
LB 1893-1928 (infants)

Hillbrook Secondary School, Upper Tooting, SW17. Opened 1916; formerly Derinton Road School; then Hillbrook Road School. (LMA: EO/DIV 9/HIL)
A&D 1946-63 (boys)
LB 1922-39 (girls)

Hillcroft School, Beechcroft Road, SW17. fl.1971.

Hillmartin College, Busby Place, Camden Road (Independent) (boys). Opened 1867.

Hill Mead School, Sussex Road, SW9. fl.1971.

Hitherfield Road School, Streatham, SW16. Opened 1910; renamed Hitherfield School, 1951. (LMA: EO/DIV 9/HIT)
A&D 1899-1910 (boys); 1899-1938 (girls) (evacuated to Ashtead during World War II; *see* Surrey History Centre, Woking for this period)
LB 1899-1910 (boys); 1899-1913 (girls); 1913-32 (mixed)

Hither Green School, Beacon Road, SE13. Opened 1885. (LMA: EO/DIV 7/HIT)
A&D 1882-1934, 1940-44 (boys); 1893-1946 (girls); 1897-1939, 1942-44 (infants)
LB 1882-1936 (boys); 1883-1939 (girls); 1885-1939 (infants)

Holbeach Road School, Rushey Green, SE6. Opened 1901; renamed Holbeach School, 1951. (LMA: EO/DIV 7/HLB)
A&D 1898-1925 (infants); 1901-35 (boys); 1901-35 (girls); 1914-27, 1935-39 (mixed)
LB 1901-35 (boys); 1901-24 (girls); 1914-27 (mixed)

Holden Street School, Greyshott Street, Lavender Hill, SW11. Opened 1877; renamed Shaftesbury Park School, 1951. (LMA: EO/DIV 9/HOD)
A&D 1877-1927 (boys); 1895-1939, 1941-58 (infants); 1911-39 (girls); 1940-43 (mixed)
LB 1877-1940 (boys); 1877-98, 1908-13, 1920-38 (girls); 1877-1939 (infants)

Holland Park School, Campden Hill Road, W8.

Holland Road Roman Catholic School, W14. (LMA: EO/DIV 1/HOL)
LB 1870-1901 (boys)

Holland Street School. SE8. Stanley Street School 1908-13; renamed Caldwell Primary School, 1951; closed 1960. (LMA: EO/DIV 8/HLS)
A&D 1918-26 (boys); 1926-39 (junior mixed); 1943-60 (girls)
LB 1908-34 (junior mixed); 1913-30, 1946-48 (infants); 1926-38, 1943-60 (mixed)
Misc punishment 1947-54

Holloway Literary Institute, Hilldrop Road, N7. (LMA: EO/DIV 3/HLI)
LB 1919-38

Holloway School, Hilldrop Road, N7. Opened 1907. (LMA: EO/DIV 3/HOL)
A&D 1907-11, 1924-34, 1939-60 (boys)

Holly Bush Vale School *see* **Hampstead Parochial School**

Holly Court Open Air School, Merton Lane, West Hill, Highgate, N6. Opened 1927. (LMA: EO/DIV 2/HOC)
A&D 1927-39 (mixed)

Hollydale Road School, Nunhead, SE15. Opened 1877; renamed Hollydale School, 1951. (LMA: EO/DIV 7/HOD)
A&D 1877-86, 1898-1929 (boys); 1912-29 (girls)
LB 1877-1929 (boys); 1877-1929 (girls); 1877-1936 (infants); 1936-39 (mixed)

Holman Hunt School, New Kings Road, SW6. Opened 1905 as New Kings Road School; renamed 1951; merged into New Kings School, 1991. (LMA: EO/DIV 1/HOL)
A&D 1943-53 (junior mixed)

Holmewood School, Upper Tulse Hill, SW2. fl.1971.

Holmleigh Primary School, Dunsmure Road, N16. Opened 1970.

Holy Child Roman Catholic School, Grundy Street or Upper North Street, E14. fl.1936/71.

Holy Cross Roman Catholic School, Ashington Road, SW6. Previously known as Ashington Road School, renamed 1951.

Holy Family Convent High School, Tooting High Street, SW17. fl.1971.

Holy Family Roman Catholic School,
Saffron Hill, Holborn, EC1. fl.1905/15.

Holy Family School, West Cromwell Road,
SW5.

Holy Ghost School, Balham *see*
Nightingale Square School

Holy Name Roman Catholic School,
Bow Common Lane, E3. Opened 1903.

Holy Trinity Clapham Church Schools see
Clapham Parochial School

Holy Trinity School, Bishops Bridge Road, W2.
(LMA: P87/TRI)
A&D 1899
Misc minute books 1864-83

Holy Trinity School, Blackheath Hill, SE10.
Opened 1847; closed 1950s.
(LMA: EO/DIV 6/HOL)
A&D 1875-92 (girls); 1947-57 (infants)
LB 1909-13 (infants)

Holy Trinity School, Bridge Street, Mile End,
E3. Opened 1844.

Holy Trinity School, Cadogan Gardens, SW3.
Opened 1873.

Holy Trinity School, Carlisle Street,
Westminster Bridge Road, SE1. Opened
1850.
A&D 1896-1946 (infants); 1909-39 (boys);
1942-85 (junior mixed) (Church of England
Records Centre); 1927-39 (girls)
(LMA: EO/DIV 8/HOL)
LB 1932-39 (boys) (LMA: EO/DIV 8/HOL);
1933-35 (infants) (Church of England
Records Centre)
Misc punishment 1947-65 (Church of England
Records Centre)

Holy Trinity School, Cloudesley Square, N1.
(LMA: P83/TRI)
Misc minute books 1875-1909

Holy Trinity School, Dartmouth Road,
Forest Hill, Sydenham, SE6. Opened 1872.
(LMA: EO/DIV 7/HOL)
A&D 1887-1931 (infants)
LB 1874-1932 (infants)

Holy Trinity School, College Crescent,
Kilburn, NW3. Opened 1859; closed 1940.
A&D 1915-25, 1928-39 (boys); 1906-27 (girls)
(Church of England Records Centre)
Misc minute books 1891-1931 (LMA: P90/TRI)

Holy Trinity School, Beechfield Road and
Mayfield Road, Dalston, E8. Also known
as Woodland Street National School.
Opened 1850. (LMA: EO/DIV 4/HOL and
P79/JNJ)
A&D 1884-1930 (boys)
LB 1866-73, 1883-1930 (boys);
1900-06 (evening)

Holy Trinity School, Russell Place,
Westminster, SW1. Opened 1875.
(LMA: EO/DIV 2/HOL 1)
A&D 1883-99, 1912-27 (infants)
LB 1862-1927 (boys); 1862-1927 (infants);
1895-1927 (girls)

Holy Trinity School, Sedding Street, SW1.
Opened 1873 (boys) and 1889 (girls), but
earlier school.

Holy Trinity School, Upper Tooting, SW2.
Opened 1862.
A&D 1901-39 (girls); 1912-39 (infants);
1926-39 (boys) (LMA: EO/DIV 9/HOL);
1942-44 (senior mixed)
(LMA: EO/DIV 9/TRI)
LB 1870-1913 (infants); 1872-1939 (boys);
1898-1939 (girls) (Church of England
Records Centre)

Holy Trinity School, Upper Tulse Hill, SW2.
fl.1966.

Holy Trinity School, West Cromwell Road,
SW5.

Holy Trinity with St Paul School, Harrow Road
previously Trinity Church of England and
St Paul's Church of England Schools;
opened 1868; merged 1954.
(LMA: EO/DIV 2/HOL 2)
A&D 1886-1911, 1930-54 (infants); 1887-1939
(boys); 1906-63 (mixed); 1908-39 (girls)
LB 1913-27 (infants - St Paul); 1914-39 (infants
- Holy Trinity); 1914-39 (girls - Holy
Trinity); 1921-53 (mixed - St Paul);
1954-63 (mixed)
Misc minute books 1852-91, 1908-14
(Westminster Archives)

Homer Row Roman Catholic School, Crawford
Street, St Marylebone, W1.

Homerton House Comprehensive School, E9.
Opened 1982.

Homerton Parochial School, High Street, E9.
Opened 1819; closed 1893.
(LMA: EO/DIV 4/HOM 1)
LB 1863-88 (boys)

Homerton Row School, Homerton High
Street, E9. Opened 1882; renamed
Templars Secondary School, 1950.
(LMA: EO/DIV 4/HOM 2)
A&D 1889-1932 (boys); 1938-39 (junior girls)
LB 1883-1927 (boys); 1906-38 (infants);
1933-39 (junior girls)

Homerton Wesleyan School, Church Road, E9.
Opened 1868; closed by 1899.

Honeywell Road School,
Wandsworth Common, SW11. Opened
1893; renamed Honeywell School, 1951;
closed 1957. (LMA: EO/DIV 9/HON)
A&D 1890-1931 (boys); 1890-1931 (girls);
1930-39 (infants); 1952-57 (secondary
boys)
LB 1913-26 (infants); 1914-56 (boys)

Honor Oak School, Homestall Road, SE22.
Opened 1906; merged into Waverly
School, 1978.

Horizon School *see* **Wenlock Road School**

Horn Park School, Alnwick Road, SE12.
fl.1971.

Hornsey Road Wesleyan Day School, N7.
Opened 1871; closed 1893.

Horseferry Road School, SW1.
(LMA: EO/DIV 2/HOR)
LB 1877-1904, 1913-15 (boys); 1877-1915
(girls); 1896-1915 (infants)

Horsley Street School, SE17.
(LMA: EO/DIV 8/HOR)
A&D 1897-98 (boys)

Hortensia Road School, SW10.
(LMA: EO/DIV 1/HOT)
LB 1907-13 (infants)

Hotham Road School, Charlwood Road,
Putney, SW15. Opened 1906.

Hoxton Academy Chapel Sunday School
A&D 1841-51 (girls) (Hackney Archives)
Misc minute books 1814-1935; cashbooks
1826-1901 (Hackney Archives)

Hoxton House School, Shoreditch, E9.
Opened 1907; renamed Burbage Primary
School, 1951.

Hughes Fields School, Creek Road or Benbow
Street, Deptford, SE8. Opened 1874.
(LMA: EO/DIV 6/HUG)
LB 1927-30 (boys)

Hugh Myddleton School,
Corporation Row, EC1. Opened 1893;
renamed Hugh Myddleton (North)
Secondary School, 1951; closed 1971.
(LMA: EO/DIV 3/HUG 1)
A&D 1893-1939 (boys); 1899-1937 (girls);
1908-39 (senior boys); 1908-39 (senior
girls); 1924-39, 1945-61 (infants); 1939,
1940-71 (mixed); 1941-57 (junior mixed)
LB 1893-1929 (infants); 1894-1937
(deaf - mixed); 1901-71 (mixed); 1907-49
(senior mixed)
Misc honours 1896-1924, 1931-38, 1948-55;
punishment 1945-71

Hugh Myddleton Central School,
Corporation Row, EC1. Opened 1911;
renamed Hugh Myddleton (South)
Secondary School, 1951.
(LMA: EO/DIV 3/HUG 2)
LB 1908-27, 1940-55 (mixed); 1919-39
(handicrafts centre)

Hugh Myddleton Junior School,
Bowling Green Lane, EC1. Opened 1875.

Hugon Road School, Hugon Road, SW6.
Opened 1894; renamed Hurlingham
School, 1936.

Hungerford Road School,
York Road, Camden Road, N7. Opened
1896; renamed Hungerford School, 1951.
(LMA: EO/DIV 3/HUN)
A&D 1927-39 (boys); 1927-46 (girls);
1930-39 (infants)
LB 1912-27 (boys); 1934-39 (infants)

Huntingfield Road School, Roehampton, SW15.
Opened 1922; renamed Huntingfield
School, 1933. (LMA: EO/DIV 9/HUN)
A&D 1925-59 (junior mixed and infants)
LB 1922-39 (junior mixed)

Hurlingham School, Peterborough Road, SW6. Opened 1894 as Hugon Road School, renamed 1936; primary school moved and renamed Sulivan School, 1951; senior school moved to Peterborough Road, 1956.

Hutton Poplars Residential School, Poplar.
LB 1930-36 (Hackney Archives)
Misc punishment 1930-67 (Hackney Archives)

Hyde Farm School, Telferscot Road, SW12.
A&D 1965-95 (Lambeth Archives)

Ibstock Place - The Froebel School, Clarence Lane, Roehampton, SW15. Opened 1894.

Ilderton Road School, Rotherhithe New Road, SE16. Opened 1893; renamed Ilderton School, 1951. (LMA: EO/DIV 7/ILD)
A&D 1889-1912 (boys); 1899-1920 (infants); 1910-30 (girls)
LB 1889-1929 (boys); 1889-1913, 1929-30 (girls); 1889-1908 (infants)

Immanuel Church of England Primary School, Factory Square, Streatham Common, SW16. Opened 1860.
A&D 1839-1939 (infants); 1866-84, 1891-1954 (boys); 1892-1930 (girls) (Church of England Records Centre)
LB 1872-1913 (boys); 1886-1912 (infants); 1913-76 (junior mixed) (Church of England Records Centre)

Imperial Street School, E3. Opened 1915; closed 1928. (LMA: EO/DIV 5/IMP)
A&D 1915-28 (mixed)
LB 1915-28 (physically defective)

Industrial Schools. These were established for children found committing crimes, out of parental control, etc. General records are noted here; there are also records of individual industrial schools, approved schools, etc.; see Brixton Hill; Cumberlow Lodge; Finley Street; Goburne House; Highbury; Mayford; Mile Oak; Upton House (LMA: LCC/EO/SS/6 and LCC/CH/D/GR)
A&D 1874-1938; case files 1910-59

Invicta Road, Westcombe Hill, SE3. Opened 1900; renamed Invicta Primary School, 1951. (LMA: EO/DIV 6/INV)
A&D 1900-32 (boys)
LB 1900-31 (boys); 1900-38 (girls); 1900-32 (infants)

Isaac Newton School, Upper School in Wornington Road, W10; Secondary School in Lancaster Road, W11. Opened 1958; merged with Holland Park School, 1983; now a college. (LMA: EO/DIV 1/ISA)
A&D 1958-72, 1979, 1981 (boys)
Misc visitors 1939-42, 1958

Isledon Secondary School, N7. Opened 1897 as Upper Hornsey Road School; renamed Isledon School, 1951. (LMA: EO/DIV 3/ISL)
LB 1952-53 (girls); 1953-57 (mixed)

Isle of Dogs School, Glengall Road, Poplar, E14. Opened 1897 as Millwall School; renamed 1928. (LMA: EO/DIV 5/ISL)
LB 1938-39 (mixed)

Islington and North London Shoe-Black Brigade School, York Road, N1. Opened 1857; closed after 1912.

Islington Chapel School, Church (later Gaskin) Street, N1. Opened 1801; closed by 1871.

Islington Green School
see **Queen's Head Street School**

Italia Conti Academy of Theatre Arts, Goswell Road, EC1. Opened 1911.

Iverson Road School, Kilburn, NW6. Opened 1899; closed c1903.

Ivydale Road School, Nunhead, SE15. Opened 1888; renamed Ivydale Primary School, 1951. (LMA: EO/DIV 7/IVY)
A&D 1888-1939 (boys); 1915-38 (girls); 1939-46 (mixed)
LB 1888-1939 (boys); 1888-1911 (mixed); 1900-10 (manual training centre); 1911-39 (girls); 1939 (senior mixed)

Jack Ashley School, Blackstock Road, Finsbury Park, N4. Until 1976 Edward Seguin School (q.v.). (LMA: EO/DIV 3/JAC)
A&D 1976-77 (senior mixed) (deaf)
LB 1976-79 (senior mixed - deaf)

James Allen's Girls' School, East Dulwich Grove, SE22. Opened 1741.

James Pascall Secondary School, SE1. formerly Westminster Bridge Road School. (LMA: EO/DIV 8/JAM)
A&D 1952-56 (mixed)

James Street School, WC2.
Renamed Buckingham Gate School, 1900.
(LMA: EO/DIV 2/JAM)
LB 1878-1905 (boys); 1879-1905 (girls);
1884-1913 (infants)

James Wolfe School *see* **Randall Place School**

Janet Street School, E14. Opened 1893 in
Bristol Street; moved 1907; closed 1939.
(LMA: EO/DIV 5/JAN)
A&D 1893-1939 (mixed)
LB 1913-31 (mentally defective)

Jessop Road School, Milkwood Road,
Herne Hill, SE24. Opened 1876; renamed
Jessop Primary School, 1951.
(LMA: EO/DIV 8/JES)
A&D 1876-1906 (boys); 1894-1935 (infants);
1897-1934 (girls); 1935-41 (junior mixed)
LB 1898-1925 (evening); 1900-37 (infants);
1903-34 (girls); 1935-39 (junior mixed)

Jewish Orphanage, Knight's Hill, SE27.

Jewish Preparatory School, Andover Place,
NW6.

Jewish Secondary School, Amhurst Park, N16.

Jew's College, Woburn House,
Tavistock Square, WC1.

Jews' Free School, Bell Lane, Spitalfields, E1.
Founded 1731; opened 1891; moved 1958
to Camden Road, NW1. (LMA:
ACC/4046)
A&D c1868-1939
LB 1863-99
Misc minute books 1818-1953

Jews' Infants School, Commercial School,
Spitalfields, E1. Opened 1883.

Johanna Street School, Lower Marsh, Lambeth,
SE1. Opened 1874 later Johanna School.
(LMA: EO/DIV 9/JOA)
A&D 1874-81 (boys)

John Aird School, Cobbold Road, W12
(partially sighted). Opened 1925. Moved
from Paddington to Kenmont School, 1954
and to Wendell Park School, 1961.

John Ball School, Southvale, Tranquil Vale,
SE3. fl.1971.

John Betts School, Paddenswick Road, W6.
Previously known as St Peter's Free
Schools, renamed 1951.

John Burgess School, Surrey Lane,
Battersea, SW11. Opened 1885 as Surrey
Lane School; renamed 1951.
(LMA: EO/DIV 9/JOH)
A&D 1942-54 (infants)
LB 1928-55 (infants)

John Burns School, Hanbury Road, SW11.
fl.1971.

John Donne School, Woods Road, SE15.
fl.1971.

John Evelyn School, Alverton Street, SE8.
Opened 1875 as Alverton Street School;
renamed Duke Street School, 1919; John
Evelyn School, 1930; closed 1986.
(LMA: EO/DIV 6/JOH)
A&D 1930-39 (girls)

John Griffiths Roman Catholic School,
Prince's Way, SW10. fl.1971.

John Harvard School, Copperfield Street,
Gravel Lane, SE1. Opened 1874 as Orange
Street School; renamed 1937.
(LMA: EO/DIV 8/JHH)
A&D 1872-80 (junior mixed); 1937-39
(senior boys)
LB 1931-35 (senior boys); 1932-40 (boys)

John Howard School see
Clapton Park Secondary School

John Keats School, Adelaide Road, NW3.
Opened 1958.

John Milton School *see* **Sleaford Street School**

John Rennie School. Opened 1878.

John Ruskin School, John Ruskin Street,
Walworth Road, SE5. Opened 1899;
renamed Whitney School, 1950.
(LMA: EO/DIV 8/JHR)
A&D 1909-32 (mixed)

John Scurr School, Cephas Street, E1.
Opened 1873 as Essex Street School;
renamed 1938. (LMA: EO/DIV 5/JOH)
A&D 1940 (mixed); 1951-60 (junior mixed)

Johnson Street Roman Catholic School, E1. Opened 1905; later St Joseph; renamed Bishop Challoner School, 1951. (LMA: EO/DIV 5/JSN)
A&D 1931-39 (infants)
LB 1914-36 (infants)

John Stainer School, St Asaph Road, SE4. fl.1971.

John Street, Kent Road, Sunday School
Misc minute books 1818-1943; staff 1858-1901; pensioners 1822-97 (Southwark Local Studies Lib)

John Wesley School, SE27. Opened 1893 as Eden Road; closed 1960. (LMA: EO/DIV 8/JHW)
A&D 1946-60 (junior mixed and infants)
Misc 1952-60 (absences of teachers)

Joseph Lancaster School, Harper Road, SE1. Opened 1874 (senior).

Joseph Lancaster School, Rockingham Street, SE1. Opened 1885 (junior). (LMA: EO/DIV 8/JOS)
A&D 1945-60 (infants); 1946-64 (junior mixed)

Joseph Priestley Secondary School, Morning Lane, E9. Opened 1951; merged into Brooke House School, 1960.

Joseph Tritton School, Wynter Street, SW11. fl.1971.

Jubilee School, Filey Avenue, N16. Opened 1972.

Julians School, Leigham Court Road, SW16. fl.1971.

Keeton's Road School, Rotherhithe, SE16. Opened 1876.

Kelvin Grove School, Kirkdale, Sydenham, SE26. Opened 1876 as Sydenham Hill Road School; renamed 1937. (LMA: EO/DIV 7/KEL)
A&D 1941-61 (infants)
LB 1939 (infants)

Kemble School, Amberley Road, W9. Opened 1951 as senior department of Amberley Road School; closed by 1958.

Kender Street School, New Cross Road, Deptford, SE14. Opened 1874; renamed Kender Primary School, 1951. (LMA: EO/DIV 6/KEN)
LB 1928-39 (junior mixed and infants)

Kenmont Gardens School, Harrow Road, NW10. Opened 1880; renamed College Park Secondary School and Kenmont Primary School, 1950/1. (LMA: EO/DIV 1/KEN)
A&D 1880-1939 (girls); 1882-1939 (boys); 1884-1938 (infants)
LB 1880-1928 (girls); 1880-1933 (infants); 1882-1928 (boys); 1889-1909 (evening); 1928-39 (mixed)

Kennington Oval School, Harleyford Road, SE11. Opened 1860.

Kennington Pupil Teachers Centre see **Charles Edward Brooke School**

Kennington Road School, Kennington Park, SE11. Opened 1897; renamed Kennington Manor School, 1951. (LMA: EO/DIV 8/KEN 2)
A&D 1904-33 (mixed); 1928-38 (infants)
LB 1904-39 (mentally defective - mixed); 1933-39 (senior boys); 1933-39 (junior mixed and infants)

Kensal House School, Paddington, W10. Opened 1911; closed after 1939. (LMA: EO/DIV 2/KEN)
LB 1928-39 (girls)

Kensington and Chelsea School District. Constituted by Chelsea and Kensington Boards of Guardians 1876-1930 and St Marylebone Board of Guardians 1920-30. (LMA: KCSD)
A&D 1878-1933
LB 1927-33
Misc minute books 1876-1930

Kensington Boards of Guardians see **Kensington and Chelsea School District; North Surrey School District**.

Kensington High School, Upper Phillimore Gardens, W8. (girls). Opened 1873.

Kensington Preparatory School, Holland Road, Kensington, W8. (Independent). Opened 1873.

Kensington School of Music, High Street, Notting Hill Gate, W11.

Kensington Square Roman Catholic School, Ansdell Street, W8.

Kentish Town Church of England School, Islip Street, Kentish Town Road, NW5. Founded 1815; opened 1847.

Kentish Town Wesleyan School. fl.1905.

Kent Road School, Lewisham.
(LMA: EO/DIV 7/KEN)
A&D 1869-77 (boys)

Kenworthy Road School, Homerton, E9.

Keyworth School, Faunce Street, SE17. fl.1971.

Kidbrooke Park School, Hargood Road, SE3. fl.1971.

Kilburn Grammar School, Salusbury Road, NW6.

Kilburn Lane School, Kensal Green, W10. Opened 1885; closed 1936. (LMA: EO/DIV 2/KIL)
A&D 1892-1936 (infants)
LB 1885-1924 (boys); 1885-1926 (girls); 1886-1936 (infants); 1920-36 (junior mixed); 1924-26 (senior mixed)

Kilburn Polytechnic, Priory Park Road, NW6.

Killick Street School see **Winchester Street School**

Kilmorie Road School, Forest Hill, SE23. Opened 1903; renamed Kilmorie School, 1931; closed 1960s. (LMA: EO/DIV 7/KIL)
A&D 1918-31 (boys); 1925-39 (girls)
LB 1903-39 (infants); 1903-13 (senior mixed); 1903-39 (manual training centre); 1913-31 (boys); 1915-28 (evening)

King Alfred Girls' School, Holbeach Road, SE6. fl.1971.

King Alfred School Society, Ellerdale Road, Hampstead, NW11. (Independent) (mixed). Opened 1897; moved to Hendon, 1919.

King and Queen Street School, Walworth, SE17. Opened 1883; renamed Robert Browning School, 1933. (LMA: EO/DIV 8/KIN)
A&D 1887-91, 1899-1926 (infants); 1909-32 (girls)
LB 1913-39 (boys)

King's Acre School, King's Avenue, SW4. fl.1971.

Kingsgate Road School, Messina Avenue, Kilburn High Road, NW6. Opened 1903; renamed Kingsgate Primary School, 1951. (LMA: EO/DIV 2/KIS)
A&D 1914-42 (infants)
LB 1914-39 (infants)
Misc Honours book 1931-40 (Camden Local Studies Library)

Kingsland Birkbeck School, Colverstone Crescent, E8. In 1905 taken over by LCC, later Dalston County Secondary School; merged into Edith Cavell School, 1963.

Kingsland British School, Stoke Newington Road, N16. Opened 1808; closed c1865.

Kingsland Roman Catholic School, Tottenham Road, Kingsland, N1. Opened 1855; later renamed Our Lady and St Joseph School.
LB 1871-1913 (Hackney Archives)

Kingsley Secondary School, SW3. Opened 1874 as Cook's Ground School and Park Walk School which amalgamated 1905 and renamed Park Walk School; renamed 1951. (LMA: EO/DIV 1/KIN)
A&D 1948-68 (mixed)

Kingsmead School, Kings Mead Way, E9. Opened 1953.

King's Park School. Opened 1934.

King Street School, Camden Street, NW1. Opened 1874 as Camden Street School; renamed 1919; renamed Richard Cobden School, 1937. (LMA: EO/DIV 2/KIN)
A&D 1883-91, 1904-22 (boys); 1931-36 (junior boys); 1933-36 (junior girls); 1936-39 (junior mixed)
LB 1931-36 (junior boys); 1936 (junior mixed)

King Street Sunday School (Methodist)
Misc minute books 1817-18 (Southwark Local Studies Lib)

King's Warren School, The, Old Mill Road, Plumstead Common, SE18. Opened 1898.

Kingswood Primary School, Gypsy Road, SE27.

Kingwood Road School, Fulham Palace Road, SW6. Opened 1898; became part of Henry Compton School, 1951. (LMA: EO/DIV 1/KSW)
A&D 1919-31 (boys); 1924-31 (girls); 1931-39 (senior girls)
LB 1898-1923 (boys); 1909-17, 1920-25 (mixed)

Kirby Grove School see **Snowsfields School**

Knapp Road School, Bow, E3. Opened 1876; renamed Knapp Secondary School, 1951. (LMA: EO/DIV 5/KNA)
A&D 1883-1934 (infants); 1901-31 (girls); 1909-28, 1942-44 (boys); 1928-39, 1943-52 (senior boys)
LB 1876-1907, 1913-34 (infants); 1876-1929 (girls); 1890-1913 (evening); 1928-31 (senior girls); 1928-50 (senior boys); 1949-52 (boys)

Laburnum Street School, Kingsland Road, E2. Opened 1908; renamed Laburnum Primary School, 1951. (LMA: EO/DIV 4/LAB)
A&D 1908-36 (boys); 1908-25, 1933-39 (girls); 1925-39 (infants); 1926-36 (junior girls); 1933-39 (junior boys)
LB 1908-26 (boys); 1908-26 (girls); 1915-34 (evening); 1926-34 (junior girls); 1926-39 (junior boys)

Ladbroke School, Upper School in Lancaster Road, W11; Lower School in St Marks Road, W10. Opened 1958; merged with Holland Park and Isaac Newton Schools, 1987 (LMA: EO/DIV 1/LAD)
A&D 1958-83 (senior girls)

Lady Eden's School, Victoria Road, W8. Opened 1947.

Lady Holles School *see* **St Giles Cripplegate Girls' School**,

Lady Margaret School, Parsons Green, SW6. Opened 1917.

Lambeth Boys' Parochial School
Misc minute books 1814-53 (Lambeth Archives)

Lambeth Chapel Wesleyan School. fl.1905.

Lambeth Orphans' Asylum, Westminster Bridge Road, SE1.
Misc apprenticeship indentures 1775-1800 (Lambeth Archives)

Lambeth Ragged School see **Borough Beaufoy School**

Lamb Lane School, London Fields, Hackney, E8. Opened 1873; closed 1925. (LMA: EO/DIV 4/LAM)
A&D 1899-1925 (mixed)
LB 1873-1913 (infants); 1916-25 (mixed)

Lancaster Road School, Wandsworth Bridge Road, SW6. Opened 1914. (LMA: EO/DIV 1/LAN)
A&D 1914-58 (senior boys); 1914-39, 1954-58 (girls); 1914-25, 1935-39, 1954-58 (infants); 1942-47 (mixed); 1948-57 (class registers)
LB 1913-26, 1933-39 (senior boys); 1914-33, 1946-58 (boys); 1914-33 (girls); 1927-39, 1947-58 (infants); 1931-45 (evening)
Misc punishment 1946-55; staff 1950-58

Lancing Street School, NW1. *see* **St Pancras Church of England School**

Langbourn Ward School, City. Opened 1702; amalgamated with Cornhill and Lime Street Wards School, 1874.
Misc minute books 1738-1875 (Guildhall Library)

Langbourne School, Lyall Avenue, SE21.

Langford Park School, Byron Street and Farrance Street, E14. fl.1971.

Langford Road School, Wandsworth Bridge Road, SW6. Opened 1890; renamed Langford Primary School, 1951. (LMA: EO/DIV 1/LFD)
A&D 1886-1939 (infants)
LB 1886-1950 (infants); 1886-90 (mixed)

Lansdowne Place Half Time School, SE1. Opened 1878; closed 1879. (LMA: EO/DIV 8/LAN)
LB 1878-79 (mixed)

Lansdowne School, SW8. (ESN) *see also* Shillington Street School. (LMA: EO/DIV 9/LAN)
A&D 1946-66 (senior mixed)

Lant Street School, SE1. Opened 1877;
renamed Charles Dickens School, 1909.
(LMA: EO/DIV 8/LAT)
LB 1900-13 (infants); 1901-13 (boys)

La Retraite High School, Atkins Road, SW12.

Larkhall Lane School, Union Street,
Clapham, SW4. Opened 1877.
(LMA: EO/DIV 9/LAR)
A&D 1887-1906 (girls); 1889-1915 (infants);
1922-39 (boys); 1933-39 (junior girls)
LB 1933-39 (infants)

Larmenier Roman Catholic Infants' School,
Great Church Lane, W6. Infants' section of
Sacred Heart High School; renamed 1963.

La Sainte Union Convent School,
Croftdown Road, NW5.

Latchmere School, Battersea Park Road, SW11.
Opened 1883. (LMA: EO/DIV 9/LAT)
A&D 1891-1932 (junior mixed); 1931-39
(senior girls)

Latimer Road School, Notting Hill, North
Kensington, W10. Opened 1880, rebuilt
1907; renamed Thomas Jones School,
1951. (LMA: EO/DIV 1/LAT)
LB 1901-07 (evening)

Latymer's Endowed Foundation,
Hammersmith Road, W6. Founded 1624;
renamed Latymer Foundation School,
1951; closed 1963.
(LMA: EO/DIV 1/LTF)
A&D 1857-1962 (boys)
LB 1872-1962 (boys)
Misc punishment 1908-34; also at
Hammersmith and Fulham Archives list of
admissions 1624-1878; other records
1938-56

Latymer Upper School, King Street, W6.
(Independent) (boys). Opened 1895.

Launcelot Road School, Downham, Bromley.
Opened 1928.

Laura Place School, E5. Emergency School on
site of Clapton County Secondary School
(LMA: EO/DIV 4/LAU)
A&D 1940 (mixed)

Lauriston County Secondary School,
Derby Road, E9. (LMA: EO/DIV 4/LAU)
LB 1892-1926 (boys); 1893-1906 (evening);
1913-29, 1932-51 (senior mixed); 1953-57
(mixed)

Lauriston Road Central School, E9. Junior
school opened 1892; senior school opened
1910; 1913 changed name to South
Hackney Central School; moved to
Cassland Road, 1917; renamed Cassland
Secondary School, 1951.
A&D 1945-56 (junior mixed)
(Hackney Archives)
LB 1910-13 (LMA: ACC/3454/1); 1927-62
(women's evening institute) (Hackney
Archives)

Lavender Hill School, Amies Street, SW11.
Opened 1892; closed 1970s.
(LMA: EO/DIV 9/LAV)
A&D 1892-1915 (boys); 1908-31 (junior boys);
1917-38, 1945-79 (girls); 1929-39 (infants);
1938-39 (junior mixed); 1943-57 (boys)
LB 1927-39 (infants); 1931-40 (senior girls);
1946-56 (boys)

Lawn Lane School,
South Lambeth Road, SW18. Opened 1908.
(LMA: EO/DIV 8/LAW)
A&D 1915-25 (mixed); 1932-42 (junior mixed)
LB 1915-25 (myopic)

Lawrence School, The, Mansford Street,
Old Bethnal Green Road, E2. Opened
1883. (LMA: EO/DIV 5/LAW)
A&D 1902-33 (girls); 1940 (mixed)
(emergency)
LB 1883-1933 (girls); 1914-25 (boys)

Laxon Street School, Long Lane, SE1.
Opened 1874. (LMA: EO/DIV 8/LAX)
A&D 1874-1910, 1934-39 (boys); 1874-1934
(girls); 1888-1939 (infants); 1931-39
(senior girls); 1931-50 (mixed)
LB 1874-1925 (boys); 1874-1931 (infants);
1924-34 (girls)
Misc honours 1925-39 (senior girls)

Laycock Junior School, Laycock Street, N1.
Opened 1915; amalgamated 1967 into
Highbury Grove School.

Laycock Secondary School, Upper Street, N1.
Opened 1885 as Station Road School;
renamed 1927. (LMA: EO/DIV 3/LAY 1)
A&D 1932-47 (girls); 1933-39, 1947-67 (boys)
Misc punishment 1962-65

LONDON SCHOOL RECORDS

Laystall Street School, Grays Inn Road, EC1.
Opened 1876; renamed Rosebery Avenue
School, 1899; Christopher Hatton School,
1951. (LMA: EO/DIV 3/LAS)
A&D 1886-1902 (boys); 1890-1903 (infants);
1891-1908 (girls)
LB 1876-1907 (boys); 1876-1913 (girls);
1876-1913 (infants)

Laysterne School, Shoreditch, N1. Opened as
Catherine Street School, 1887; renamed
1932. (LMA: EO/DIV 4/LAY)
LB 1932-29 (junior mixed)

Lea Marsh School, E9. Opened 1899 as
Windsor Road 1899; renamed Berkshire
Road, 1906; renamed 1951, closed 1966.
(LMA: EO/DIV 4/LEA)
A&D 1941-66 (mixed)
LB 1948-66 (mixed)
Misc punishment 1963

Leathersellers' College, Tower Bridge, SE1.

Lee Church of England School,
Lee Church Street, SE13. Opened 1835.
A&D 1849-62, 1895-1940 (mixed); 1869-1908
(boys); 1877-1902 (girls); 1885-1929
(infants) (Lewisham Local History Lib)
LB 1863-1906 (boys); 1863-1906 (girls);
1863-1928 (infants); 1906-40 (mixed)
(Lewisham Local History Lib)

Lee Manor School, Leahurst Road, SE13.
Opened 1911 as Manor Lane School;
renamed 1951. (LMA: EO/DIV 7/LEE)
A&D 1945-65 (boys)

Lena Gardens School, W6. Opened 1928.

Leo Street School, Asylum Road,
Peckham, SE15. Opened 1899; renamed
Leo Secondary School, 1951; closed 1960s.
(LMA: EO/DIV 7/LEO)
A&D 1898-1928, 1941-44 (mixed); 1899-1938,
1945-58 (boys); 1913-39 (girls)
LB 1899-1913 (infants)

Lewisham Boards of Guardians see
North Surrey School District.

Lewisham Bridge School, Elmira Road, SE13.
Opened 1875. (LMA: EO/DIV 7/LEW)
A&D 1887-1935 (girls); 1903-36 (boys);
1904-29 (infants)
LB 1872-1936 (boys); 1872-1919, 1925-39
(girls); 1875-1925 (infants); 1896-1913
(evening); 1900-39 (manual training centre)

Lewisham Grammar School, Catford, SE6.
Opened 1890.
Misc records at Lewisham Local History Lib

Lewisham Park School, Lewisham
(Independent) (boys). Opened 1854.

Lewisham Prendergast School, Rushey Green,
SE6.

Lexden House School, Heybridge Avenue,
Streatham, SW16.

Licensed Victuallers' School, Upper
Kennington Lane, Lambeth, SE11.
(Independent) (boys). Opened 1803.
A&D list of pupils 1865 (Guildhall Library)
Misc estate records 1837-57; administrative
records 1865-93 (Guildhall Library)

Lillie Road School, SW6. Opened 1893;
renamed Sir John Lillie School, 1951.
LB 1891-1912 (Hammersmith and Fulham
Archives)

Linden Lodge School, Battersea. (blind boys).
Opened 1902.

Lindisfarne School, Blackheath
(Independent) (boys).

Lingham Street Church of England School,
Lambeth, SW9. fl.1952.

Linton House School, Holland Park Avenue,
Notting Hill Gate, W11. (Independent)
(boys).

Littleton Street School, Littleton Street, SW18.
Later Greenmead School.

Livingstone Primary School, Australia Road,
W12. White City No.2 Primary School to
1951; closed 1965. (LMA: EO/DIV 1/LIV)
A&D 1953-65 (infants)
LB 1951-65 (infants)
Misc punishment 1962

Lollard Street School, Lambeth, SE11.
Opened 1880.

Lombard Wall School, Woolwich Road, SE7.
Opened 1884; closed 1940s.
(LMA: EO/DIV 6/LOM)
LB 1884-1910, 1913-32 (boys); 1884-1912,
1924-29 (girls), 1910-13 (junior mixed);
1907-39 (infants); 1929-39 (mixed)

Lomond Grove School, Camberwell Road, SE15. Opened 1878 as George Street School; Lomond Grove School to 1931; Oliver Goldsmith School 1931-38; reverted to original name, 1938. (LMA: EO/DIV 7/LOM)
A&D 1916-31 (boys); 1931-36 (junior boys); 1916-39 (infants)
LB 1917-35 (junior girls)

London College of Divinity, Aubert Park, N5.

London College of Music, Great Marlborough Street, W1.

London County Council Technical Institute Day Secondary School, Saltram Crescent, Paddington, W9. Opened 1905.
see **Paddington**

London Fields School, Westgate Street, The Triangle, E8. Opened 1874. (LMA: EO/DIV 4/LON)
LB 1874-1913 (boys); 1898-1913 (girls); 1900-13 (infants)

London Oratory Roman Catholic School, Seagrave Road, SW6. Founded 1863; moved to Fulham, 1970.

London School of Printing, Stamford Street, SE1.

London Street School, E1. Opened 1876; renamed Somerford Street School, 1881. (LMA: EO/DIV 5/LON)
LB 1876-1905 (boys); 1876-91 (girls)

Loudoun House School, Loudoun Road, NW8. (Independent) (boys).

Loughborough Central School, Minet Road, Loughborough Road, SW9. Opened 1928. (LMA: EO/DIV 8/LOU)
A&D 1928-60 (mixed)
LB 1928-39, 1947-52 (mixed)

Lower Chapman Street School, Bigland Street, St George in the East, E1. Opened 1874; renamed Chapman School, 1935. (LMA: EO/DIV 5/LOW)
A&D 1874-1930 (boys); 1877-87, 1900-06 (infants); 1905-30 (girls); 1930-39 (senior boys); 1930-39 (junior mixed and infants)
LB 1874-1908, 1918-30 (boys)

Lowood School, Shadwell, E1. Opened 1914. (LMA: EO/DIV 5/LWD)
LB 1933-39 (mentally defective)

Lubavitch House School, Clapton Common, E5. (boys).

Lubavitch House School, Stamford Hill, N16. (girls).

Lucas Street School, Lewisham High Road, SE8. Opened 1879 as Gainsford School; renamed 1938; later Lucas Vale School. (LMA: EO/DIV 6/LUC)
A&D 1879-98, 1909-30 (girls); 1879-1913, 1922-33 (infants); 1892-1930 (boys); 1930-36 (junior mixed); 1936-40 (junior girls)
LB 1898-1938 (evening); 1913-30 (girls); 1913-39 (infants); 1930-36 (junior mixed); 1936-40 (junior girls)

Lyham Road School, Lambeth, SW2. Opened 1878; renamed Parkside School, 1935.
LB 1873-1912 (Lambeth Archives)

Lyndhurst Grove School, SE15. Opened 1883; renamed Lyndhurst School, 1951. (LMA: EO/DIV 7/LYN)
A&D 1890-1933 (infants); 1906-39 (girls); 1932-39 (junior boys); 1942 (mixed)
LB 1883-1929 (boys); 1883-1938 (infants); 1911-32 (girls)

Lyndhurst House Preparatory School, Lyndhurst Gardens, Hampstead, NW3. Opened 1952.

Lyulph Stanley Central School, Camden Street, St Pancras, NW1. Opened 1910; renamed Stanley School, 1927.

Macaulay School, Victoria Rise, SW4 see **Clapham Parochial School**

Macklin Street Roman Catholic School, Drury Lane, WC2. Opened 1858; renamed St Joseph School, 1951.
A&D 1908-69 (girls and boys); 1908-28 (infants); (LMA Modern Records Section)
LB 1901-30 (LMA Modern Records Section)

Macmurdo Road School, Lysia Street, SW6. Opened 1901; renamed Queensmill Road School, 1905; Queens Manor School, 1951; amalgamated with Peterborough School, 1992. (LMA: EO/DIV 1/MAC)
LB 1901-13 (boys); 1901-13 (girls)

Magdalen Road School, Wandsworth, SW18.
Opened 1927; later Beatrix Potter School.
(LMA: EO/DIV 9/MAG)
A&D 1911-29 (mixed); 1929-39
(junior mixed and infants)
LB 1913-29 (mixed)

Magdalen Street School, Rotherhithe, SE1.
Opened 1907.

Maidstone Street School,
Goldsmiths Row, Hackney Road, E2.
Opened 1874; renamed Sebright School,
1951. (LMA: EO/DIV 4/MAI)
A&D 1868-1946 (girls); 1874-1931 (boys);
1931-46 (junior boys)
LB 1872-1932 (boys); 1932-39 (junior boys);
1887-1939 (girls); 1899-1913 (evening
boys); 1903-13 (evening girls)

Malmesbury Road School,
Coburn Road, Bow Road, E3. Opened
1885; renamed Malmesbury School, 1951.
(LMA: EO/DIV 5/MAL)
A&D 1885-1936 (boys); 1899-1929 (junior
mixed); 1929-39 (junior girls); 1934-39
(infants); 1936-39 (junior boys)
LB 1885-1933 (boys); 1885-1913 (girls);
1913-39 (junior girls); 1933-39 (junior
boys)
Misc honours 1929-39 (junior boys); 1930-39
(junior girls)

Malory School, Launcelot Road, Bromley.
fl.1971.

Manchester Street School, Kings Cross, NW1.
Opened 1881; renamed Argyle Street
School, 1937. (LMA: EO/DIV 2/MAN)
A&D 1873-89, 1903-38 (boys); 1879-1915
(infants); 1904-30 (girls)
LB 1878-88, 1914-38 (boys); 1878-1913
(infants); 1902-31 (girls); 1903-36 (senior
girls)

Mander Portman Woodward, Elvaston Place,
SW7. Opened 1973.

Mandeville Street School, Millfields Road, E5.
Opened 1902; renamed Clapton Park
School, 1951. (LMA: EO/DIV 4/MAN)
A&D 1902-31 (infants); 1942-45 (boys)
LB 1913-31, 1946-53 (boys); 1913-36 (infants)

Manorfield School, Wyvis Street, E14. fl.1971.

Manor House School, Clapham (Independent)
(boys). Opened 1876.

Manor Lane School, Leahurst Road, SE13.
Opened 1911; renamed Lee Manor Primary
School, 1951. (LMA: EO/DIV 6/MAN)
LB 1911-13 (girls)

Manorway Primary School, SE2. Opened 1903;
renamed Church Manorway Primary
School, 1951; closed 1960s.
(LMA: EO/DIV 6/MAN)
LB 1932-56 (infants)

Mansfield Road Special School,
St Pancas, NW3. Opened 1900;
later Gospel Oak School.
(LMA: EO/DIV 2/MAS)
A&D 1900-40 (mixed)
LB 1932-39 (mixed)

Mansford Street Secondary School, Bethnal
Green Road, E2. Opened 1883; Mansford
Street Central School, 1896; renamed
Mansford Secondary School, 1951.
(LMA: EO/DIV 5/MAN)
A&D 1946-56 (boys)
LB 1928-39 (mixed)

Mantle Road School, Brockley, SE4. Opened
1885; renamed Brockley Central School,
1914; Thomas Wolsey Secondary School,
1951. (LMA: EO/DIV 7/MAN)
LB 1888-95 (evening)

Mantua Street School, York Road, Clapham
Junction, SW11. Opened 1876; renamed
Falconbrook Primary School, 1951.
(LMA: EO/DIV 9/MAN)
A&D 1876-85, 1923-39 (boys); 1876-99 (junior
boys); 1876-1909, 1933-39 (girls);
1893-1900 (senior girls); 1900-27 (junior
mixed)
LB 1876-1939 (boys); 1876-1937 (girls);
1876-1927 (infants)
Misc punishment 1902-38 (infants)

Marianne Thornton School, Clapham Common
West Side, SW4. (LMA: EO/DIV 9/MAR)
A&D 1960-67

Marion Richardson School *see* **Senrab Street
School**

Marist Convent School, Fulham Road, SW6.
Opened 1895; closed 1995.

Marlborough Grove School, SE1. Opened
1874; renamed Elfrida Rathbone School,
1951. (LMA: EO/DIV 7/MAR)
A&D 1920-40 (senior mixed)

Marlborough Road School, SW1.
(LMA: EO/DIV 2/MAR)
LB 1900-38 (manual training centre)

Marlborough School, Draycott Avenue, SW3.
Opened 1878 as Marlborough Road School;
renamed 1907. (LMA: EO/DIV 1/MAR)
A&D 1877-1902, 1917-39 (girls); 1878-88
(boys); 1903-17 (junior mixed); 1903-14
(senior mixed); 1914-17 (mixed); 1945-48
(senior boys)

Marner Street School,
St Leonards Street, Bow, E3. Opened
1873; renamed Marner Primary School,
1951. (LMA: EO/DIV 5/MAR 1)
A&D 1873-1939 (boys); 1876-1939 (infants)
LB 1896-1906 (evening)

Marsh Lane School, SE10. Opened 1888.
(LMA: EO/DIV 6/MAS)
A&D 1904-36 (infants)
LB 1888-1910 (girls)

Martin Frobisher Secondary School,
E14. Opened 1874 as Halley Street
Secondary School; renamed 1951.
(LMA: EO/DIV 5/MAR 2)
A&D 1945-63 (mixed)
LB 1952-58 (senior mixed)

Marvels Lane School, Grove Park, SE12.
Opened 1929. (LMA: EO/DIV 7/MAV)
A&D 1930-48 (infants)
LB 1930-57 (infants)

Mary Boon School, Earsby Street, W14.
Previously Hammersmith Secondary
Technical School for Girls; renamed 1951.

Mary Datchelor School, Grove Lane,
Camberwell, SE5. Opened 1877.
(LMA: EO/DIV 8/MAR)
A&D 1930-33, 1941-53, 1966-79 (senior girls)
(LMA)
Misc administrative records 1875-1909
(Guildhall Library)

Maryfields Primary School, W9. Opened 1913
as Bravington Road Special School;
renamed 1950; closed *c*1960.
(LMA: EO/DIV 2/MAR)
A&D 1941-60 (mixed)

Marylebone Commercial Institute,
New Cavendish Street, W1.

Maryon Park School, Woolwich Road,
Old Charlton, SE7. Opened 1896; closed
1960s. (LMA: EO/DIV 6/MAY)
A&D 1896-1938 (boys); 1922-28 (infants);
1938-58 (junior mixed); 1955-58 (junior
mixed and infants)
LB 1896-1943 (boys); 1896-1946 (infants);
1913-39, 1945-49 (girls); 1932-39 (junior
mixed)
Misc visitors 1896-1924; list of old boys
1914-18; medical exams 1947-48 (girls);
1949-50 (junior mixed and infants)

Mary Ward School, St Pancras. Opened 1899.
(LMA: EO/DIV 2/MAY)
A&D 1918-39 (mixed)

Matthias Road Deaf School, Stoke Newington,
N16. closed 1903; transferred to Hugh
Myddleton Deaf Centre.
(LMA: EO/DIV 3/MAT)
LB 1895-1903 (mixed)

Mawbey Road School, Old Kent Road, SE1.
Opened 1884; closed 1940s.
(LMA: EO/DIV 7/MAW)
A&D 1874-1935 (girls); 1884-1935 (boys)

Mayford Approved School, Woking, Surrey.
(LMA: LCC/CH/D/MAY)
A&D 1909-28
LB 1884-1954

Meadway School, Waldron Road, SW18.
fl.1971.

Metropolitan Asylums Board Training Ship
Exmouth (LMA: MAB)
A&D 1876-1947
Misc minute books 1875-1930; staff 1900-45

Meyfield School, West Hill, SW15. fl.1971.
Records Some at Wandsworth Library

Mayflower School, Upper North Street, E14.
fl.1971.

Maze Hill School, Woodland Place, Trafalgar
Road, Greenwich, SE10. Opened 1876.

Mazenod Roman Catholic School, Mazenod
Avenue, Kilburn, NW6. Opened 1967.

Medburn School,
Charrington Street, Crowndale Road,
St Pancras, NW1. Opened 1877; renamed
Sir William Collins Secondary School,
1951. (LMA: EO/DIV 2/MED)

Medburn School [*continued*]
A&D 1898-1936 (boys); 1910-38 (girls); 1911-31 (junior boys); 1916-28 (infants); 1929-40 (senior boys)
LB 1895-1913, 1925-31 (junior boys); 1912-39 (manual training centre); 1913-36 (senior boys); 1913-31 (senior girls); 1913-38 (infants)
Misc 1874-94 (pupil leavers)

Meeting House Lane School (ESN), Peckham High Street, SE15. Opened 1916. (LMA: EO/DIV 7/MEE)
A&D 1906-35, 1946-50 (mixed)
LB 1913-39 (mixed)

Meeting House School, Downham, Bromley. fl.1971.

Melcombe School, Fulham Palace Road, W6. Previously Fulham Palace Road School; renamed 1951.

Melior Street Roman Catholic School, SE1. Opened 1864; renamed La Salette Roman Catholic Primary School, 1951. (LMA: EO/DIV 8/MEL)
LB 1866-1907 (girls); 1901-24 (mixed)

Mellitus Street School, Mellitus Street, W12. Opened 1913 as Old Oak Estate School renamed 1921; Old Oak School, 1932.

Mercers' School, Barnard's Inn, Holborn, EC1. (Independent) (boys). Opened 1447.

Merchant Taylors' School, Charterhouse Square, EC1. (Independent) (boys). Opened 1561 in Suffolk Lane; to Charterhouse 1875; later moved to Northwood, Middlesex.
Registers Register of Scholars admitted into Merchant Taylors' School from 1562-1874 (C.J. Robinson, 1882-3); Additons and Corrections to Robinson's Register (E.P. Hart, 1933); School Register 1561-1934 (E.P. Hart, 1934); School Register 1851-1920 (E.P. Hart, 1921)

Meridian School, Old Woolwich Road, SE10. Opened 1889 as Old Woolwich Road School; renamed 1951. (LMA: EO/DIV 6/MER)
A&D 1929-32 (senior girls)

Merton Road School, Putney, SW18. Opened 1891. (LMA: EO/DIV 9/MER)
A&D 1891-1932 (infants); 1918-21 (boys); 1932-39 (senior mixed)

Michael Faraday School, Faraday Street, Portland Street, SE17. Opened 1897; formerly Westmoreland Street. (LMA: EO/DIV 8/MIC)
A&D 1897-1939 (senior boys); 1920-35 (infants)

Middle Park School, Gregory Crescent, SE9. Opened 1937.

Middle Row School, Kensal New Town, W10. Opened 1878; renamed Brunel Secondary School, 1951. (LMA: EO/DIV 1/MID)
A&D 1893-1958 (boys); 1898-1932, 1946-66 (junior mixed); 1910-40 (girls)
LB 1934-58 (boys)

Middlesex Society Charity School, St George in the East.
Misc minute books 1806-19 (Tower Hamlets Library)

Middlesex Street Presbyterian School, Somers Town
LB 1864-74 (Camden Local Studies Library)

Midway Place School also known as Rotherhithe Nautical School, Bush Road, Rotherhithe New Road, SE8. Opened 1877. (LMA: EO/DIV 8/MID)
A&D 1891-1914 (boys); 1895-1905 (infants); 1944-45 (girls)
LB 1910-13 (boys); 1945-47 (girls)
Misc punishment 1941-46

Mile End Central School, Myrdle Street, Commercial Road East, E1. Opened 1905. (LMA: EO/DIV 5/MIE)
A&D 1930-39 (mixed - class registers)

Mile End Old Town Charity School *see* **Red Coat School**

Mile Oak Approved School, Portslade, Sussex. Replaced Chailey Industrial School. (LCC/CH/D/MIL)
A&D 1875-1944

Miles Coverdale School, Coverdale Road, W12. Amalgamation of Thornfield Road School, Coverdale Road School and Coverdale School, 1960.

Millbank School, Erasmus Street, Millbank
Estate, SW1. Opened 1902; closed 1960
reopened as Millbank Primary School
1970. (LMA: EO/DIV 2/MILL)
A&D 1902-45 (girls); 1902-47 (infants);
1914-45 (boys); 1941-43 (mixed)
LB 1901-11 (mixed); 1901-55 (manual training
centre); 1901-55, 1959-60 (senior mixed);
1902-39, 1941-45 (boys); 1902-35 (girls);
1902-32 (infants); 1935-39 (senior girls);
1940-45 (mixed - emergency)
Misc visitors 1902-39

Millfields Road School, Lower Clapton Road,
E5. Opened 1895; renamed Millfields
School, 1938. (LMA: EO/DIV 4/MIL)
A&D 1903-16 (junior mixed)

Millfields Road Central School, E5. Opened
1911; renamed North Hackney Central
School, 1927.

Milson Road School, Milson Road, W14.
Opened 1915; closed 1933; demolished
c1937. (LMA: EO/DIV 1/MIL)
LB 1915-33 (girls); 1915-33 (infants)

Millwall Central School, Poplar. Opened 1928.

Millwall School, Glengall Road, Poplar, E14.
Opened 1897; renamed Isle of Dogs
School, 1928. (LMA: EO/DIV 5/MIL)
A&D 1907-32 (mixed)
LB 1907-13 (mixed)

Mina Road School, SE17.
(LMA: EO/DIV 8/MIN)
A&D 1889-1934 (girls); 1890-1939 (boys);
1892-1920, 1928-35 (infants); 1900-24
(junior girls); 1930-34 (mixed)

Miss Edge's School, Tooting Bec Gardens,
SW17.

Miss Pace's School, Camberwell, SE5.
Misc accounts 1844-52 (Southwark Local
Studies Lib)

Mitcham Lane School, Penwortham Road,
Streatham, SW16. Opened 1908; renamed
Estreham Secondary School and
Penwortham Primary School, 1951.
(LMA: EO/DIV 9/MIT)
A&D 1902-12, 1934-54 (senior boys); 1902-11
(infants); 1906-15 (mixed); 1913-37 (boys);
1922-54 (senior girls)
LB 1902-35 (mixed); 1908-34 (handicrafts);
1926-34 (girls); 1932-60 (secondary girls)

Moatbridge School, Eltham Palace Road, SE9.
fl.1971.

Moberley School, Harrow Road, W9.
Opened 1884 as Harrow Road School;
renamed 1913; closed 1957.
(LMA: EO/DIV 2/MOB)
A&D 1884-1926 (infants); 1893-1957 (girls);
1896-1932 (boys); 1930-57 (junior mixed);
1942-45 (mixed and infants)
LB 1930-39, 1942-57 (junior mixed and infants)

Modern School, Paradise House,
Stoke Newington (Independent) (boys).
Opened 1876.

Modern School, Streatham High Road, SW16.

Monnow Road School, Southwark, SE1.
Opened 1874; renamed Monnow Road
Central School, 1910; Bermondsey Central
School, 1915. (LMA: EO/DIV 8/MON)
LB 1895-1909, 1913-20 (boys); 1900-13
(manual training centre)

Monson Road School,
New Cross Road, SE14. Opened 1882 as
Cold Blow Lane School; renamed 1895;
renamed Monson School, 1951. (LMA:
EO/DIV 6/MON & EO/DIV 7/MON)
A&D 1895-1913 (boys)
LB 1904-30 (girls); 1932-41 (junior mixed)

Montbelle School, Montbelle Road, SE9.
fl.1971.

Montem Street School, Marriott Road,
Tollington Park, N4. Opened 1886;
renamed Montem Primary School. 1949;
removed to Hornsey Road, 1957.
(LMA: EO/DIV 3/MON)
A&D 1942-71 (infants)

Montieth Road School, Old Ford Road, E3.
Opened 1873. (LMA: EO/DIV 5/MON)
A&D 1881-1939 (boys); 1905-33 (infants)
LB 1873-97, 1913-33 (infants); 1889-1915
(laundry centre); 1890-1913 (girls);
1892-1939 (boys); 1913-29 (mentally
defective)

Montrose College, Streatham Hill (Independent)
(boys).

Moorfields School, Radnor Street, EC1.

Moorhouse Road Emergency School *see*
St Mary of the Angel School

Moorside Road Roman Catholic School,
(later Pastor Bonus School), Downham
Estate, Lewisham.

Morden Terrace School, Orchard Hill, SE3.
Opened 1880; later Morden Mount School.

More House School, Pont Street, SW1.
Opened 1953.

Moreland Street School, Goswell Road, EC1.
Opened 1877; renamed Moreland Primary
School 1951. (LMA: EO/DIV 3/MOR)
A&D 1877-1914, 1953-71 (infants); 1892-1939
(girls); 1956-73 (junior)
LB 1877-1903, 1913-38 (boys); 1902-28 (girls);
1902-25, 1937-54 (infants); 1945-83
(primary mixed)
Misc miscellaneous book 1895-1912;
punishment 1943-66

Morning Lane School, Mare Street, E9. Opened
1884; renamed Morningside Primary
School and Joseph Priestley Secondary
School, 1951. (LMA: EO/DIV 4/MOR)
A&D 1873-92, 1908-30 (boys); 1894-1939
(girls); 1940-44 (mixed)
LB 1884-1939 (boys); 1884-1913, 1920-44
(girls); 1884-1922 (infants); 1913-38
(junior mixed - blind)

Morpeth Street Central School, Bethnal Green,
E2. Opened 1910.
A&D 1943-87 (Tower Hamlets Library)
LB 1944-92 (Tower Hamlets Library)

Mount Carmel Roman Catholic School, Eden
Grove, N7. Opened 1967.

Mount Pleasant County Secondary School,
Upper Clapton, Hackney, E5. Opened
1935; merged into Brooke House School,
1960.

Mowlem Street School, Bishop's Road,
Cambridge Heath, E2. Opened 1887;
renamed Mowlem Primary School, 1951.
(LMA: EO/DIV 5/MOW)
A&D 1887-1939 (boys); 1887-1920 (infants);
1899-1939 (girls); 1940, 1943-45 (mixed)
LB 1887-1939 (boys); 1887-1939 (girls);
1887-1939 (infants); 1921-27 (mentally
defective)
Misc visitors 1887-1939; honours 1930-39
(senior girls)

Mulgrave Place Myopic School, Wellington
Street, SE18. Opened 1894; renamed
Mulgrave Primary School, 1951.
(LMA: EO/DIV 6/MUL)
A&D 1921-32 (mixed); 1935-39 (infants)
LB 1917-43 (evening)

Munster Road School,
Fulham Road, SW6. Opened 1893;
renamed Munster School, 1938; closed
1992. (LMA: EO/DIV 1/MUN)
A&D 1893-1931 (boys); 1893-1937 (girls);
1893-1939 (infants); 1931-39 (junior boys);
1937-39 (junior girls); 1940-48 (senior
mixed)
LB 1893-1939 (boys); 1893-1939 (girls);
1913-38 (infants); 1916-42 (evening)

Myrdle Street School, Commercial Road East,
E1. Opened 1905; renamed Grenfell
School, 1950. (LMA: EO/DIV 5/MYR)
A&D 1905-30, 1940 (boys); 1905-30 (infants);
1905-25, 1943 (mixed); 1930-32, 1942-43
(senior girls); 1932-39 (junior girls); 1940
(girls)

Nansen School, Pendragon Road, Bromley.
fl.1971.

Napier Street School,
Shepherdess Walk, Hoxton, N1. Opened
1885; renamed Napier School, 1938;
Thomas Fairchild Primary School, 1951.
(LMA: EO/DIV 4/NAP)
A&D 1885-1939, 1944-45 (boys); 1885-1901,
1912-39, 1941-42 (girls); 1903-56 (infants)
LB 1885-1939 (boys); 1885-1939 (girls);
1885-1939 (infants); 1900-34 (training
centre)

Nathaniel Heckford School, Cable Street, E1.
fl.1971.

National Society's Central School, Baldwins
Garden's, Holborn, EC3. Opened 1812.
Misc minute books 1813-28 (Church of England
Records Centre)

Neale's Mathematical School, St Dunstan in the
West, EC4.
A&D 1931-35, 1939-40 (Guildhall Library)
Misc administrative records 1924-54
(Guildhall Library)

Neckinger School, Bermondsey, SE1.
(LMA: EO/DIV 8/NEC)
A&D 1893-1928 (boys); 1923-33 (infants);
1928-34 (junior mixed)

Nelson Street School,
Trafalgar Street, Walworth, SE17. Opened
1891 as Sandford Row School; renamed
1932. (LMA: EO/DIV 8/NEL)
A&D 1870-82 (boys); 1930-35 (girls); 1930-39
(junior mixed); 1941-45 (emergency);
1945-62 (senior mixed)
LB 1930-39, 1942-44 (junior mixed);
1945 (secondary modern mixed)
Misc staff 1949-62

Netherwood Street School, Kilburn, NW8.
Opened 1881; renamed Harben School,
1931. (LMA: EO/DIV 2/NER)
A&D 1881-1939 (boys); 1881-1939 (girls)
LB 1881-1931 (boys); 1881-1929 (girls)
(evening class 1885-1933 at (Camden Local
Studies Library)

Netley Street School, Hampstead Road, NW1.
Opened 1884 as St John Netley Street;
renamed, 1879; renamed Netley Primary
School, 1951. (LMA: EO/DIV 2/NET)
A&D 1929-39 (boys); 1945-64 (junior mixed)
LB 1879-1939 (boys); 1921-39 (infants);
1945-59 (junior mixed)

New Castle Street School, Bethnal Green, E2.
later Virginia Road School; renamed
Virginia Primary School, 1951.
(LMA: EO/DIV 5/NEW)
LB 1875-1913 (boys); 1875-1913 (girls);
1875-1900 (infants); 1893-1913 (special)

Newcomen's Domestic Trade School for Girls,
Borough, SE1.

New Cross Sunday School. (Methodist)
A&D 1938 (Southwark Local Studies Lib)
Misc minute books 1839-49, 1906-39; accounts
1933-44 (Southwark Local Studies Lib)

New End School, Heath Street, NW3.
Opened 1906. (LMA: EO/DIV 2/NEE)
A&D 1940-52 (junior mixed and infants)

Newington Green School, N16. Opened 1884 as
Matthias Road School; renamed by 1893.

Newington Junior School (temporary)
Opened 1932.

New Jerusalem School, St Pancras. Opened as
New Jerusalem British School.
(LMA: EO/DIV 2/NEJ)
A&D 1869-79 (infants)
LB 1865-78 (boys); 1870-78 (infants)

New Kings Road School, SW6. Opened 1905;
renamed Holman Hunt School, 1951.
(LMA: EO/DIV 1/NEW)
LB 1914-39 (junior mixed)

New Kings School, New Kings Road, SW6.
Formed 1991 from Holman Hunt and
Munster Road Schools.

New Park Road School, Brixton Hill, SW2.
Opened 1897; renamed Richard Atkins
School, 1951. (LMA: EO/DIV 9/NEP)
A&D 1896-1934, 1940 (boys); 1913-34 (girls);
1931-50 (junior boys); 1934-39 (infants)
LB 1894-1939 (infants); 1896-1933 (boys);
1898-1913 (mixed); 1913-39 (girls);
1913-46 (evening); 1934-39 (junior boys);
1942-58 (junior girls)

New River School, Clissold Road, N16.
fl.1971.

New Road School, Thessaly Road,
Wandsworth Road, SW8. Opened 1874;
renamed Bradmede School, 1951.
(LMA: EO/DIV 9/NEW)
A&D 1879-1912 (infants); 1917-39 (girls);
1925-33 (boys)
LB 1874-92, 1932-33 (boys); 1874-1931 (girls);
1903-13, 1934-39 (infants); 1931-39 (junior
girls); 1933-39 (junior boys)

Newton Preparatory School, Battersea Park
Road, SW8. Opened 1991.

Nicholas Gibson School, The Highway, E1.
Opened 1885 formerly Broad Street School;
renamed 1951. (LMA: EO/DIV 5/NIG)
A&D 1895-1907, 1945-52 (boys); 1941-55
(infants); 1945-52 (girls); 1945-56 (junior
mixed)
LB 1945-56 (junior mixed)

Nicholl Street School,
Bethnal Green, E2. Opened 1879;
transferred to New Castle Street School,
1888. (LMA: EO/DIV 5/NIC)
LB 1872-88 (boys); 1884-88 (girls)

Nightingale Square Roman Catholic School,
(later Holy Ghost School), Endlesham
Road, Balham, SW12. Opened 1903.

Nightingale Street School, St Johns Wood,
NW8. Renamed Capland Street School,
1887. (LMA: EO/DIV 2/NIG)
LB 1874-98 (infants); 1876-93 (girls);
1878-99 (boys)

Norland Place School, Holland Park Avenue, W11. Opened 1876.

Normand Park School, Lillie Road, W14. Opened 1959. (LMA: EO/DIV 1/NOM)
A&D 1959-70 (mixed)

Northampton Polytechnic, St John Street, EC1.

Northampton Secondary School, Chequer Street, EC1. Opened 1877 as Chequer Street School; renamed 1951. (LMA: EO/DIV 3/NOR)
A&D 1956-59 (boys)

North Bridge House School, Netherhall Gardens, NW3. Private. Opened by 1960.

Northbrook Church of England School, Hedgley Street, SE12. Opened 1871 as Hedgley Street School; renamed 1904.
A&D 1884-1939 (boys); 1893-1930 (girls); 1877-1936 (infants) (Lewisham Local History Lib)
LB 1884-1909, 1917-40 (boys); 1884-1939 (girls); 1877-1940 (infants) (Lewisham Local History Lib)
Misc minute books 1870-81, 1902-18 (Lewisham Local History Lib)

Northcote Lodge School, Bolingbroke Grove, SW11. fl.1971.

North Croft School, Shepherds Bush Road, W6 (maladjusted). Opened 1958.

North End Road School, Lillie Road, SW6. Opened 1881; destroyed 1944. (LMA: EO/DIV 1/NER)
A&D 1891-1909 (girls)
LB 1881-97, 1913-31 (boys); 1913-20 (girls); 1931-40 (senior girls)

North End School, Sandy Road, NW3. Opened 1840; closed 1907.

Northern Polytechnic Day School, Holloway Road, N7. Opened 1896.

Northey Street School, Limehouse, E14. Opened 1874; renamed Cyril Jackson School, 1925. (LMA: EO/DIV 5/NOR)
A&D 1893-1924 (infants); 1903-39 (girls)
Misc visitors 1886-1927; punishment 1912-33

North Hackney Central School, Hilsea Street and Elmcroft Street, E5. Opened 1911; closed c1958/63.
A&D 1928-51 (Hackney Archives)
LB 1928-58 (Hackney Archives)

North Hammersmith Central School, Bryony Road, W12. Opened 1931; renamed North Hammersmith Secondary Boys School, 1946.

North Hammersmith Secondary Boys School, Mellitus Street, W12. Opened 1931 as North Hammersmith Central School; renamed 1946; amalgamated with Christopher Wren School, 1956 and premises taken over by Old Oak School.

North Hammersmith Secondary School for Girls, Bryony Road, W12. Opened 1946; moved to The Curve and renamed Hammersmith County School, 1957.

North Kensington Central School, St Marks Road, St Charles Square, W10. Opened 1911 as St Marks Road Central School; renamed 1921; Answorth Nursery School, 1951. (LMA: EO/DIV 1/NOR)
A&D 1911-39 (mixed)
LB 1913-33 (mixed)

North London College, Sandall Road, NW5. Opened 1850.

North Paddington Central School, Kilburn Lane, Kensal Green, W10. Opened 1885 as Kilburn Lane School; renamed 1926; merged to form Paddington School, 1972. (LMA: EO/DIV 2/NOR)
A&D 1926-48 (girls); 1940-45 (emergency); 1945-48 (boys); 1945-58 (mixed)
LB 1945-72 (mixed)
Misc punishment 1946-73

North Surrey School District. Constituted by Chelsea Board of Guardians 1850-76, Kensington Board of Guardians 1870-1876, Lewisham Board of Guardians 1849-1930 and Wandsworth and Clapham Board of Guardians 1849-1930 (LMA: NSSD)
A&D 1850-1931
Misc minute books 1849-1930; staff 1850-1930

North-Western Polytechnic, Kentish Town Road and Prince of Wales Road, NW5.

North West London Jewish School, Minster Road, Cricklewood, NW2. Opened 1945; moved to Willesden 1958.

Northwold Road School, Upper Clapton Road, E5. Opened 1902; renamed Northwold Primary School and Northwold Secondary School, 1951. (LMA: EO/DIV 4/NOR)
A&D 1902-37 (infants); 1902-30, 1942-51 (senior mixed); 1902-29 (junior mixed); 1903-32 (mixed); 1929-39 (girls); 1930-39 (boys)
LB 1884-88, 1913-39 (girls); 1902-32 (infants); 1902-13 (mixed); 1903-26 (mentally defective - mixed and infants); 1913-51 (senior mixed)

North Woolwich Secondary School, Woodman Street, E16. Opened 1891 as Dock Street Temporary School; renamed Elizabeth Street School, 1894; again renamed 1951 (LMA: EO/DIV 6/NOR)
A&D 1945-62 (mixed)

Norwood School or **Norwood Park School**, Gypsy Road, SE27.

Notre Dame Convent Commercial School for Girls, Eglinton Road, Plumstead, SE18.

Notre Dame School, Battersea Park Road, SW8.
A&D 1904-75 (LMA Modern Records Section)

Notre Dame Secondary School, St George's Road, SE1.

Nunhead Passage School, SE15. Opened 1884; renamed Peckham Rye School; renamed Nunhead Secondary School, 1951; closed 1960s. (LMA: EO/DIV 7/NUN)
A&D 1893-1920 (infants)
LB 1884-1911 (girls)

Nynhead Street School, SE14. Opened 1883; closed 1930s. (LMA: EO/DIV 6/NYN)
A&D 1883-1928 (infants); 1893-1928 (girls); 1923-28 (boys); 1928-32 (junior mixed and infants)

Oakfield Preparatory School, Thurlow Park Road, Dulwich, SE21. Opened 1887.

Oak Lodge, Nightingale Lane, SW12. (Deaf).

Oakmere Secondary School, Wickham Lane, SE2. Opened 1903 as Wickham Lane School; renamed 1959; closed 1960s. (LMA: EO/DIV 6/OAK)
A&D 1944-66 (boys)
LB 1943-66 (senior boys)

Oban Street School, Bromley, E14. Opened 1883. (LMA: EO/DIV 5/OBA)
A&D 1883-1931 (boys); 1883-1933 (girls); 1883-1933 (infants)
LB 1883-1933 (boys); 1883-1933 (girls); 1893-1913 (evening); 1900-33 (infants)

Ocean Street School, E1. Opened 1908; renamed Raleigh School, 1933. (LMA: EO/DIV 5/OCE)
A&D 1931-39 (infants)
LB 1932-39 (senior girls)

Offord Road Special School, N1. Opened 1905; renamed Offord Primary School, 1950; special unit closed c1967. (LMA: EO/DIV 3/OFF)
LB 1905-13 (mixed)

Old Battersea Roman Catholic School, Trott Street, SW11. Opened 1903; later Sacred Heart of Jesus School.

Old Castle Street School, Old Castle Street, E1. Opened 1873; closed 1917. (LMA: EO/DIV 5/OLD 1)
A&D 1902-17 (infants)

Oldfield Road School, Kynaston Road, Stoke Newington High Street, N16. Opened 1882; renamed Daniel Defoe Secondary School, 1951. (LMA: EO/DIV 4/OLD)
A&D 1888-1913 (boys); 1901-39 (junior mixed and infants); 1913-31 (mixed)
LB 1914-31 (junior mixed and infants); 1931-39 (senior girls); 1932-39 (evening)

Old Ford School, E3. *see also* Roman Road School. (LMA: EO/DIV 5/OLD 3)
LB 1872-90 (infants); 1873-89 (girls)

Old Kent Road Ragged and Industrial Schools, Park Road, SE1. (LMA: P73/CTC)
Misc minute books 1871-89

Old Kent Road Special School, Southwark, SE1. Opened 1903; bombed 1940.
LB 1938-40 (boys)

Old Montague Street School, E1.
Opened 1903; closed 1926.
(LMA: EO/DIV 5/OLD 2)
A&D 1903-26 (boys); 1903-26 (girls);
1903-26 (infants)

Old Oak School, Mellitus Road, W12.
Opened 1913 as Old Oak Estate School;
renamed Mellitus Street School, 1921 and
renamed Old Oak School, 1932.
(LMA: EO/DIV 1/OLD)
A&D 1913-43 (junior mixed); 1921-43 (infants)
LB 1913-47 (infants)

Old Palace Road School,
St Leonard's Street, E3. Opened 1896.
(LMA: EO/DIV 5/OLD 3)
A&D 1932-39 (junior mixed and infants);
1940-46 (emergency)

Oldridge Road School, Balham, SW12. Opened
1882; school for deaf opened 1934;
renamed Alderbrook School, 1951.
(LMA: EO/DIV 9/OLD)
LB 1882-1903, 1913-34 (boys); 1882-1929
(girls); 1882-97, 1913-37 (infants)

Old Woolwich Road or Trafalgar Road School,
SE10. Opened 1889; renamed Meridian
School, 1951. (LMA: EO/DIV 6/OLD)
A&D 1933-39 (senior mixed)
LB 1913-33 (girls); 1929-31 (infants); 1933-36
(junior mixed)

Olga Street School, Medway Road, Roman
Road, E3. Opened 1874; renamed John
Bartlett Primary School, 1951.
(LMA: EO/DIV 5/OLG)
A&D 1875-1928 (infants); 1893-1933 (boys);
1897-1933 (girls); 1926-39 (junior mixed)
LB 1874-1930 (boys); 1874-1933 (girls);
1874-1927 (infants); 1946-48 (mixed - in
EO/DIV 5/BOW 4/LB/2)

Oliver Goldsmith School, Cork Street,
Waterloo Street, SE5. Opened as Acorn
Street School, 1895; part of Southampton
Street School 1895-1931; renamed
Southampton Way School, 1938; Dovedale
School, 1951. (LMA: EO/DIV 7/OLI)
A&D 1914-31 (girls); 1931-50 (junior girls);
1950-60 (junior mixed)
LB 1900-23 (manual training centre); 1931-39
(senior girls); 1936-39 (junior girls)

Orange Street School, SE1. Opened 1874;
renamed John Harvard School, 1937.
(LMA: EO/DIV 8/ORA)

Orange Street School [*continued*]
A&D 1889-1936 (infants); 1931-36
(senior boys)

Oratory Roman Catholic School, Bury Street,
SW3. Opened 1856.

Oratory Roman Catholic School, Ixworth Place,
SW3. Opened 1881.

Oratory Roman Catholic Central Schools,
Stewart's Grove, SW3. Opened 1857.

Orchard House School see **Prendergast School**

Orchard Primary School, Well Street, Hackney,
E9. Opened 1926 as Holcroft Road School;
renamed 1927.

Osbourne Place School. Opened 1908; closed
1936. (LMA: EO/DIV 5/OSB)
A&D 1905-36 (mixed)

Ottaway Street School, Lower Clapton, E5.

Our Lady and St Philip Neri School,
Sydenham Road, SE26. fl.1969/71.

**Our Lady of Assumpton Roman Catholic
School**, Copenhagen Place, E14. Opened
1926. (LMA: EO/DIV 5/OUR)
A&D 1926-39 (mixed and infants)
LB 1930-39 (girls); 1930-39 (infants)

**Our Lady of Assumpton Roman Catholic
School**, Bonner Road, Old Ford Road, E2.

Our Lady of Dolours Roman Catholic School,
Desborough Street, Paddington, W2.
Opened 1867 as Harrow Road Vine Court
Roman Catholic School, name changed
*c*1907.

Our Lady of Grace Roman Catholic School,
Charlton Road, SE7.

Our Lady of Sion School, Eden Grove, N7.
Opened 1903; closed 1967 replaced by
Mount Carmel School.

Our Lady of Sion School, Denbigh Road, W11.

**Our Lady of The Angels Roman Catholic
School**, Nine Elms Lane, SW8.
(LMA: EO/DIV 9/OUR)
LB 1930-39 (infants)

Our Lady of the Sacred Heart Roman Catholic School, Eden Grove, Holloway, N7. Opened 1868.

Our Lady of Victories Roman Catholic School, Clarendon Drive, SW15. fl.1971.

Our Lady of Victories Roman Catholic School, Warwick Road, West Kensington, W14. Opened 1882 as St Edward's, Holland Street; renamed 1906.
(LMA: EO/DIV 1/OUR)
A&D 1879-1939 (boys)
LB 1901-39 (boys)

Our Lady Queen of Heaven Roman Catholic School, Victoria Drive, SW19. fl.1971.

Overhill School, SW11. Opened 1890; formerly Plough Road School.
(LMA: EO/DIV 9/OVE)
A&D 1945-62 (girls)

Owen's School, Owen's Row, Islington, EC1. (Independent) (boys). Opened 1613.
see A History of Owen's School (R.A. Dare, 1963)

Oxford Gardens School, Ladbroke Grove, W10. Opened 1884.
(LMA: EO/DIV 1/OXF)
A&D 1884-1935 (junior girls); 1884-1931 (infants); 1892-1939 (junior boys)
LB 1884-1939 (boys); 1884-1937 (girls); 1913-48 (infants)

Oxford House School, Junction Road, Upper Holloway (Independent) (boys). Opened 1864.

Paddenswick Road School, Goldhawk Road, W6. *see* **St Peter's Free School**

Paddington and Maida Vale High School, Elgin Avenue, W9. Opened 1884; independent until 1913; merged into Paddington School, 1972. (LMA: EO/DIV 2/PAD 1)
A&D 1905-45 (girls)

Paddington Green School, Park Place Villas, W2. fl.1971.

Paddington School, Oakington Road, W9. Opened 1972.

Paddington Technical Institute, Saltram Crescent, W9. Opened 1903; renamed Paddington Technical College, 1948. (LMA: EO/DIV 2/PAD 2)
A&D 1912-36, 1940-52 (boys); 1912-44 (girls)
LB 1911-12 (Technical Institute); 1924-36 (Literary Institute)

Paddington Wharf School, Church Place, W2. Opened 1848; probably closed by 1880.

Page's Walk School, Old Kent Road, SE1. Opened 1897. (LMA: EO/DIV 8/PAG)
A&D 1913-39 (infants); 1917-31 (mixed); 1924-36 (junior boys); 1936-39 (senior girls)
LB 1913-33 (infants); 1917-27 (evening)

Pakeman Street School, Holloway, N7. Opened 1888.

Paradise House School, Paradise Row, N16. Opened 1876; closed 1929.

Paragon School, New Kent Road, SE1. Opened 1900; renamed Borough Paragon School, 1951; closed 1960. (LMA: EO/DIV 8/PAR)
A&D 1932-46 (infants)
LB 1900-10 (boys); 1900-09 (girls); 1900-10 (infants)
Misc punishment 1943-59

Parayhouse School, King's Road, SW10. Opened 1964.

Park Chapel School, Chelsea. fl.1904.

Parkside School, Bartley Road, Lambeth. SW2. Opened 1878 as Lyham Road School; renamed 1935. (LMA: EO/DIV 8/PAS)
A&D 1948-70 (girls)

Park Walk Primary School, Kings Road, SW10. Opened 1882 (see Cooks Ground for earlier). (LMA: EO/DIV 1/PAR)
LB 1924-39 (evening)

Parkwood Primary School, Queen's Drive, N16. Opened 1969.

Parliament Hill School, Highgate Road, NW5. Opened 1906. (LMA: EO/DIV 2/PLM)
A&D 1957-76 (girls)

Parliament Street Roman Catholic School, Cambridge Road, E2. Opened 1869.

Parmiter's School, Victoria Park, E2.
(Independent) (boys). Opened 1681.
A&D 1892-95 (Tower Hamlets Library)
LB 1939-40 (Tower Hamlets Library)
Misc minute books 1884-1956
(LMA: ACC/1844)

Parsons Green School, Ackmar Road, SW6.
Previously part of Ackmar Road School,
renamed 1951; closed 1962. (LMA:
EO/DIV 1/PAR and EO/DIV 1/PAS)
A&D 1931-46 (mixed); 1946 (senior boys);
1946-61 (children over compulsory leaving
age)
Misc punishment 1949-62 (boys)

Pastor Bonus Roman Catholic School
(previously Moorside Road School,
Bromley. (LMA: EO/DIV 7/PAS)
A&D 1942-46, 1957-58 (mixed)

Paxton School, Woodland Road, SE19.

Peckham Central School, Choumert Road,
SE15 (boys). Opened 1894.

Peckham Central School, Peckham Road, SE15
(girls). Opened 1894.

Peckham Park School, Friary Road,
Peckham, SE15. Opened 1876.
(LMA: EO/DIV 7/PEC 1)
A&D 1876-1929 (boys); 1888-1923 (girls);
1903-39 (junior boys); 1929-39 (junior
girls); 1945-60 (junior mixed)

Peckham Rye School, Whorlton Road, SE15.
Opened 1884 as Nunhead Passage School;
renamed Nunhead Secondary School, 1951;
closed 1960s. (LMA: EO/DIV 7/PEC 2)
A&D 1913-36 (boys); 1913-39 (infants);
1935-39 (girls); 1936-59 (mixed)
LB 1912-13, 1917-39, 1948-50 (girls);
1938-39 (boys)
Misc punishment 1936-59

Peckham Secondary School Opened 1905;
closed 1958. (LMA: EO/DIV 7/PEC 3)
A&D 1946-58 (girls)

Peckham Wesleyan School. Opened 1834;
renamed Stafford Street School, 1923;
closed 1930. (LMA: EO/DIV 7/PEC 4)
A&D 1900-13 (boys); 1900-07, 1913-29
(mixed); 1908-19 (girls)

Pell Street School, St George in the East, E1.
Opened 1903; closed 1906.
(LMA: EO/DIV 5/PEL)
A&D 1903-06 (infants)

Pembridge Hall School, Pembridge Square,
W1. Opened 1979.

Pendragon Road School,
Downham Estate, Bromley. Opened 1929;
renamed Pendragon School, 1951; closed
1970s. (LMA: EO/DIV 7/PEN)
A&D 1922, 1941-43 (junior); 1929-39 (junior
boys); 1929-38 (infants); 1940 (girls)
LB 1929-38 (junior girls)

Pennoyer's Free School, Whitechapel, E1.
A&D 1788-98 (Guildhall Library)
Misc administrative records 1701-1900
(Guildhall Library)

Penrose School, SE17. Opened 1875.

Penton Grove School, N1. Opened 1875;
renamed White Lion Street School, 1899.
(LMA: EO/DIV 3/PEN)
A&D 1888-1900 (infants)
LB 1875-93 (boys)

Penton Primary School *see* **Richard Street
School**

Pentonville Charity School, Finsbury, N1.
(LMA: A/PCS and P76/JS2)
LB 1894-1900
Misc minute books 1819-74; accounts 1802-96

Penwortham School, Penwortham Road, SW16.
fl.1971.

Peterborough Lodge School, Finchley Road,
Hampstead. Opened 1898; closed 1940.

Peterborough School, Clancarty Road, SW6.
Opened 1901. (LMA: EO/DIV 1/PET)
A&D 1927-38 (infants); 1928-42 (boys);
1940-45 (mixed)
LB 1930-39, 1943-64 (junior boys);
1940-46 (mixed)

Peter Hills School, St Marychurch Street,
Rotherhithe, SE16. Previously Amicable
Society School; united to St Mary and
St Paul Schools, 1983.

Peter Joye's Charity School, St Ann
Blackfriars, EC2.
A&D 1705-44 (Guildhall Library)
Misc estates records 1611-1734; administrative
records 1707-1892 (Guildhall Library)

Philological School see
St Marylebone Grammar School

Phoenix School, Bow Road, E3. fl.1971.

Pigot Street School, E14. Opened 1910.
(LMA: EO/DIV 5/PIG)
A&D 1910-38 (mixed)

Pilgrim School see **Globe Terrace School**

Pimlico School, Lupus Street, SW1. fl.1971.

Pitfield School, Shoreditch, N1. Opened 1883
as St Johns Road School; renamed 1938;
closed 1959. (LMA: EO/DIV 4/PIT)
A&D 1952-59 (boys)

Pitman Street Roman Catholic School,
Wyndham Road, Camberwell, SE5.
Opened 1861.

Plassy Road School, Rushey Green, SE6.
Opened 1884; renamed Rushey Green
School, 1951. (LMA: EO/DIV 7/PLA)
A&D 1884-1929 (boys); 1884-96, 1905-17
(infants); 1894-1928 (girls); 1941-43
(mixed)
LB 1884-1908, 1913-28 (girls); 1884-1913
(infants); 1909-15 (evening); 1913-29
(boys); 1951-66 (physically defective)
Misc medical register 1912; punishment 1947

Plough Road School, St John's Hill, Clapham
Junction, SW11. Opened 1890; later
Overhill School. (LMA: EO/DIV 9/PLO)
A&D 1884-1927, 1940-49 (boys); 1912-31
(girls); 1936-39 (infants)
LB 1884-1913, 1932-53 (girls);
1926-36 (infants)

Plumcroft School see **Plum Lane School**

Plum Lane School, Plumstead Common, SE18.
Opened 1903; renamed Plumcroft School,
1951. (LMA: EO/DIV 6/PLL)
A&D 1895-1921 (infants); 1921-31 (girls);
1944-55 (mixed); 1954-60 (boys)
LB 1903-32 (infants); 1913-39 (boys);
1931-39 (senior girls)
Misc punishment 1950-60

Plumstead Central School, Plumstead High
Street, SE18. Opened 1879.

Plumstead High Street School see **High Street
School, Plumstead**

Plumstead Road School, High Street.
Opened 1878; closed 1920s.
(LMA: EO/DIV 6/PLU)
A&D 1897-1920 (infants)
LB 1878-1920 (infants); 1886-1915 (evening)

Pocock Street School, Blackfriars Road, SE1.
Opened 1885 as Friar Street School;
renamed 1915. (LMA: EO/DIV 8/POC)
A&D 1890-1913 (infants)
LB 1885-97, 1913-36 (infants); 1904-13 (boys)

Poland Street School, W1. (Belgian Refugees)
(LMA: EO/DIV 2/POL)
LB 1914-19 (mixed and infants)

Polytechnic School of Architecture, Regent
Street, W1.

Polytechnic School of Art, Regent Street, W1.

Polytechnic School of Engineering, Regent
Street, W1.

Polytechnic School of Photography, Regent
Street, W1.

Polytechnic Secondary Boys School,
Regent Street (boys)

Ponton Road School, Battersea, SW8.
(LMA: EO/DIV 9/PON)
A&D 1895-1928 (infants)

Pooles Park School, Lennox Road,
Seven Sisters Road, N4. Opened 1876.
(LMA: EO/DIV 3/POO)
A&D 1903-47 (boys)
LB 1892-1930 (boys)

Pope John Roman Catholic School,
Commonwealth Avenue, W12. Opened
1966.

Pope Street School, Foots Cray Road,
New Eltham, SE9. Opened 1887; renamed
Wyborne Primary School, 1951.
(LMA: EO/DIV 6/POP)
LB 1888-1919 (evening)

Popham Road School, New North Road, N1.
Opened 1875 as Anglers Gardens; renamed
1895; renamed Charles Lamb School,
1949. (LMA: EO/DIV 3/POP)
A&D 1897-1965 (infants); 1899-1939 (boys);
1914-27, 1943-57 (junior mixed); 1916-32
(girls); 1927-39 (junior girls)
LB 1876-1927 (boys); 1893-1931 (girls);
1900-38 (infants); 1914-39 (junior mixed);
1933-39 (senior boys)

Poplar and Blackwall National School, Bow
Lane now Bazely Street, later Poplar High
Street, E14. Founded 1711
Misc minute books 1804-31, 1857-80 (Tower
Hamlets Library)

Poplar Board of Guardians see
Forest Gate School District

Poplar High Street School see
High Street School, Poplar.

Poplar Technical College, Poplar High Street,
E14. Formerly LCC School of Marine
Engineering. (LMA: EO/DIV 5/POP)
A&D 1955-62 (boys)

Portland Town Church of England School,
St Marylebone, W1. Opened 1864.

Portland Town Roman Catholic School, Upper
William Street, St Marylebone, W1.
Opened 1903.

Portman Chapel School, W1.
(LMA: EO/DIV 2/POR)
LB 1863-94 (girls)

Portman Place School, Globe Road, Bethnal
Green, E2. Opened 1878.
(LMA: EO/DIV 5/POR)
A&D 1894-1900, 1917-39 (infants); 1898-1925
(junior mixed ESN); 1915-27 (senior mixed
myopic); 1915-24, 1943-45 (junior mixed);
1919-37 (girls); 1930-39 (junior girls)
LB 1898-1925 (mentally defective); 1904-29
(infants); 1904-15 (evening); 1915-27
(myopic); 1930-39 (junior girls)

Portobello Road, Notting Hill, W11.
Opened 1876. (LMA: EO/DIV 1/POR)
A&D 1878-1906 (girls); 1919-39 (infants)
LB 1876-1913 (girls); 1876-1913, 1935-39
(infants); 1914-33 (boys)

Portsoken Street School, Minories, E1.

Powis Street School, SE18. Opened 1872 as
Union Street School; renamed 1938.
(LMA: EO/DIV 6/POW)
A&D 1895-1928 (mixed)
LB 1894-1929 (blind - mixed)
Misc minute book 1873-74 (pupil teachers)

Prendergast School, Hawstead Road, SE6.
Known as Orchard House School until 1889
Misc staff 1890-1912 (Lewisham Local
History Lib)

Preparatory School, Queen's Gate, Kensington
(Independent).

Preparatory School, Sloane Street (Independent)
(boys). Opened 1899.

Primrose Hill School *see* **Princess Road School**

Princess May Road School,
Stoke Newington, N16. Opened 1892;
renamed Princess May Primary School,
1951. (LMA: EO/DIV 4/PRI)
A&D 1896-1935 (mixed; special school);
1930-39 (junior girls); 1945-56 (junior
boys)
LB 1896-1913 (mixed - physically and mentally
defective); 1913-35 (junior mixed)

Princess Road School, Regents Park Road,
NW1. Opened 1885; renamed Primrose
Hill Primary School, 1951.
(LMA: EO/DIV 2/PRI)
A&D 1885-1939 (infants); 1922-35 (girls);
1935-39 (junior mixed)
LB 1885-1935 (boys); 1885-1935 (girls);
1935-68 (junior mixed)
Misc punishment 1942-45

Princeton Street School, Bedford Row, WC1.
Opened 1877; renamed Princeton School,
1951; closed 1955. (LMA: EO/DIV 3/PRI)
A&D 1898-1931 (girls); 1911-39 (boys);
1911-39, 1948-55 (infants); 1931-48 (junior
mixed); 1939-48 (mixed)
LB 1877-1936, 1941-54 (infants)
Misc punishment 1948-55

Prior Weston School, Whitecross Street, EC1.
fl.1971.

Priory Grove School, Wandsworth, SW8.
Opened 1886; renamed Priory School,
1933. (LMA: EO/DIV 8/PRI)
A&D 1892-1933 (boys); 1934-48 (girls)
LB 1886-1931 (boys); 1932 (special); 1934-46
(senior girls)

Priory House School, The Common, Upper Clapton, E5. (Independent) (boys). Opened 1846.

Pritchard's Road School, Hackney Road, Bethnal Green, E2. Opened 1875. (LMA: EO/DIV 5/PRI)
A&D 1875-1939 (infants); 1889-1931 (boys); 1900-31, 1934-39 (girls)
LB 1875-1913 (boys); 1913-31, 1934-39 (girls)

Prospect House School, Putney Hill, SW15. Opened 1991.

Prospect Terrace School, Sidmouth Street, Grays Inn Road, St Pancras WC1. Opened 1890. (LMA: EO/DIV 2/PRO)
A&D 1890-1925 (boys); 1890-1924 (junior boys); 1890-1925 (girls); 1890-1924 (junior girls); 1924-39 (infants); 1925-39 (junior mixed)
LB 1890-1939 (infants)

Pulteney Street School, Peter Street, Wardour Street, W1. Opened 1881. (LMA: EO/DIV 2/PUL)
A&D 1904-39 (infants); 1909-39 (girls); 1912-39 (boys)
LB 1875-98, 1901-27 (infants); 1881-98 (girls); 1884-1910 (evening); 1913-39 (boys)

Purcell School, Lyndhurst Terrace, NW3. Opened 1972.

Purrett Road School, Plumstead High Street, SE18. Opened 1888; renamed Gallions Mount School, 1951. (LMA: EO/DIV 6/PUR)
A&D 1895-1918 (infants)
LB 1885-1909 (boys); 1885-1923 (girls); 1888-1956 (infants)

Putney Church of England School, Lower Common and Felsham Road, SW15. (LMA: EO/DIV 9/PUT)
LB 1866-94 (junior girls); 1892-1911, 1932-39 (girls); 1894-99 (evening - girls); 1929-39 (senior girls)

Putney County Secondary School, Mayfield, West Hill, SW15. Opened 1907. (LMA: EO/DIV 9/PCS)
A&D 1907-42 (girls)

Putney High School, Putney Hill, SW15. (girls). Opened 1893.

Putney Park School, Woodborough Road, SW15. Opened 1953.

Putney Roman Catholic School, Clarendon Road, SW15. (LMA: EO/DIV 9/PRC)
A&D 1925-49 (mixed and infants)

Putney School of Art, Oxford Road, SW15.

Queenhithe Ward School, EC4.
Misc minute books 1862-71 (Guildhall Library)

Queensbridge Road School, Dalston, E8. see **Queen's Road School**

Queen's College, Harley Street, W1. (Independent). Opened 1848.
see Queen's College 1848-1948 (R.G. Grylls, 1948)

Queen's Court School, Greyhound Road, W14. Previously known as Star Road School, renamed 1955; merged into Gilliatt School, 1961 and buildings handed over to West London College.

Queen's Crescent School, St Pancras, NW5. Opened 1884 as Carlton Road School; renamed 1937. (LMA: EO/DIV 2/QUC)
LB 1911-54 (manual training centre)

Queen's Gardens School, SW7. (LMA: EO/DIV 2/QUG)
LB 1876-92, 1913-31 (infants); 1878-86 (boys); 1881-96 (girls); 1882-1906 (evening)

Queen's Head Street School, Essex Road, N1. Opened 1886; renamed 1951 at Tudor Secondary School; renamed 1965 Islington Green Comprehensive School. (LMA: EO/DIV 3/QUE)
A&D 1894-1926, 1932-39 (girls); 1911-32 (mixed); 1932-39 (boys); 1934-39 (infants)
LB 1901-13, 1927-34, 1937-42 (girls); 1913-31 (infants); 1932-39 (boys)

Queen's House School, Fitzjohn's Avenue, NW3. Opened 1947; closed c1964.

Queen's Manor School, Lysia Street, SW6. Previously known as Queensmill Road School; renamed 1951.

Queensmill Road School, Fulham Palace Road, SW6. Opened 1901 as Macmurdo Road School; renamed, 1905; Queens Manor School, 1951; amalgamated with Peterborough School, 1992. (LMA: EO/DIV 1/QMR)
A&D 1901-11 (junior mixed & infants)
LB 1913-39 (boys); 1913-31 (girls)

Queen's Park Primary School, Droop Street, W10. Opened 1877 as Droop Street School; renamed 1951. (LMA: EO/DIV 2/QUE)
A&D 1944-60 (infants); 1953-58 (junior mixed)

Queen's Road School, Dalston, E8. Opened 1898; renamed Queensbridge School, 1951. (LMA: EO/DIV 4/QUE)
A&D 1923-34 (girls)
LB 1913-23 (junior mixed); 1923-32 (girls); 1937-39 (senior boys)

Queens Road Wesleyan Methodist Sunday School, SE15.
A&D 1866-83, 1913-29, 1934-46 (Southwark Local Studies Lib)
Misc minute books 1915-70 (Southwark Local Studies Lib)

Quintin Kynaston School, Marlborough Hill, NW8. fl.1971.

Radnor Street School, EC1. Closed 1903. (LMA: N/M/17)
A&D 1877-91 (Sunday)
LB 1821-35 (Sunday)

Raine's School, Cannon Street Road, St George in the East, E2. (Independent) (mixed). Opened 1719. (LMA: ACC/1811)
A&D 1736-1955
LB 1818-1949
Misc minute books 1736-1941

Raleigh Memorial School, Albion Road, N16. Opened 1880; closed 1925.

Raleigh Street School, Ocean Street, E1. Opened 1908 as Ocean Street School; renamed 1933. (LMA: EO/DIV 5/RAL)
A&D 1932-39 (senior girls)

Ram's Episcopal Chapel School, Urswick Road, Lower Clapton, E9. Founded 1792 (girls), 1801 (boys); reopened 1877; renamed Hackney Free and Parochial School (Ram's Episcopal), 1951.

Randal Cremer School, Shoreditch. Opened 1875.

Randall Place School, Roan Street, SE10. Opened 1868; renamed James Wolfe Primary School, 1951; later Beverley School. (LMA: EO/DIV 6/RAN)
A&D 1868-1915, 1931-39 (boys); 1898-1913 (infants); 1902-30 (mixed invalid); 1905-39 (mixed deaf); 1912-39 (girls)
LB 1874-1939 (boys); 1874-1939 (girls); 1875-1939 (infants); 1913-39 (mixed)

Ranelagh Road School, Pimlico, SW1. Opened 1898; renamed Warwick Junior School then Churchill Gardens School, 1929. (LMA: EO/DIV 2/RAN)
A&D 1899-1912 (infants)
LB 1876-99 (infants); 1876-80 (mixed)

Rangefield School, Downham Estate, Bromley. Opened 1925. (LMA: EO/DIV 7/RAN)
A&D 1925-34 (mixed); 1926-39 (girls); 1934-39 (boys)
LB 1925-38 (boys); 1926-39 (girls)

Ratcliff School *see* **Coopers' Company's School**

Rathfern Road School, Stanstead Road, Catford, SE6. Opened 1888; renamed Rathfern Primary School, 1951. (LMA: EO/DIV 7/RAT)
A&D 1914-39 (infants); 1928-39 (junior girls)
LB 1885-1911 (boys); 1888-1913 (girls)

Ravensbourne School, Alleyn Road, SE8. Opened 1880s; renamed St John's School, 1913 (partially sighted opened 1934); closed 1940s. (LMA: EO/DIV 6/RAV)
A&D 1886-1914 (boys); 1905-36 (girls); 1921-39 (senior mixed); 1936-44 (junior mixed)
LB 1933-39 (infants)

Ravenstone School, Balham High Road, SW12. Opened 1915 as Balham High Road School; renamed 1926; Elmfield Secondary School, 1951. (LMA: EO/DIV 9/RAV)
A&D 1915-46 (boys)
LB 1915-33 (boys); 1915-33 (girls)

Raywood Street School, Battersea, SW8. Opened 1882. (LMA: EO/DIV 9/RAY)
A&D 1893-1939 (infants)
LB 1915-63 (infants); 1941-43 (mixed)

Reay Central School, Hackford Road, Kennington, SE9. Opened 1910.

Redcliffe School, Redcliffe Gardens, SW10.
Opened 1948.

Redcoat Church of England Secondary School.
Stepney Green, E1. Opened as Parochial
Day School, 1714; known by names incl.
Charity School of Mile End Old Town;
merged with Sir John Cass School
(Secondary Dept), 1944; closed 1966.
A&D 1776-1837, 1874-1918 (Guildhall
Library); 1912-27 (mixed) (Tower Hamlets
Library); 1962-66 (mixed)
(LMA: EO/DIV 5/RED)
LB 1863-89, 1913-39 (girls); 1883-1936
(infants); 1930-39 (boys) (Guildhall
Library)
Misc minute books 1795-1809 (Tower Hamlets
Local History Library and Archives);
1811-22, 1851-89 (Guildhall Library); roll
of service 1914-18 (LMA: P93/DUN/368)

Reddins Road School, Glengall Road, SE15.
Opened 1881; closed 1940s.
(LMA: EO/DIV 7/RED)
A&D 1918-44 (infants); 1929-39 (junior mixed)
LB 1913-44 (infants); 1929-44 (mixed)

Redman's Row School,
Jubilee Street, Mile End, E1. Opened 1909;
renamed Redman School, 1951.
(LMA: EO/DIV 5/RED 2)
LB 1917-21 (myopic)

Redriff School, Rotherhithe Street, SE16.
Opened 1910.

Redvers Street School, Kingsland Road, N1.
Opened 1877; formerly Wellington Street
School. (LMA: EO/DIV 4/RED)
A&D 1919-39 (infants)
LB 1902-13 (evening); 1913-34 (girls); 1913-36
(infants); 1934-39 (junior girls)

Regent's Park School, Grove Road, NW8.
Opened 1887 as Capland Street School;
Central School, 1912; renamed 1928.

Regent Street School, St Marylebone, W1.
(LMA: EO/DIV 2/REG)
LB 1902-09 (manual training centre);
Regent Street School *see*
Frankham Street School

Rhyl Street School, Malden Road, Kentish
Town, NW5. Opened 1898; renamed Rhyl
School, 1951. (LMA: EO/DIV 2/RHY)
A&D 1928-39 (infants); 1937-46 (junior mixed)
LB 1913-28 (infants)

Ricardo Street School, Kerbey Street, East India
Dock Road, E14. Opened 1874; renamed
Susan Lawrence Primary School, 1951.
(LMA: EO/DIV 5/RIC)
A&D 1883-1935 (infants); 1887-1926 (boys);
1900-15 (girls); 1929-39 (senior girls)
LB 1914-35 (infants)

Richard Atkins School, Kingswood Road, SW2.
Opened 1897 as New Park Road School;
renamed 1951. (LMA: EO/DIV 9/RIC)
A&D 1945-61 (junior girls); 1950-61
(junior boys)
LB 1942-65 (mixed); 1955-65 (boys);
1955-65 (girls)

Richard Cobden School, St Pancras, NW1.
Opened 1874 (infants); 1895 (junior) *see*
King Street School

Richard Street School, Liverpool Road, N1.
Opened 1891; renamed Ritchie School,
1938; Penton Primary School, 1971.
(LMA: EO/DIV 3/RIC)
A&D 1905-39 (boys); 1918-39 (infants);
1922-39 (girls)
LB 1891-1936 (boys); 1904-13 (infants)

Richmond Street Roman Catholic School. Now
St John's Wood Roman Catholic School;
opened 1903. (LMA: EO/DIV 2/RIC)
A&D 1914-39 (infants)
LB 1911-13 (boys); 1913-39 (infants)

Richmond Street Roman Catholic School
closed 1892. (LMA: EO/DIV 6/RIC)
LB 1875-92 (infants)

Riley Street School, Bermondsey, SE1.
renamed Tower Bridge Secondary School,
1935. (LMA: EO/DIV 8/RIL)
A&D 1934-39 (junior girls)

Ring Cross School, Eden Grove, Holloway,
N7. Opened 1931. (LMA: EO/DIV 3/RIN)
A&D 1950-60 (junior mixed and infants)

Risinghill Comprehensive School, N1. Opened
1885 as Risinghill Street School; renamed
1951. (LMA: EO/DIV 3/RIS 2)
A&D 1960-65 (senior mixed)

Risinghill Street School, N1. Opened 1885;
renamed Risinghill Primary School, 1951;
closed 1955. (LMA: EO/DIV 3/RIS 1)

Risinghill Street School [*continued*]
A&D 1906-12, 1929-39, 1943-56 (infants);
1943-56 (junior mixed)
LB 1920-39 (infants); 1929-39 (girls); 1930-39
(boys); 1944-56 (junior mixed and infants);
1960-65 (senior mixed)
Misc visitors 1885-1937; honours 1933-36;
punishment 1943-56

Ritchie School, Liverpool Road, Islington, N1.
Opened 1891 as Richard Street School;
renamed 1938; closed 1960.
(LMA: EO/DIV 3/RIT)
A&D 1945-60 (girls)

Riversdale School, Merton Road,
Southfields, SW18. Opened 1909.
(LMA: EO/DIV 9/RIV)
LB 1913-33 (mixed)

Riverside School, Farncombe Street,
Rotherhithe, SE16. Junior School opened
as Farncombe Street Junior School, 1874;
renamed 1931; Senior School opened as
East Lane Senior School, 1882; renamed
1931.
LB 1931-34 (senior girls)

Riverston School, Eltham Road, Lee, SE12.
Opened 1927.

Riverway Secondary School, Blackwall Lane,
SE10. Opened 1893 as Blackwall Lane
School; renamed Dreadnought ESN School
1918; Riverway Secondary, 1950.
(LMA: EO/DIV 6/RIV)
A&D 1944-75 (mixed)
LB 1944-52, 1959-76 (ESN)
Misc 1946-76 (ESN)

Roan School, Devonshire Drive, Greenwich,
SE10. (Independent) (girls).
Misc 1473-1963 (LMA: AC69-70 not yet fully
listed)

Roan School, Maze Hill, SE3. (Independent)
(boys). Opened 1643.
Misc 1473-1963 (LMA: AC69-70 not yet fully
listed)

Robert Blair School, N7. Opened 1873.
see **Blundell Street School**

Robert Browning School, King and Queen
Street, SE17. Opened 1883.

Robert Louis Stevenson School, NW1. Opened
as Great College Street School, 1874;
renamed 1951; closed 1965.
(LMA: EO/DIV 2/ROB)
A&D 1931-39, 1941-65 (infants)
LB 1930-65 (infants)
Misc visitors 1948-55; punishment 1958

Robert Montefiore School, Vallance Road, E1.
Opened 1899 as Deal Street School;
renamed Vallance Street School, 1915;
renamed 1951. (LMA: EO/DIV 5/ROB)
A&D 1925-31, 1950-83 (senior mixed);
1945-57 (junior mixed and infants)
LB 1916-21 (evening)

Robert Street School, Upper Earl
Street, Plumstead. Opened 1873.
(LMA: EO/DIV 6/ROB)
LB 1873-1904 (boys)

Robinsfield School, Ordnance Hill, NW8.
fl.1971.

Rochelle Street School, Mount Street, E2.
Opened 1879; renamed Rochelle School,
1951. (LMA: EO/DIV 5/ROC)
A&D 1877-1936 (boys); 1897-1933 (infants);
1931-36 (junior girls); 1945-76 (junior
mixed and infants ESN)
LB 1873-1905, 1913-33 (infants); 1914-39
(boys); 1928-39 (junior girls); 1951-68
(primary)
Misc punishment 1926-33

Rockliffe Manor School, Bassant Road, SE18.

Roehampton Gate School, Danebury Avenue,
SW15. fl.1971.

Roehampton Parochial School, Putney Heath
West, SW15. Opened 1828.
A&D 1850-80, 1898-1939 (boys); 1869-1939
(girls and infants); 1945-64 (junior mixed
and infants); 1962-75 (waiting list) (Church
of England Records Centre)
LB 1869-1939 (boys); 1869-1939 (girls and
infants); 1909-38 (handicrafts centre)
(Church of England Records Centre)
Misc punishment 1906-38; visitors 1850-73;
minute books 1865-1905, 1945-88 (Church
of England Records Centre)

Roger Manwood School, Brockley Rise and
Kilmorie Road, SE23. fl.1971.

Rolls Road School, Bermondsey, SE1. Opened 1874; closed 1930s. (LMA: EO/DIV 7/ROL)
A&D 1874-1937 (infants); 1884-1935 (girls); 1887-1935 (boys)

Roman Road School, Old Ford, E3. Opened 1877 as Old Ford School; renamed 1951 Bow County Secondary School for Girls; 1957 merged with Cranbrook County to become Bowbrook Girls' School (LMA: EO/DIV 5/ROM)
A&D 1893-1931 (girls); 1897-1939, 1942-60 (infants); 1926-47 (boys); 1931-39 (junior girls)
LB 1896-1913, 1945-64 (infants)

Romilly Road School, N4. Opened 1902. (LMA: EO/DIV 3/ROM)
LB 1913-30 (boys)

Ronald Ross School, Beaumont Road, SW19. fl.1971.

Roper Street School later Grange Hill Road; renamed The Gordon School, 1904. (LMA: EO/DIV 6/ROP)
LB 1900-15 (evening)

Rosa Bassett School, Welham Road, SW17. fl.1971.

Rosaline Road School, Fulham, SW6.

Rosary Roman Catholic School, Haverstock Hill, NW3. Opened 1867 as Bartram's Roman Catholic School; renamed after World War II.

Rosebery Avenue School, EC1. Opened 1876 as Laystall Street School; renamed 1899; renamed Christopher Hatton Primary School, 1951; closed 1968. (LMA: EO/DIV 3/ROS)
A&D 1876-88, 1895-1929 (boys); 1903-20, 1932-46 (infants); 1908-29 (girls); 1932-46 (junior mixed)
LB 1907-29 (boys); 1913-29 (girls); 1913-35 (infants); 1929-38 (mixed)

Rose Cottage School, Welton Road, SE18. fl.1971.

Rosemary School, Prebend Street, N1. Opened 1970 (special).

Rosemead Preparatory School, Thurlow Park Road, SE21. Opened 1942.

Rosemount School, New Kings Road, SW6. Previously part of New Kings Road School; renamed 1950; closed 1957.

Rosendale Road School, Turney Road, SE21. Opened 1900; renamed Rosendale Primary School, 1951. (LMA: EO/DIV 8/ROS)
A&D 1897-99 (girls); 1906-39 (mixed); 1914-36 (infants); 1915-26 (junior mixed)
LB 1903-30, 1933-39 (mixed)

Rosslyn Hill British School, Willoughby Road, NW3. Opened mid 1860s; closed 1906.

Rotherfield Street School, Essex Road, N1. Opened 1898; renamed Rotherfield Primary School, 1951. (LMA: EO/DIV 3/ROT)
A&D 1898-1911, 1937-45 (boys); 1898-1938 (girls)
LB 1898-1952 (infants); 1909-45 (girls)
Misc honours 1933-38; punishment 1940-57

Rotherhithe Charity School
Misc lists of subscribers 1743-1818 (LMA: A/RCS); minute books 1777-1870; accounts 1746-1869 (Southwark Local Studies Lib)

Rotherhithe New Road School, SE16. Opened 1876; renamed Rotherhithe School, 1951. (LMA: EO/DIV 8/ROT)
A&D 1906-21, 1933-39 (boys); 1899-1939 (girls); 1889-1939 (infants)
LB 1876-1901, 1913-31 (girls); 1876-1925 (infants); 1891-1939 (boys); 1913-37 (evening); 1932-39 (junior girls)

Royal Academy of Dramatic Art, Gower Street, WC1.

Royal Academy of Music, Marylebone Road, NW1.

Royal Air Force Memorial School, Vanbrugh Castle, Maze Hill, SE3.

Royal Ballet School, Colet Gardens, W14. Previously known as Sadler's Wells Ballet School; renamed 1956.

Royal College of Art, Exhibition Road, SW7.

Royal College of Music, Prince Consort Road, SW7.

Royal College Street School, NW1. Renamed Cantlowe Secondary School, 1951.

Royal Hill School, SE10. Opened 1899; closed 1957. (LMA: EO/DIV 6/ROY)
A&D 1951-56 (infants)
LB 1954-56 (infants)

Royal Sailors' Orphan Girls' School, Fitzjohn's Avenue, NW3. Opened 1829; closed 1957

Royal School of Needlework, Exhibition Road, SW7.

Royal Soldiers' Daughters' Home, Rosslyn Hill, NW3. Opened 1855; closed c1951.

Royal Victoria Patriotic School, Trinity Road, SW18. Opened 1907. (LMA: EO/DIV 9/ROY)
A&D 1932-39 (girls)
LB 1913-39 (girls)

Ruby Street School, Old Kent Road, SE5. Opened 1885; renamed Watling School, 1951; later Woodstock School. (LMA: EO/DIV 7/RUB)
A&D 1885-1921 (boys); 1885-1929 (girls); 1921-32 (junior mixed); 1943-47 (mixed)
LB 1936-39 (infants)
Misc punishment 1908-37

Rushey Green School, *see* **Plassy Road School**

Rushmore Road School, Chatsworth Road, Lower Clapton, E5. Opened 1877; renamed Rushmore Primary School, 1951.
A&D 1940 (mixed); 1944-61 (infants) (LMA: EO/DIV 4/RUS); 1877-1938 (Hackney Archives)
LB 1877-1904, 1913-30 (boys); 1885-1907 (evening); 1930-30 (senior boys); 1931-39 (infants) (LMA: EO/DIV 4/RUS); 1877-1938 (girls) (Hackney Archives)

Rushworth School, Webber Street, SE1. Opened 1897; renamed Friars ESN School, 1950. (LMA: EO/DIV 8/RUS)
A&D 1946-53 (mixed)

Russian Soviet Embassy School, Heath Drive, NW3.

Rutherford School, Penfold Street, NW1. fl.1971.

Rutland Street School, Bedford Street, E1. Opened 1885; renamed Rutland School, 1938. (LMA: EO/DIV 5/RUT)
A&D 1885-90, 1899-1910, 1938-39 (infants)
LB 1912-39 (infants); 1930-39 (junior mixed)

Ruxley Manor School, Milverton Way, SE9. fl.1971.

Ryland Secondary School, Prince of Wales Road, NW5. (LMA: EO/DIV 2/RYL)
A&D 1958-66 (senior girls)
Misc punishment 1961-63

Sacred Heart of Jesus School, Battersea *see* **Old Battersea Roman Catholic School**

Sacred Heart Roman Catholic School, Hammersmith Road, W6. Opened 1871 as Hammersmith Roman Catholic School for Girls. Infants School moved to Great Church Lane, 1963 and renamed Larmenier Roman Catholic Infants' School.

Sacred Heart Roman Catholic School, Roehampton Lane, SW15. Opened 1870.

Sacred Heart Roman Catholic School, Willow Row, Three Colt Street, E14. Opened 1903.

St Agnes Church of England School, Farmers Road, Kennington Park, SE11. Opened 1875.

St Agnes Roman Catholic School, Arrow Road or Botolph Road, Bow, E3.

St Alban's Church of England School, Manor Place, Walworth, SE17.

St Alban's Roman Catholic School, Herring Street, Camberwell, SE5.

St Alban's School, Baldwin's Gardens, EC2. Opened 1874. (LMA: EO/DIV 3/ST.ALB)
A&D 1885-1924 (boys); 1924-32 (mixed)

St Alfege with St Peter, Creek Road, SE10. Opened 1849 as St Peter School (q.v.).

St Aloysius College, Hornsey Lane, N6. Opened 1879.

St Aloysius Roman Catholic School, Aldenham Street, Somers Town, NW1. Opened 1903/5 as **Aldenham Street Roman Catholic School**. (LMA: EO/DIV 2/ST.AL)
A&D 1883-1912 (boys); 1886-1900 (girls); 1896-1920 (infants)
LB 1880-1910 (mixed); 1910-15 (infants); 1913-33 (girls)

St Andrew's and St Philip's School,
Bosworth Road and Appleford Road, W10.
Opened 1872; renamed St Thomas, 1976.

St Andrew's Parochial School, Hatton Garden,
EC1. Founded early 18th century.
(LMA: EO/DIV 3/ST.AND; P82/AND)
A&D 1790-1844, 1848-80 (boys); 1858-1939
(girls); 1916-39 (infants)
LB 1862-1913 (boys); 1863-1905 (girls);
1895-1905, 1913-35 (infants)
Misc administrative records 1824-1938
(Guildhall Library); minute books 1726-85,
1801-99; accounts 1803-37, 1866-1902;
subscribers 1716-1871; punishment
1828-42 (LMA: P82/AND)

St Andrew's National School, Haverstock Hill.
(LMA: P90/AND)
Misc minute books 1856-78

St Andrew's Roman Catholic School, Polworth
Road, Hopton Road, Streatham, SW16.
Opened 1896. (LMA: EO/DIV 9/ST.AND)
A&D 1885-1933 (infants)

St Andrew's School, Colmer Road,
Wandsworth, SW16. fl.1905/13.

St Andrew's School, Matilda Street, Barnsbury,
N1. Formerly St Thomas, Islington.
Founded c1857.

St Andrew's School, Roupell Street, Exton
Street, Waterloo Road, SE1. Opened 1867.
(LMA: EO/DIV 8/ST.AND and P85/AND)
A&D 1882-1939 (boys); 1887-1903 (lower
boys); 1900-39 (girls); 1904-39 (infants);
1955-79 (junior mixed and infants)
LB 1953-71 (junior mixed and infants)
Misc cash accounts 1926-30; punishment
1948-68; minute books 1867-1902

St Andrew's School, Wells Street, W1. Opened
1870. (LMA: EO/DIV 2/ST.AND)
LB 1869-1920 (girls); 1870-1920 (boys);
1870-1920 (infants)

**St Andrew's Stockwell Church of England
School**, Lingham Street, SW9. Opened
1815.

St Andrew Undershaft School, EC3.
Misc estate records 1634-1805
(Guildhall Library)

St Anne's National School, East Hill, SW18.
Opened 1858. (LMA: EO/DIV 9/ST.ANN;
P95/ANN)
A&D 1902-39 (junior boys)
LB 1900-39 (infants)
Misc accounts 1920-52

St Anne's Roman Catholic School,
Buxton Street and Underwood Road, Mile
End New Town, E1. Opened 1856.

St Anne's School, Brookfield, Chester Road,
Dartmouth Park Hill, N19. Opened 1870.
(LMA: EO/DIV 2/ST.AN 1)
A&D 1881-1906 (girls); 1892-1906 (boys);
1899-1939 (infants); 1907-38 (junior
mixed)
LB 1895-1907 (girls); 1896-1930 (infants);
1907-39 (mixed)

St Anne's School, Dean Street, Soho, W1.
Opened 1872. (LMA: EO/DIV 2/ST.AN 2)
A&D 1896-1930 (boys); 1904-30 (girls);
1914-30 (infants)
LB 1913-29 (boys); 1913-39 (girls); 1913-25
(junior mixed and infants)

St Anne's School, Dixon Street, E14.
Opened 1840.

St Anne's Tollington Park School, Pooles Park.
N4. Opened 1870; closed 1898.

St Ann's Roman Catholic Boys' School,
Spitalfields, E1.
A&D 1886-1946 (Tower Hamlets Library)

St Ann's Roman Catholic School, Croom's Hill,
SE10. Opened 1856.

St Ann's Roman Catholic School,
Kennington Lane, SE11. Opened 1900;
closed 1960s. (LMA: EO/DIV 6/ST.ANN)
A&D 1900-07, 1914-15 (infants); 1907-45
(mixed); 1937-63 (mixed and infants)
LB 1872-1963 (infants); 1907-63 (mixed)

St Anselm's Convent School, Tooting Bec
Road, SW17.

St Anselm's School, Gilbert Street, St George
Hanover Square, W1. Opened 1889.
(LMA: EO/DIV 2/ST.ANS)
LB 1907-11

St Anthony's, Fitzjohns Avenue, NW3.
Opened 1952.

St Anthony's Roman Catholic School,
Lordship Lane, East Dulwich, SE22.

St Augustine Church of England School,
Kilburn Park Road, NW6. Opened 1871.
(LMA: EO/DIV 2/ST.AU)
A&D 1874-1939, 1945-52 (boys); 1940-45
(emergency); 1952-96 (secondary mixed)
LB 1874-1909, 1913-25 (boys)
Misc punishment 1948-69

St Augustine's Roman Catholic School
(LMA: EO/DIV 7/ST.AUG)
A&D 1928-39 (mixed and infants)

St Augustine's Roman Catholic School,
Beckenham Hill Road, SE6.

St Augustine's Roman Catholic School,
Disbrowe Road, W6. Opened 1965.

**St Barnabas' and St Philip's Church of England
School,** Addison Road, Earls Court Road,
W8. Opened 1869. (LMA: P84/BAN)
LB 1862-90 (girls)
Misc minute books 1924-62 (minute book
1904-23 with incumbent of St Philip, Earls
Court); cash 1853-64

St Barnabas Gomm School,
Plough Road, SE16. Opened 1872.
(LMA: EO/DIV 8/ST.BAR)
A&D 1886-1902 (infants)

St Barnabas' School, Bethnal Green. fl.1904.

St Barnabas School, Ebury Street, Pimlico,
SW1. Opened 1846.

St Barnabas' School, Kennington. fl.1905/6.

St Barnabas School, Queens Road (later Berger
Road), Homerton, E9. Opened 1855;
closed 1878. (LMA: EO/DIV 4/ST.BAR)
LB 1875-78 (girls)

St Barnabas School, Sherburne Road, N1.
Opened 1837. (LMA: EO/DIV 3/ST.BAR)
LB 1888-1901 (infants)

St Bartholomew Church of England School,
Shepperton Road, N1. Opened 1856; closed
1911.

St Bartholomew School, Coventry Street,
Bethnal Green, E1. Opened 1844.
(LMA: EO/DIV 5/ST.BAR and P72/BAT)

St Bartholomew School [*continued*]
A&D 1915-39 (infants)
LB 1932-39 (mixed)
Misc minute books 1933-36, 1963-69

St Bartholomew School, The Peak, Sydenham,
SE26. Opened 1815.

St Bartholomew the Great School,
West Smithfield, EC1. Opened 1888?.
A&D 1867-72 (Guildhall Library)
Misc estate records 1627-1918; administrative
records 1728, 1780-1932 (Guildhall
Library)

St Bede's Roman Catholic Infants' School,
Thornton Road, SW12.

St Bernardette Roman Catholic School,
Cavendish Road, SW12. fl.1971.

St Bernard's Roman Catholic Central Schools,
Baker Street, Stepney, E1.
A&D 1929-61 (Tower Hamlets Library)

St Bernard's Roman Catholic Central Schools,
Old Bethnal Green Road and Mansford
Street, E2. fl.1971.

St Boniface Roman Catholic School,
Adler Street, E1.

St Boniface Roman Catholic School,
Undine Street, SW17. fl.1952/71.

St Botolph Aldgate Parochial School. Opened
c1665 Little Tower Hill; amalgamated with
Billingsgate and Tower Wards School,
1905 to form Sir John Cass Junior School
(q.v.).
A&D 1896-1906 (boys) (Guildhall Library)
LB 1899-1906 (Guildhall Library)
Misc minute books 1729-1904 (Guildhall
Library)

**St Botolph Bishopsgate Parochial Charity
School,** EC2.
Misc administrative records 1758-1800
(Guildhall Library)

St Brides School Opened 1848; closed 1936.
(LMA: EO/DIV 5/ST.BRI)
A&D 1878-1936 (mixed and infants)
Misc administrative records 1865-1949
(Guildhall Library)

St Catherine Laboure School, Herbal Hill,
EC1. Opened as St Peters Italian Church
School, 1867; renamed 1953.
(LMA: EO/DIV 3/ST.CAT)
A&D 1957-67 (mixed)

St Charles Roman Catholic School, Ogle Street,
St Marylebone, W1. Opened 1903.

St Charles Roman Catholic School,
St Charles Square, W10. Opened 1907.
(LMA: EO/DIV 1/ST.CH)
A&D 1940-54 (class registers)
LB 1907-39 (girls); 1907-39 (infants)

St Christopher's School, Belsize Lane,
Hampstead, NW3. Opened 1883 in
Hampstead Hill Gardens, moved 1919.

St Clement and St James School, Penzance
Place, W11. Founded by 1861.

St Clement Danes Boys Grammar School,
Du Cane Road, W12. Opened 1862; moved
to Hammersmith 1928; also known until
1951 as St Clement Danes Holborn Estate
Grammar School; merged with Burlington
School, 1957. (LMA: EO/DIV 1/ST.CL 1)
A&D 1862-1950 (boys)

St Clement Danes Grammar School, Aldwych
(Independent) (boys). Opened 1864.

St Clement Danes School, Drury Lane, WC2.
Opened 1872. (LMA: EO/DIV 2/ST.CL 1)
A&D 1892-1900 (girls); 1899-1925 (boys);
1902-39 (infants)
LB 1872-1940 (boys); 1872-1913 (girls);
1881-1929 (infants)
Misc staff 1887-1944

St Clements Road School, Notting Hill, W11.
Opened 1880; 1904 Sirdar Road &
Avondale Park Schools 1936.
(LMA: EO/DIV 1/ST.CL 2)
A&D 1880-1916 (boys); 1880-1907 (girls)
LB 1880-1905 (girls); 1895-1913 (mentally
defective); 1896-1903 (deaf); 1899-1939
(evening); 1900-48 (manual training centre)

St Clements School, Cumberland Street,
Barnsbury, N7. Opened 1861.
(LMA: EO/DIV 3/ST.CLE)
A&D 1906-54 (boys); 1913-54 (girls); 1924-73
(infants); 1956-73 (junior mixed)
LB 1902-39, 1946-55 (girls); 1905-54 (boys);
1913-49 (infants); 1956-73 (junior mixed
and infants)

St Clements School [*continued*]
Misc punishment 1958-72

St Columba's School, Kingsland Road,
Shoreditch, E2. Opened 1866.
(LMA: EO/DIV 4/ST.COL)
A&D 1879-92, 1911-39 (boys); 1908-26,
1933-39 (girls); 1940-42 (junior mixed and
infants)
LB 1873-1913 (girls); 1873-1905 (infants);
1913-35 (boys)

St Cuthbert with St Matthias, Warwick Road,
SW5. Founded 1871.

St Dominic's Roman Catholic Primary School,
Ballance Road, E9. Opened 1873.

St Dominic's Roman Catholic School,
Southampton Road, Haverstock Hill, NW5.
Opened 1867. (LMA: EO/DIV 2/ST.DO)
A&D 1904-70 (infants)
LB 1871-1935, 1939-46 (infants)

**St Dunstan in the West Parochial Charity
School**, EC4.
A&D 1868-99 (boys); 1878-1939 (girls);
attendance: 1923-30 (boys); 1891-1909,
1912-40 (girls); 1925-30 (infants)
(Guildhall Library)
LB 1863-1939 (girls); 1863-1940 (boys);
1900-38 (infants) (Guildhall Library)
Misc estate records 1709-1934; administrative
records 1609, 1632, 1771-1949 (Guildhall
Library)

St Dunstan's College, Catford (Independent)
(boys). Opened 1888.
Misc minute books 1866-1977 (Lewisham Local
History Lib)

St Dunstan's Road School, W6. Opened 1886;
renamed Captain Marryat's Infant School,
1951.

**St Edmund's Roman Catholic Secondary
School**, St Dunstan's Road, W6. Previously
known as St Thomas' Roman Catholic
Secondary School; renamed 1949; closed
1991.

St Edmund's Roman Catholic School,
Westferry Road, E14. Opened 1903.

St Edwards Roman Catholic School,
Broad Street, Westminster later Lisson
Grove, NW1. Opened 1857.

LONDON SCHOOL RECORDS

St Edwards Roman Catholic School,
Dufour's Place, Strand, W1. fl.1905/12.

St Edwards Roman Catholic School,
St Marylebone *see* **Blandford Square School**

St Ethelburga's Society School. Opened 1720.
A&D 1824-73 (mixed) (Tower Hamlets Library)

St Etheldreda's Roman Catholic School,
Saffron Hill, EC1.

St Faith's Church of England School,
Alma Road, East Hill, Wandsworth, SW18. Opened 1889.

St Francesca Cabrini Roman Catholic School,
Honor Oak Park, SE23. fl.1957.

St Francis' Roman Catholic School,
Friary Road, Peckham, SE15. Opened 1856.

St Francis Roman Catholic School, Pottery Lane, Kensington, W11. Opened 1861.

St Francis Roman Catholic School, Silchester Road, Kensington, W10. Opened 1857.

St Francis Xavier Roman Catholic School,
Upper William Street, Marylebone. fl.1904/5.

St Gabriel's College, Cormont Road, SE5.

St Gabriel's School. (LMA: EO/DIV 4/ST.GA)
LB 1898-99 (evening)

St Gabriel's School, Glasgow Terrace, Pimlico, SW1. Opened 1862. (LMA: EO/DIV 2/ST.GA)
A&D 1909-40 (boys); 1916-40 (infants)
LB 1888-1936 (boys); 1894-1914, 1921-39 (girls)

St Gabriels School, Morris Road, Bow, E14. Opened 1871; closed 1937. (LMA: EO/DIV 5/ST.GAB)
A&D 1890-1937 (infants); 1905-24 (girls); 1924-37 (mixed)
LB 1890-1909, 1913-37 (infants); 1901-13 (girls); 1913-37 (mixed)

St George Botolph Lane School, City.
A&D 1849 (boys) (Guildhall Library)

St George Hanover Square Board of Guardians see **West London School District**

St George Hanover Square School,
South Street, W1. Opened 1898. (LMA: EO/DIV 2/ST.GEO)
LB 1913-27 (boys)
Misc 1935-45 (care committee minute book); punishment 1948-52

St George in the East Central School,
Cable Street, E1. Opened 1899 as Cable Street School; renamed 1929. (LMA: EO/DIV 5/ST.GEO)
A&D 1930-39 (senior mixed); 1942-63 (mixed)
LB 1942-45 (mixed)
Misc 1947-52 (school association); 1962-63 (governors' meetings)

St George in the East National School. Founded 1820; merged with Raine's School, 1877. (LMA: ACC/1811)
A&D 1858-74
LB 1863-80
Misc minute books 1865-77

St George Roman Catholic School,
Lanark Road, W9. Opened 1956.

St George's German Lutheran Church School,
Cleveland Street, Fitzroy Square, W1.
A&D 1828-1917 (Tower Hamlets Library)

St George's Row School, SW1. Opened 1898; renamed Warwick Senior School, 1929. (LMA: EO/DIV 2/ST.GR)
A&D 1895-1929 (boys); 1911-29 (infants); 1923-39 (mixed)
LB 1895-1923 (boys); 1895-1925 (girls); 1895-1920 (infants); 1926-29 (senior mixed)

St George's School, Edge Street, W8. fl.1905/50.

St George's School, New Church Road, Camberwell, SE5. Opened 1826. (LMA: P73/GEO)
LB 1863-90 (infants)
Misc minute books 1871-1951; accounts 1904-18

St George's School, Thessaly Road, SW8. Opened 1857. (LMA: EO/DIV 9/ST.GEO)
A&D 1878-99, 1916-54 (boys); 1923-39 (infants); 1942-45 (mixed)
LB 1877-85 (infants); 1909-54 (boys); 1935-39 (girls)

St George's School, Westminster Bridge Road, SE1. (LMA: EO/DIV 8/ST.GEO)
LB 1862-1933 (girls); 1890-1918, 1924-33 (infants)

St George the Martyr Parochial School, Queen Square, Holborn, WC1. Opened 1859.
LB 1910-13 (boys).
(LMA: EO/DIV 2/ST.GM); 1928-39 (girls); 1928-39 (infants); 1945-60 (junior) (P82/GEO 2/95/1)
Misc minute books 1904-29

St George the Martyr School, Borough Road, SE1. Opened 1698; boys only until 1747.
A&D 1868-70, 1872-1985 (girls) (Church of England Records Centre); 1946-66 (junior mixed and infants) (LMA: EO/DIV 8/ST.GEO 1)
LB 1863-1901 (girls); 1863-1910 (infants) (Church of England Records Centre)
Misc minute books 1836-1946 (Church of England Records Centre)

St Gerard's Roman Catholic School, Clapham Common. fl.1964.

St Giles Cripplegate Boys' School, Red Cross Street, EC1.
A&D 1707-48 (Guildhall Library)
Misc estate records 1527-1852; administrative records 1690-1905 (Guildhall Library)

St Giles Cripplegate Girls' School (Lady Holles School), EC1.
Misc estate records 1527-1852; administrative records 1690-1969 (Guildhall Library)

St Giles' Greencoat and National Schools, Camberwell. Opened 1709; closed 1958.
LB 1862-1943 (boys); 1872-81, 1913-39 (girls); 1913-39 (infants) (Church of England Records Centre)
Misc minute books 1709-1958 (Church of England Records Centre)

St Giles in the Fields School, Endell Street, WC2. Opened 1859. (LMA: EO/DIV 3/ST.GIL)
A&D 1930-39, 1951-63 (infants); 1951-63 (junior mixed)
LB 1951-63 (junior mixed and infants)
Misc punishment 1953-60

St Gregory the Great Secondary School, Bethnal Green.
A&D 1953-64 (Tower Hamlets Library)

St Helen's Church of England School, Latimer Road, W10. Opened 1875.

St Helen's Roman Catholic School, Brook Green, Hammersmith, W6.
LB 1872-1907 (infants); 1873-1913 (girls) (Hammersmith and Fulham Archives)

St Helen's School, North Side, Streatham Common, SW16.

St Hubert's School, Mellitus Street, W12. Previously part of Brook Green School, renamed c1908; transferred to Old Oak School, 1957.

St Ignatius' College, Stamford Hill (Roman Catholic Independent) (boys). Opened 1894.

St James and St Michael School see **St James School**, Craven Terrace

St James and St Peter School, Great Windmill Street, W1. fl.1904/71.

St James Church of England School, Thurland Road, Rotherhithe, SE16. Founded 1812; opened 1841.

St James Independent Junior School for Boys, Queen's Gate, SW7. Opened 1975.

St James Independent School for Girls, Pembridge Villas, W11. Opened 1975.

St James Myopic School. Opened 1898; closed 1918. (LMA: EO/DIV 5/ST.JAM)
A&D 1915-18 (mixed)

St James Roman Catholic School, Marylebone Lane, W1. Opened 1862; renamed St James Spanish Place, 1951. (LMA: EO/DIV 2/ST.JA)
A&D 1877-1966 (boys); 1903-20 (girls and infants)
LB 1863-1968 (boys); 1863-1906, 1914-20 (girls); 1895-1904, 1914-20 (infants)
Misc punishment 1960-68

St James School, Craven Terrace, Hyde Park, W2. Opened 1862; later St James and St Michael.

St James School, George's Road, Holloway, N7. Opened 1838; closed 1950. (LMA: EO/DIV 3/ST.JAM)

St James School [*continued*]
A&D 1893-1905, 1920-47 (senior mixed);
1895-1925 (girls); 1903-39 (infants);
1905-20 (boys); 1925-39 (junior mixed)
LB 1862-1904, 1913-22 (boys); 1877-1927
(girls); 1879-1921 (infants); 1923-39
(senior mixed); 1927-44 (junior mixed and
infants); 1945-49 (mixed)

St James School, New Cross Road, Hatcham,
SE14. Opened 1846. (LMA: P75/JS 1)
LB 1862-84
Misc accounts 1901-42; minute books 1904-37

St James School, Regency Place, Kennington
Opened 1852. (LMA: EO/DIV 8/ST.JAM)
A&D 1904-06 (mixed and infants)

St James's Norland Church of England School,
Penzance Place, W11. Opened 1861.

St James's School, Powell Road,
Lower Clapton, E5. Opened 1857;
reorganised, 1898. (LMA: P79/JSG)
LB 1913-39 (boys)
Misc accounts 1895-97; minute books 1904-28

**St James the Less Church of England Primary
School**, Thorndike Street, Westminster,
SW1. Opened 1864; closed 1898.
A&D 1875-1939 (boys); 1890-1939 (girls);
1902-39 (infants); 1940-69 (junior mixed)
(Church of England Records Centre)
LB 1859-1939 (girls); 1865-1939 (boys);
1888-1939 (infants) (Church of England
Records Centre)
Misc punishment 1915-66
(Church of England Records Centre)

St Joan of Arc Roman Catholic Primary School,
Northolme Road, N5. Opened 1956.

St John and All Saints School,
Waterloo Road, SE1. Opened 1900.
(LMA: EO/DIV 8/ST.JOH)
A&D 1864-1939 (boys); 1876-1939, 1942-51
(infants); 1880-1939 (girls); 1924-27
(junior mixed)
LB 1862-1939 (boys); 1862-1924 (girls);
1867-93, 1913-24, 1927-38, 1942-51
(infants); 1924-27 (junior mixed and
infants)

St John and St Clement's School, East Dulwich,
SE15. Founded 1837; opened 1873
A&D 1873-78, 1890-1977
(infants); 1888-1932 (girls); 1912-31
(boys); 1932-77 (senior mixed) (Church of
England Records Centre); 1926-40 (boys)
(LMA: EO/DIV 7/ST.JOH 2)
LB 1886-1939 (infants); 1932-72 (junior mixed
and infants) (Church of England Records
Centre)
Misc punishment 1925-69 (Church of England
Records Centre)

St John Church of England Primary School,
Kilburn. Opened 1882; closed 1979.
A&D 1882-1939 (girls); 1909-39 (boys);
1919-39 (infants); 1947-79 (junior mixed
and infants) (Church of England Records
Centre)
LB 1949-68 (junior mixed and infants) (Church
of England Records Centre)
Misc punishment 1947-68 (Church of England
Records Centre)

St John Church of England School,
Glenthorne Road, later Macbeth Street,
W6. Founded 1864 in Bradmore Lane;
moved to Glenthorne Road, 1871;
destroyed 1944; moved to part of Waterside
School; closed 1983.
A&D 1941-45 (mixed).
(LMA: EO/DIV 1/ST.JO 2); 1933-71
(boys); applications for admission 1942-68
(Hammersmith and Fulham Archives)
LB 1863-1983 (mixed); 1863-85, 1904-64
(girls); 1870-1935 (infants); 1913-30 (boys)
(Hammersmith and Fulham Archives)

**St John Clarendon Road Church of England
Secondary School**, W11. Became a
Secondary Modern, 1948 and younger
children moved to Heathfield Street School.
(LMA: EO/DIV 1/ST.JO 1)
A&D 1902-38 (boys); 1929-39 (infants);
1929-39 (junior mixed); 1930-62 (mixed)
LB 1930-62 (boys)
Misc punishment 1949-62

St John Evangelist School, Tottenham Court
Road, St Pancras, W1. Opened 1860.

St John Kensal Green School, W10.
Opened 1849; closed 1930.
(LMA: EO/DIV 2/ST.JO 1)
LB 1862-80 (boys); 1862-1930 (girls); 1862-96,
1913-30 (infants)

St John of Jerusalem School, Kingshold Road, E9 see **South Hackney Parochial School**

St John School, Titchborne Row, Edgware Road, W2. Opened c1830; closed 1940. (LMA: EO/DIV 2/ST.JO 2)
A&D 1875-1913 (boys); 1887-1913 (girls); 1898-1916, 1926-39 (infants); 1905-39 (junior mixed)
LB 1928-39 (mixed)

St John's Church of England School, Dawes Road, SW6. Founded 1836; moved from Walham Green to Dawes Road, 1894; moved to Munster Road School premises, 1997.

St John's Church of England (Bowyer) School, Gaskell Street, Larkhall Lane, SW4. Opened 1893.

St John's Church of England School, Heathfield Street, W11. Opened 1862. (LMA: P84/JN)
Misc minute books 1845-62, 1910-28

St John's Church of England School later **St John the Baptist School**, New North Road, Hoxton, N1. Opened 1842. (LMA: EO/DIV 4/ST.JOH 1)
A&D 1903-39 (infants); 1905-32 (girls); 1909-29, 1932-39 (mixed); 1928-39 (senior mixed)
LB 1899-1913 (boys), 1909-28 (girls); 1938-39 (junior mixed and infants)

St John's Church of England School, Pemberton Gardens, Upper Holloway, N19. Opened 1830. Also known as Holloway and Highbury National School. (LMA: P83/JNE)
A&D 1875-96 (boys)
LB 1862-81, 1916-39 (boys); 1885-1939 (girls); 1913-39, 1946-48 (infants); 1940-45 (emergency)
Misc minute books 1828-67, 1870-71; accounts 1926-44; staff 1955-63

St John's College, Angell Road, Brixton, SW9. Founded 1852; opened 1880.

St John's College, Green Lanes, Stoke Newington (Independent) (boys). Opened 1881.

St John Servant Training School, Great Western Road. Opened 1862 (girls); closed c1933.

St John's Lane School, EC1. (LMA: EO/DIV 3/ST.JOH 1)
LB 1912-18 (infants)

St John's National School, East Dulwich, SE22. Opened 1850s. (LMA: EO/DIV 7/ST.JOH 1)
A&D 1855-61, 1865-69, 1873-77, 1883-86 (boys)

St John's Road School, Hoxton, N1. Opened 1883; renamed Pitfield School, 1938; closed 1959. (LMA: EO/DIV 4/ST.JOH 2)
A&D 1898-1929 (mixed); 1899-1931 (girls); 1906-39 (infants)
LB 1883-1938 (infants); 1899-1932 (girls); 1899-1929 (mentally defective); 1908-13 (mixed)

St John's School, Canterbury Road, Brixton, SW9. Opened 1852.

St John's School, Park Place later Conewood Street, Highbury Vale, N5. Founded 1810.

St John's School, Larcom Street, Walworth, SE17. Opened 1865.

St John's School, Peel Grove, Bethnal Green, E2. Founded c1839; opened 1858.

St John's School, Roserton Road, Poplar, E14. Opened 1870. (LMA: EO/DIV 5/ST.JOH 1)
A&D 1927-39 (infants)

St John's School, St John's Row, Deptford Opened 1856. (LMA: EO/DIV 6/ST.JOH)
LB 1885-1913 (infants)

St John's School, Usk Road, SW11. Opened 1865. (LMA: EO/DIV 9/ST.JOH and P70/JN)
A&D 1895-1939 (girls); 1899-1939 (boys); 1905-39 (infants); 1941-48 (mixed); 1949-62 (junior mixed)
LB 1874-97, 1913-40 (boys); 1897-1932 (girls); 1867-1939 (infants); 1942-55 (junior mixed and infants)
Misc minute books 1900-12

St John's Wood Roman Catholic School, Orchardson Street, NW8. Formerly Richmond Street Roman Catholic School; opened 1903. (LMA: EO/DIV 2/ST.JO 3)
LB 1863-89 (mixed); 1913-39 (boys)

St John the Baptist School, Beachborough Road, Downham, Bromley, Kent. Founded before 1850.

St John the Baptist Roman Catholic School, Bonner Road, E2. fl.1971.

St John the Baptist Roman Catholic School, King Edward's Road, E9. Opened 1849 as Triangle School.
(LMA: EO/DIV 4/ST.JOH 3)
A&D 1926-39 (girls)

St John the Baptist Roman Catholic School, Mare Street, E8.

St John the Divine School, Warham Street, Camberwell New Road, SE5. Founded *c*1867.
A&D 1872-1939 (boys); 1878-1922 (mixed); 1884-1956 (infants); 1885-1939 (girls); 1939-44 (emergency); 1950-73 (boys and girls) (Lambeth Archives)
LB 1872-1902 (boys); 1886-1905 (junior mixed); 1898-1913 (girls); 1906-13 (infants); 1949-73 (mixed) (Lambeth Archives)
Misc punishment 1905-34 (Lambeth Archives)

St John the Evangelist School, Red Lion Square, Holborn, WC1. Opened 1872. (LMA: EO/DIV 3/ST.JOH 2)
A&D 1874-1904 (infants); 1940 (mixed)

St John the Evangelist Roman Catholic School, Duncan Street, Islington, N1. Opened 1839.

St Joseph Roman Catholic School, Highgate Hill, N19. Opened 1860. (LMA: EO/DIV 3/ST.JOS 1)
A&D 1884-1933 (infants); 1893-1912 (girls); 1906-37 (boys)
LB 1891-1913 (infants); 1940 (emergency)
Misc 1919-36 (confirmations) (mixed)

St Joseph Roman Catholic School, Lambs Passage, Bunhill Row, EC1. Opened 1901.
(LMA: EO/DIV 3/ST.JOS 2)
A&D 1945-76 (junior mixed)
LB 1945-71 (junior mixed and infants)

St Joseph Roman Catholic School, Lanark Road, W9. Opened 1959.

St Joseph's Academy, Lee Terrace, SE3. fl.1971.

St Joseph's Roman Catholic School, Battersea Park Road, SW8. Opened 1871.

St Joseph's Roman Catholic School, Borough High Street, SE1. Opened 1862.

St Joseph's Roman Catholic School, Brook Green, W6. Opened 1892; closed 1919.

St Joseph's Roman Catholic School, Cadogan Street, SW3. Opened 1903.

St Joseph's Roman Catholic School, Deptford High Street, SE8. Opened 1850 as Deptford Roman Catholic School.

St Joseph's Roman Catholic School, George Road, Dockhead, SE1. Opened 1839.

St Joseph's Roman Catholic School, Gun Street, Spitalfields, E1.

St Joseph's Roman Catholic School, Macklin Street, WC2. fl.1971.

St Joseph's Roman Catholic School, Paradise Street, Jamaica Road, Rotherhithe, SE16. Opened 1865.

St Joseph's Roman Catholic School, Pelton Road, Greenwich, SE10. Opened 1869.

St Joseph's Roman Catholic School, Putney Bridge Road, SW18. Opened 1875.

St Joseph's Roman Catholic School, Pitman Street, SE5.

St Joseph's School, Crispin Street, Whitechapel, E1. Opened 1866. (LMA: EO/DIV 5/ST.JOS)
A&D 1887-1972 (girls and infants)
LB 1955-72 (girls); 1955-72 (infants)

St Jude's Church of England School, Old Bethnal Green Road, E2. Opened 1848. (LMA: EO/DIV 5/ST.JUD and P72/JSG)
LB 1936-39 (girls); 1936-39 (infants)
Misc minute books 1967-78; accounts 1970-77

St Jude's Church of England School, Railton Road, Herne Hill, SE24. Founded 1834; opened 1890.

St Jude's District Church of England School, Ball's Pond Road, N1. Opened 1857.

St Jude's School, Colnbrook Street, SE1.
Opened 1852. (LMA: EO/DIV 8/ST.JUD)
A&D 1930-39 (junior boys)
LB 1933-39 (junior boys); 1940 (senior boys)
Misc minute books 1965-83 (Church of England
Records Centre)

St Jude's School, Grays Inn Road, WC1.
Opened 1872.

St Jude's School also known as **St Jude and
St Paul School**, Mildmay Park, N1. Opened
1857.
LB 1863-1913 (Islington History Collection)
Misc minute books 1908-72 (LMA: P83/JUD)

St Katharine's School, St Katharine by the
Tower, EC3.
A&D 1859-64 (boys) (Guildhall Library)

St Leonard's Church of England School,
Mitcham Lane, SW16. Founded 1837.

St Leonard Shoreditch Infants' School, EC2.
Misc administrative records 1837-54
(Guildhall Library)

St Leonard's Road School, Poplar, E14.
Opened 1885. (LMA: EO/DIV 5/ST.LEO)
A&D 1885-1931 (boys); 1896-1914 (girls);
1931-39 (junior mixed); 1932-39 (infants);
1933-39 (junior girls)
LB 1896-1906 (boys)

St Luke and Camden School, Sumner Road,
SE15.
LB 1845-1979 (LMA: ACC/2630)
Misc minute books 1845-1979
(LMA: ACC/2630)

St Luke Church of England School, Fernhead
Road, West Kilburn, W9. Opened 1877.
A&D 1877-90 (boys) (Church of England
Records Centre)
LB 1877-1931 (boys); 1877-1925 (infants);
1893-1925 (girls) (Church of England
Records Centre)
Misc minute books 1877-98, 1904-11, 1921-37
(LMA: P87/LUK 1)

St Luke's Church of England School,
Canal Road, Mile End, E3. Opened 1872.

St Luke's Parochial School, Old Street, EC1.
Founded 1698 (boys), 1761 (girls); opened
1881 as St Luke's Parochial Primary
School; renamed 1951; moved to Radnor
Street, 1973. (LMA: EO/DIV 3/ST.LUK)

St Luke's Parochial School [*continued*]
A&D 1897-1939 (infant girls); 1902-16 (girls);
1918-39 (infant boys)
LB 1900-13 (infants); 1911-13 (girls);
1933-39 (boys)

St Luke's School, Elder Road, West Norwood,
SE27. Opened 1899.

St Luke's School, Nutford Place, W1.
Opened 1859. (LMA: EO/DIV 2/ST.LU)
LB 1900-25 (girls); 1901-35 (infants);
1906-25 (boys)

St Luke's School, St Luke's Street, Chelsea,
SW3. (LMA: EO/DIV 1/ST.LU)
LB 1935-39 (girls); 1935-39 (infants)

St Luke's School, Westferry Road, Milwall,
E14. Opened 1872.

St Margaret Pattens School, City.
A&D 1848-50 (boys) (Guildhall Library)

St Margaret's Church of England School,
Dean Farrar Street, SW1. Opened 1859.
(LMA: EO/DIV 2/ST.MAG)
LB 1931-39 (senior mixed)

St Margaret's Church of England School,
St Margaret's Grove, Plumstead, SE18.
Opened 1856.

St Margaret's School, Kidderpore Gardens,
NW3. Opened 1884 in Oak Hill Park;
incorporated Threave House School,
1932; moved c1948.

St Mark's Church of England School, Bishops
Avenue, SW6. Founded 1843; moved to
Fulham 1954; closed 1995.

St Mark's Church of England School,
Royal Mint Street, E1. Opened 1841.

**St Mark's Church of England School for Girls
and Infants**, St James Street, W6. Opened
c1877; closed 1906.

St Mark's College School, Chelsea
(Independent) (boys). Opened 1867.

St Mark's Practising School, Fulham Road,
SW10. Opened 1842.

St Mark's Road School *see* **St Quintin Park
School** and **North Kensington Central
School**

St Mark's School, Battersea Rise, SW11.
Opened 1866. (LMA: EO/DIV 9/ST.MRK)
A&D 1942-60 (infants)
LB 1942-60 (infants)

St Mark's School, Brewer Street and Old Street,
North Goswell Street, EC1. Opened 1856.
(LMA: EO/DIV 3/ST.MAR)
LB 1890-1907 (boys - Old Street); 1896-1907
(infants - Brewer Street)

St Mark's School, Grove Road,
Holloway Road, N7. Opened 1836.

St Mark's School, Hamilton Terrace, NW8.
(LMA: EO/DIV 2/ST.MK.1)
A&D 1873-1939 (boys); 1889-1939 (infants);
1901-39 (girls)
LB 1863-1913, 1929-39 (boys); 1863-1913
(girls); 1873-1939 (infants)

St Mark's School, Harleyford Road,
Kennington, SE11. Founded *c*1820.
(LMA: A/KNS)
A&D 1881-1968
LB 1862-1976
Misc minute books 1824-62

St Mark's School, Marylebone Road, NW1.
(LMA: EO/DIV 2/ST.MK 2)
LB 1882-1922 (boys); 1882-1922 (infants);
1899-1913 (mixed); 1913-39 (girls)

St Mark's School, St Mark's Road,
Notting Hill, W11. Opened 1868.
(LMA: P84/MRK)
Misc minute books 1868-89

St Mark's School, Sussex Way, Tollington
Park, N19. Founded 1863.

St Martin in the Fields High School, Tulse Hill,
SW2. Opened in Hungerford Market, 1699.
A&D 1850-69, 1883-1945 (girls)
(Church of England Records Centre)
LB 1901-13 (infants)
(LMA: EO/DIV 8/ST.MAR)
Misc minute books 1701-1913; staff 1880-1952
see A Short History of St Martin in the Fields
High School for Girls (D.H. Thomas,
1929)

St Martin in the Fields Board of Guardians see
Central London School District

St Martin in the Fields School,
Adelaide Place, WC2. Opened 1833.
(LMA: EO/DIV 2/ST.MR)

St Martin in the Fields School [*continued*]
A&D 1875-1935 (boys); 1878-1935 (girls);
1878-1939 (infants); 1935-39 (mixed);
1948-65 (senior mixed)
LB 1881-1901, 1913-29 (infants); 1905-27
(girls); 1913-36 (boys); 1954-66 (senior
mixed)
Misc punishment 1952-66
(LMA: EO/DIV 2/ST.MR); minute books
1844-85 (Westminster Archives)

St Martin in the Fields School, Shelton Street,
WC2. Opened 1858.

St Mary Abbot's School, Kensington High
Street, W8. Founded 1645; opened 1875.

**St Mary and St Dominic's Roman Catholic
Boys School**, Ballance Road, Homerton,
E9. Opened 1903 as Ballance Road School.
LB 1873-1912 (Hackney Archives)

St Mary and St Joseph Roman Catholic School,
Wade's Place, E14.

**St Mary and St Michael Roman Catholic
School**, Lucas Street and Sutton Street, E1.

**St Mary and St Pancras Church of England
School**, Polygon Road, NW1. fl.1971.

St Mary Boltons' Church of England School,
Gilston Road, SW10.

St Mary Bryanstone Square School, Enford
Street, W1. Founded 1824.

St Mary Church of England Primary School,
Barn Street, N16. Opened 1831.

St Mary Haggerston School, N1. Opened 1838.
(LMA: EO/DIV 4/ST.MRY)
LB 1873-1906 (infants)

**St Mary Islington Church of England Primary
School**, Halton Road, N1. Opened 1710.
(LMA: P83/MRY 1)
A&D 1815-29, 1849-71
Misc apprenticeship indentures 1765-1831;
baptism certificates 1796-1827; minute
books 1813-26, 1842-1939; visitors
1817-24
see History of Islington Parochial School
(T. Rutt, 1910)

St Marylebone Board of Guardians see
North Surrey School District.

St Marylebone Central School, NW1. Opened 1858. (LMA: EO/DIV 2/ST.MRY 5)
LB 1863-1913 (girls); 1863-1939 (infants)
Misc punishment 1929-57

St Marylebone Grammar School, Marylebone Road, NW1. Opened 1792 as Philological School; council 1909; others records at Westminster Archives.
(LMA: EO/DIV 2/ST.MRY 4)
A&D 1971-79 (senior boys)
LB 1980-81 (senior boys)
Misc 1979-81 (schoolkeeper's diary)

St Mary Magdalen School, Grange Walk, Tower Bridge Road, SE1. Opened 1853. (LMA: EO/DIV 8/ST.MMG)
A&D 1920-68 (applicants)
LB 1935-68 (infants)
Misc punishment 1905-45

St Mary Magdalene School, Godman Road, Peckham, SE15. Opened 1855. (LMA: EO/DIV 7/ST.MMG)
A&D 1897-1903 (infants)

St Mary Magdalene School, Lewisham *see* **Brockley School**

St Mary Magdalene's School, Harrow Road, Paddington, W2. Founded 1865 in Clarendon Street; moved 1879.

St Mary Magdalene's School, Liverpool Road, N7. Opened 1842.

St Mary Magdalene's School, Munster Square, NW1. Opened 1904. (LMA: EO/DIV 2/ST.MRY 3)
A&D 1895-1912, 1940-64 (mixed); 1911-39 (girls); 1915-39, 1963-76 (infants)
LB 1872-94 (boys); 1872-94, 1901-13 (girls); 1872-1922 (infants); 1945-77 (mixed)
Misc punishment 1915-70

St Mary Newington Board of Guardians see **South Metropolitan School District**

St Mary Newington School, Newington Butts, SE11. Opened 1851. (LMA: EO/DIV 8/ST.MRY 2, A/SMN and P92/MRY)

St Mary Newington School [*continued*]
A&D 1816-1923; 1834-52 (infants); 1940 (mixed)
LB 1863-1913
Misc minute books 1710-1963; accounts 1875-1960; Sunday School minute books 1908-15 (LMA: A/SMN and P92/MRY); Sunday School minute books 1870-73 (Southwark Local Studies Lib)

St Mary of the Angels Roman Catholic School, Westmoreland (later Moorhouse) Road, W2. Opened 1857.

St Mary Overie School. Opened 1843; united to St Saviour School, 1953.

St Mary School,
Felsham Road, Putney, SW15. Opened 1819; merged with All Saints, 1928.
A&D 1875-79, 1892-95 (infants); 1898-1927 (boys); 1927-74 (junior mixed) (Church of England Records Centre); 1867-82, 1900-05 (infants); 1913-39 (girls) (LMA: EO/DIV 9/ST.MRY 1)
LB 1891-1927 (boys); 1913-39 (infants) (Church of England Records Centre); 1913-32 (girls) (LMA: EO/DIV 9/ST.MRY 1)
Misc minute books 1849-1932 (Church of England Records Centre)

St Mary's Church of England School, Balham High Road, SW12. *see* Balham.

St Mary's Church of England School, High Street, SE13. Opened 1856.

St Mary's Church of England School, Lower Road, Rotherhithe, SE16. (LMA: EO/DIV 8/ST.MRY 4)
A&D 1841-65 (girls); 1872-78 (mixed); 1873-1901 (infants)

St Mary's Church of England School, West Hampstead, NW6. Opened 1870.

St Mary's College, Lancaster Gate, W1. Opened 1873.

St Mary's Convent School, England's Lane, NW3. Opened 1880; moved 1927 to Fitzjohn's Avenue, NW3.

St Mary's Kilburn School, West End Lane, NW6. Opened 1864.

St Mary's Parochial School, Vicarage Crescent, Battersea, SW11. see under Battersea.

St Mary's Practising Roman Catholic School, Brook Green, W6. Opened 1850; renamed St Mary's Roman Catholic Boys' School, 1953.

St Mary's Roman Catholic Girls and Infants School, Crescent Lane, SW4.

St Mary's Roman Catholic Junior Boys School, St Alphonsus Road, Clapham, SW4. Opened 1849.
(LMA: EO/DIV 9/ST.MRY 2)
A&D 1906-39 (boys)

St Mary's Roman Catholic School, Arnold's Place, Dockhead, SE1.

St Mary's Roman Catholic School, East Row, W10. Opened 1877.

St Mary's Roman Catholic School, Eltham High Street, SE9. (LMA: EO/DIV 6/ST.MRY 1)
A&D 1953-57 (infants and mixed)

St Mary's Roman Catholic School, Holly Place, NW3. Opened 1833; closed 1905.

St Mary's Roman Catholic School, Prince of Wales Drive, Battersea Park, SW11. Opened 1870.

St Mary's Roman Catholic Secondary School, South Side, SW4.

St Mary's School, Clarendon Square, Somers Town, NW1. Opened 1899.

St Mary's School, Earsby (previously William) Street, W14. Opened 1840; closed 1875 and merged into William Street School.

St Mary's School, Gate Street, Holborn, WC2.
LB 1863-1905 (LMA Modern Records Section)

St Mary's School, Hide Place, Vincent Square, SW1. Opened 1850. (LMA: EO/DIV 2/ST.MRY7)
A&D 1926-32 (infants)

St Mary's School, Kingsmead Street, SE18. Founded 1840.

St Mary's School, Paddington Gardens, Paddington Green, W2. Opened 1802. (LMA: EO/DIV 2/ST.MRY 1)
LB 1913-17, 1923-29 (boys)

St Mary's School, Princes Road, SE11. Opened 1871. (LMA: EO/DIV 8/ST.MRY 3)
A&D 1924-26 (infants)

St Mary's School, Soho, W1. (LMA: EO/DIV 2/ST.MRY 2)
LB 1875-1900 (boys)

St Mary's School, Spital Square, Whitechapel, E1. Opened 1853; closed 1907. (LMA: EO/DIV 5/ST.MRY)
A&D 1891-1907 (mixed); 1895-1907 (infants)

St Mary's School, York Street, W1. A fire in 1944 destroyed previous records. (LMA: EO/DIV 2/ST.MRY 8)
A&D 1944-60 (junior mixed and infants)

St Mary's Town and Country School, Eton Avenue, NW3. Opened 1937; closed c1983.

St Mary the Less School, Sancroft Street, Kennington, SE11. Opened 1871; renamed St Mary Secondary Boys' School, 1946. (LMA: EO/DIV 8/ST.MRY 1 and P85/MY 2)
A&D 1872-96, 1905-27, 1940-43 (girls); 1875-1901, 1940, 1946-62 (boys); 1891-92 (infants); 1902-46 (mixed)
LB 1862-90 (girls); 1913-62 (boys)
Misc punishment 1946-62

St Matthew's Church of England School, Denmark Hill, SE5. Opened 1862. (LMA: P85/MTW 2)
Misc accounts 1935-65; minute books 1943-50

St Matthew's Church of England School, New Norfolk (later Rotherfield) Street, N1. Opened 1837; closed 1901.

St Matthew's School, Camberwell New Road, SE5. Opened 1858.

St Matthew's School, Milson Road/Ceylon Road, Kensington, W14. Opened 1872; closed 1908 and children sent to Addison Gardens. (LMA: EO/DIV 1/ST.MA and P80/MTW)
LB 1896-1907 (girls); 1900-08 (boys); 1903-08 (infants)
Misc minute books 1867-1908

St Matthew's School, Nelson Place, City Road, N1. Opened 1851; closed by 1955. (LMA: EO/DIV 3/ST.MAT)

St Matthew's School [*continued*]
A&D 1874-99, 1911-32 (boys); 1886-1932 (girls); 1893-1939 (infants); 1932-48 (junior mixed)
LB 1862-1933 (mixed); 1863-90, 1899-1905, 1913-32 (boys); 1871-1913 (infants); 1896-1932 (girls); 1932-48 (junior mixed)

St Matthew's School, Queensway, Bayswater, W2. Opened 1832 as Bayswater National School and 1842 Paddington National School; merged and renamed 1868; closed 1938. (LMA: EO/DIV 2/ST.MTW 1 and P87/MTW)
A&D 1866-1938 (boys); 1874-1904 (junior boys); 1874-1904 (junior girls); 1901-38 (girls); 1904-38 (infants)
LB 1862-1933 (boys); 1876-1932 (girls); 1884-1938 (infants); 1933-38 (mixed)
Misc a few staff late 19th century

St Matthew's School, Arlington Road, Camden, NW1. Opened 1864. (LMA: EO/DIV 2/ST.MTW 2)
A&D 1917-39 (infants)

St Matthew's School, Old Pye Street or Victoria Street, SW1. Opened 1856.

St Matthias Church of England School, Grundy Street and Bullivant Street, Poplar, E14. Founded 1845; opened 1870. (LMA: EO/DIV 5/ST.MAT)
A&D 1894-1902 (infants); 1940-44 (emergency); 1946-83 (junior mixed and infants)
LB 1913-32 (boys); 1913-39, 1944-83 (infants); 1935-39 (junior boys); 1944-83 (junior mixed)
Misc minute books 1933-83 (Church of England Records Centre)

St Matthias' Church of England School, Warwick Road, SW5. Opened 1881.

St Matthias' School, Granby Street, Bethnal Green, E2. Opened 1851.

St Matthias' School, Wordsworth Road, Stoke Newington, N16. Opened 1852. (LMA: P94/MTS)
Misc minute books 1920-40

St Michael and All Angels School *see* **Bell Green School**

St Michael and All Angels Secondary Modern School, Wyndham Road (boys) and Toulon Street (girls and infants), SE5. (LMA: EO/DIV 6/ST.MIC)
A&D 1932-39 (junior mixed); 1935-63 (infants)
LB 1946-63 (junior mixed)
Misc punishment 1932-60

St Michael and All Angels School, Lamb Lane, London Fields, E8. Opened 1871 as Ada Street School. (LMA: EO/DIV 4/ST.MIC)
A&D 1931-39 (mixed and infants)

St Michael and All Angels School, Farmers Road, Camberwell, SE5. (LMA: EO/DIV 7/ST.MIC)
A&D 1875-78, 1908-39, 1946-53 (infants); 1891-1946 (boys); 1881-1946 (girls); 1946-53 (mixed)

St Michael's and All Angels' Church of England School, Borgard Road, SE18. Opened 1871.

St Michael's Church of England School, Bingfield Street, N1. Opened 1853; closed by 1878.

St Michael's Church of England School, Halstead Street, Stockwell, SW9. Opened 1901. (LMA: EO/DIV 8/ST.MIC and P85/MIC)
A&D 1903-61 (infants)
LB 1864-1961 (infants)
Misc visitors 1904-39; minute books 1894-1910, 1936-61; accounts 1909-27

St Michael's Roman Catholic School, Arnold's Place, Dockhead, SE1. Previously Dockhead Roman Catholic School.

St Michael's Roman Catholic School, Westbourne Park, W2. Opened 1874; amalgamated with St Mary of Angels by 1961. . (LMA: EO/DIV 2/ST.MIC 3)
A&D 1957-58 (junior boys)

St Michael's School, Arlington Road, Camden Town, NW1. Opened 1872.

St Michael's School, Champion Road, Sydenham, SE26. Opened 1871.

St Michael's School, Ebury Square, Pimlico, SW1. (LMA: EO/DIV 2/ST.MIC 2)
A&D 1852-1909 (boys); 1912-32 (girls); also records 1863-1977 (Westminster Archives)
LB 1863-89, 1912-39 (girls); 1910-27 (evening); 1912-27 (boys); 1913-39 (infants)

St Michael's School, Granville Road, Southfields, Putney, SW18. Opened 1879. (LMA: P95/MAA)
Misc accounts 1926-29

St Michael's School, North Road, Highgate, N5. Opened 1851.

St Michael's School, Star Street, Edgware Road, W2. Opened 1871; closed c1970. . (LMA: EO/DIV 2/ST.MIC 1)
A&D 1907-39 (infants); 1908-39 (girls); 1924-37 (mixed); 1933-46 (boys)
LB 1870-1937 (girls); 1870-1925 (infants); 1886-1939 (boys)

St Monica's Roman Catholic School, Hoxton Square, N1. Opened 1870.

St Olave's School, Tower Bridge (Independent, later State) (boys). Opened 1571, moved to Orpington, Kent, 1967.

St Pancras Church of England School, Lancing Street, NW1. Opened 1884. (LMA: EO/DIV 2/ST.PAN)
A&D 1884-1943 (infants); 1900-13 (girls); 1930-39 (junior boys); 1940-50 (mixed and infants)
LB 1863-1929 (boys); 1863-1940 (infants); 1899-1929 (girls); 1930-50 (senior girls); 1930-39 (junior boys)

St Patrick (Benevolent Society of) School, Cornwall Road, Lambeth, SE1. Opened 1897.
A&D 1905-19 (boys); 1905-19 (girls) (LMA: EO/DIV 8/ST.PAT); 1910-79 (junior mixed and infants) (LMA: EO/DIV 9/ST.PAT)
LB 1910-19 (handicraft centre); 1912-13 (boys) (LMA: EO/DIV 8/BEN)
LB 1926-43, 1946-79 (mixed); 1926-79 (infants) (LMA: EO/DIV 8/ST.PAT)

St Patrick's Roman Catholic School, Great Chapel Street, Soho, W1. Opened 1903.

St Patrick's Roman Catholic School, Green Bank, Wapping, E1.

St Patrick's Roman Catholic School, Griffin Road, SE18. Opened 1891. (LMA: EO/DIV 6/ST.PAT)
A&D 1908-49 (boys); 1908-49 (girls); 1909-30 (infants)

St Patrick's Roman Catholic School, Raglan Street, NW5. fl.1971.

St Paul's Bentinck School, Rossmore Road, Marylebone Road, NW1. Opened 1857. (LMA: EO/DIV 2/ST.PAU 1)
A&D 1867-1939 (boys); 1875-1901, 1909-47 (girls); 1913-39 (infants); 1940-47 (mixed); 1946-69 (mixed and infants)
LB 1863-1939 (boys); 1863-1947 (girls); 1863-1939, 1947-61 (infants); 1940-61 (mixed)

St Paul's Cathedral Choir School, New Change, EC4.
A&D 1879-1938, 1968-72 (Guildhall Library)
Misc administrative records 1885-1981 (Guildhall Library)
Register Register 1873-1964 (9th edition 1964; (1st edition, 1920))

St Paul School, Broke Road, Dalston, E8. Opened 1870. (LMA: EO/DIV 4/ST.PAU)
A&D 1870-79, 1889-1945 (boys); 1876-82, 1886-1951. (infants); 1910-45 (girls)
LB 1869-97, 1913-34 (girls); 1888-1924 (infants); 1913-34 (boys)

St Paul's Church of England Primary School, Winchester Road, Hampstead, NW3. Opened 1873.
A&D 1871-74 (boys); 1895-1918 (girls); 1943-72 (junior mixed and infants) (Church of England Records Centre)
LB 1903-39 (boys); 1906-28 (girls); 1913-28 (infants); 1944-82 (junior mixed and infants) (Church of England Records Centre)

St Paul's Church of England School, Queen Caroline Street, W6. Opened 1756; refounded 1836; moved to Worlidge Street, W6, 1958.
LB 1863-1913 (boys); 1863-1913 (girls); 1866-1925 (infants) (Hammersmith and Fulham Archives)
Misc staff records 1884-95 (Hammersmith and Fulham Archives)

St Paul's Church of England School, Wellclose Square, E1. Opened 1869. (LMA: P93/PAU 2)

St Paul's Church of England School [*continued*]
A&D 1954 (nursery)
LB 1864-1913 (infants); 1867-96 (girls);
1869-96 (boys); 1896-1913 (mixed)
Misc staff 1875-97 (nursery); minute books
1874-91, 1928-55; minute books 1875-98,
1920-35, 1945-50 (nursery)

St Paul's Girls' Preparatory School, Brook
Green, W6. Previously Colet Girls' School.
Opened 1904.

St Paul's School, Blenheim Road, N19. Opened
1875; closed 1901.

St Paul's National School,
Shadwell High Street, E1. Opened 1870;
closed 1906. (LMA: EO/DIV 5/ST.PAU 2)
A&D 1905-06 (mixed)
Misc 1970 (centenary report)

St Paul's Preparatory School, Colet Court
(Independent) (boys). Opened 1881.

St Paul's Road School, Burdett Road,
Mile End, E3. Opened 1873; renamed
St Paul's Way School, 1938.
(LMA: EO/DIV 5/ST.PAU 1)
A&D 1873-1931 (girls); 1905-40 (infants);
1913-32 (junior boys); 1927-37 (boys);
1931-37 (junior girls)
LB 1873-1939 (boys); 1873-91, 1905-39
(infants); 1891-1931 (girls); 1931-37
(junior girls)
Misc punishment 1905-30 (girls); 1931-54
(mixed)

St Paul's School, Clapham, SW4.
Opened 1871.

St Paul's School, Dorset Street, Essex Road,
N1. Opened 1829; closed 1971.
(LMA: EO/DIV 3/ST.PAU 1 and
P83/PAU 2)
A&D 1882-1939 (girls); 1908-42 (boys);
1909-55 (infants); 1940-70 (mixed)
LB 1867-82, 1893-1954 (boys); 1882-1955
(girls); 1888-1908, 1911-55 (infants);
1954-71 (senior mixed)
Misc minute books 1874-76, 1880-1911;
punishment 1919-69; visitors 1922-39;
school journey reports 1936-37

St Paul's School, East Street. Opened 1861;
closed 1920. (LMA: EO/DIV 2/ST.PAU 2)
LB 1863-1920 (boys); 1885-1920 (infants);
1894-1920 (girls)

St Paul's School later **St Paul with St Michael
School**, Pownall Road, Haggerston, E8.
Opened 1865.

St Paul's School, Hammersmith, W6.
(Independent) (boys). Opened 1509 at
Ludgate Hill, moved 1884; moved to
Barnes 1968.
Registers Register of Admission 1509-1748
(M. McDonnell, 1977); Admission Register
1748-1876 (R.B. Gardiner, 1884);
Admission Register 1876-1905
(R.B. Gardiner, 1906); Admission Register
1905-1985 (anon, 1990)

St Paul's School, Rotherhithe Street, SE16.
Opened 1847.

St Paul's School, Surrey Gardens, Walworth,
SE17. Opened 1884; St Alban Church of
England School, 1937; renamed St Paul
Church of England School, 1951; rebuilt on
site of Penrose Street School and renamed
St Paul's School, Walworth, 1953.
(LMA: EO/DIV 8/ST.PAU 1)
A&D 1880-1918, 1940 (boys); 1893-1933
(girls); 1906-16 (infants)
LB 1913-33 (boys); 1913-33 (girls); 1933-39
(mixed); 1946-53 (secondary modern)

St Paul's School, Sutherland Square, SE17.
Opened 1870.
(LMA: EO/DIV 8/ST.PAU 3)
A&D 1918-39, 1946-53 (senior mixed)

St Paul's School, Vauxhall, SE1. Opened 1868.
(LMA: EO/DIV 8/ST.PAU.2)
LB 1869-1916 (boys); 1899-1913 (infants)

St Paul's School, Wilton Place, SW1.
Opened 1877. (LMA: EO/DIV 1/ST.PA
and EO/DIV 2/ST.PAU 4)
A&D 1927-40 (girls); 1933-40 (boys); 1937-53
(infants); 1939-40 (senior mixed); 1939-40,
1946-53 (junior mixed) (DIV 1); 1844-74,
1879-1922 (boys); 1844-74 (girls);
1865-1935 (junior girls); 1869-1926
(infants); 1915-39 (mixed and infants)
(DIV 2); also 1844-70 (Westminster
Archives)
LB 1862-1912 (boys); 1862-1906, 1914-39
(girls); 1862-1939 (infants); 1875-95
(mixed)
Misc cash books 1844-59, 1866-1904;
ledgers 1844-61, 1866-82; weekly
payments 1902-04; punishment 1907-38
(infants); 1918-24 (boys); visitors 1911-18

St Paul's School, Waverley Terrace *see*
Holy Trinity with St Paul

St Paul's School, Westbourne Street, Pimlico,
SW1. (LMA: EO/DIV 2/ST.PAU 3)
LB 1895-1905 (infants)

St Paul's School for Girls, Brook Green, W6.
Opened 1904.

St Paul's Unit, Waverley Terrace,
Paddington, W2. Opened 1871.
(LMA: EO/DIV 2/ST.PAU 6)
A&D 1939-41 (infants)

St Paul's Way School *see* **St Paul's Road School**

St Peter's and St Paul's Roman Catholic School,
Amwell Street, EC1. Opened 1903.

St Peter's Church of England School,
King Street, W6. Opened 1849; new school
in St Peter's Grove, 1971.

St Peter's Church of England School,
Chippenham Road or Goldney Road,
Paddington, W9. Opened 1872.

St Peter's Church of England School,
Lower Belgrave Street, SW1. Founded by
1841; opened 1872.

St Peter's Church of England School,
Plough Road, Battersea, SW11. Opened
1876. (LMA: EO/DIV 9/ST.PET)
A&D 1931-39 (boys)

St Peter's College, Manor Road, Wickham
Park, Brockley, SE4. (private) (boys).

St Peter's Free Schools, Paddenswick Road,
W6. Opened 1871; closed 1883; reopened
1949; renamed John Betts School, 1951.

St Peter's Italian Roman Catholic School,
Little Saffron Hill, EC1. Opened 1867;
renamed St Catherine Laboure School,
1953. (LMA: EO/DIV 3/ST PET)
A&D 1936-57 (infants)

St Peter's Roman Catholic School, New Road,
SE18. Opened 1857.

St Peter's Saffron Hill National School,
Onslow Street, Saffron Hill, EC1.
Misc estate records 1852-1901
(Guildhall Library)

St Peter's School, Bridge Street, SE10.
Founded 1849; opened 1867; later
St Alfege and St Peter School.
A&D 1952-72 (various) (Church of England
Records Centre)
LB 1913 (infants); 1913-37 (girls); 1937-64
(junior and infants) (Church of England
Records Centre)

St Peter's School, Cephas Street, E1.
Opened 1851. (LMA: P93/DUN/369 and
EO/DIV 5/ST.PET 1)
A&D 1878-1908 (boys)
Misc accounts 1890-94

St Peter's School, Gye Street, Vauxhall, SE11.
Opened 1860. (LMA: EO/DIV 8/ST.PET
and P85/PET 1)
A&D 1881-98 (girls); 1889-1917 (boys);
1892-1939, 1943-55 (infants)
LB 1885-1934 (boys); 1908-32 (infants);
1913-37 (girls); 1943-54, 1957-80 (junior
mixed and infants) (1885-1913 in
P85/PET 1/51)
Misc honours 1940-57; minute books 1928-33
(choir school)

St Peter's School, Hackney Road, E2.
(LMA: EO/DIV 4/ST.PET)
LB 1931-38 (boys)

St Peter's School, Liverpool Grove, Walworth,
SE17. Opened 1839. (LMA: P92/PET 1)
A&D 1872-1904 (girls); 1874-1905 (boys);
1878-1938 (infants); 1905-16 (mixed)
LB 1913-26 (infants); 1913-37 (mixed)
Misc minute books 1846-70

St Peter's School, London Docks, E1. Founded
1704 as St John Wapping School.
(LMA: EO/DIV 5/ST.PET 2)
A&D 1876-83, 1902-29 (boys)

St Peter's School, Red Lion Street, E1.

St Peter's School, St Oswald's Place,
Kennington Lane, SE11. Opened 1904.

St Philip's Roman Catholic School,
Sydenham Road, SE26.

St Philip's School, Wells Park Road,
Upper Sydenham, SE26. Opened 1873.
(LMA: ACC/1879 and ACC/2049)
Misc minute books 1912-36

St Philip the Evangelist National School, Hale (later Rees) Street, N1. Opened 1856; closed 1911.

St Phillip's Church of England School, Mount Street, E2. Opened 1852.

St Phillip's School, Reedworth Street, Kennington, SE11. Opened 1871. (LMA: EO/DIV 8/ST.PHI)
A&D 1936-39 (boys)
see also Archbishop Sumner's Memorial School

St Quintin Park School, W10.
St Marks Road School until 1951. (LMA: EO/DIV 1/ST.QU)
A&D 1945-58 (girls)
LB 1942-58 (girls)

St Richard of Chichester Roman Catholic School, Reed's Place, NW1 and Prince of Wales Road, NW5. fl.1969/71.

St Saviour and St Olave School, New Kent Road, SE1. Opened 1852.

St Saviour's Junior Mixed School, Shirland Road, W9. Opened 1872. (LMA: P87/SAV)
A&D 1880-93
LB 1871-96, 1913-20 (boys); 1913-20 (girls); 1934-64 (infants); 1952-59 (junior mixed)
Misc minute books 1905-62; accounts 1925-43

St Saviour's Roman Catholic School, High Street, SE13.

St Saviour Salamanca School, Rendall Row, Vauxhall Walk, SE11. Opened 1866. (LMA: EO/DIV 8/ST.SAV 1)1
A&D 1909-33 (boys); 1915-39 (girls); 1933-39, 1944-60 (mixed)
LB 1904-13, 1943-60 (infants); 1913-34 (girls); 1943-60 (mixed)

St Saviour Church of England School, Herne Hill Road, SE24. Opened 1869. (P85/SAV 2)
Misc minute books 1867-1915; accounts 1868-69

St Saviour's School, Northumberland Street and Hobday Street, Poplar, E14. Opened 1864. (LMA: EO/DIV 5/ST.SAV)
A&D 1960-71 (mixed)
LB 1913-38 (girls); 1938-39 (boys)

St Saviour Southwark Board of Guardians see **Central London School District**

St Saviour Southwark School, Redcross Street, SE1. Opened 1717; united to St Mary Overie School, 1953. (LMA: EO/DIV 8/ST.SAV 2 and P92/SAV)
LB 1910-13, 1934-39 (mixed); 1910-13 (infants)
Misc accounts 1583-1614; punishment 1943-60; staff 1949-59

St Scholastica's Roman Catholic School, Kenninghall Road, E5.

St Sepulchre's School, Giltspur Street, Newgate Street, EC1. Opened 1860.
A&D 1861-75 (girls); 1882-96 (boys); 1911-24 (general) (Guildhall Library)
LB 1863-88 (girls); 1863-75 (boys)
Misc estate records 1916; administrative records 1700-1939 (Guildhall Library)

St Stephen's Church of England School, Jerrard Street, SE13. Opened 1866.

St Stephen's National School, Essex Road, N1. Opened 1842; closed 1880s.

St Stephen's National School, Spitalfields, E1. Opened 1872; closed 1909. (LMA: EO/DIV 5/ST.STE)
A&D 1896-1909 (girls); 1902-09 (infants)

St Stephen's Roman Catholic School, Rylett Road, W12. Opened 1850.

St Stephen's School, Albyn Road, Lewisham, SE8. Opened 1865.

St Stephen's School, Dorset Road, Kennington, SW8. Opened 1847. (LMA: EO/DIV 8/ST.STE and P85/STE)
LB 1913 (girls)
Misc minute books 1861-90; accounts 1953-68

St Stephen's School, Avenue Road, St John's Wood, NW8. Opened 1859. (LMA: P81/STE 1)
Misc minute books 1852-88

St Stephens School, Uxbridge Road, W12.
Opened 1851. (LMA: EO/DIV 1/ST.ST)
A&D 1874-79, 1883-93, 1899-1939 (boys);
1880-1961 (infants); 1883-1953 (girls)
LB 1863-1934 (girls); 1863-1933 (infants);
1911-39 (boys)
Misc visitors 1907-38

St Stephen's School, Westbourne Park Road,
W2. Opened 1859.

St Theresa's Roman Catholic School,
Belmont Hill, SE13. fl.1971.

St Thomas à Becket Roman Catholic School,
Mottisfont Road, SE2. fl.1971.

St Thomas Church of England School, Sand
Street, SE18. Opened 1855; closed 1940s.
(LMA: EO/DIV 6/ST.THO 1-2 and
P97/TMS)
A&D 1892-1908 (boys); 1906-14 (infants)
LB 1886-1908 (boys); 1932-39 (junior girls);
1932-39 (infants)
Misc minute books 1905-30; accounts 1931-33

St Thomas Colet Church of England School,
Arbour Square, E1. Opened 1854.

St Thomas More Roman Catholic School,
Appleton Road, SE9.

St Thomas' Roman Catholic School,
Dawes Road, SW6. Opened 1848.
(LMA: EO/DIV 1/ST.TH)
A&D 1917-37 (infants)
LB 1913-39 (infants)

St Thomas' Roman Catholic Secondary School,
St Dunstan's Road, W6. Originally at
Dawes Road and part of St Thomas' School
there; moved 1947; renamed St Edmund's
Roman Catholic Secondary School, 1949.

St Thomas School, Bosworth Road and
Appleford Road, W10. Opened 1872 as
St Andrew's and St Philip's School;
renamed St Thomas, 1976.

St Thomas School, Charterhouse, EC1.
(LMA: P76/TMS)
Misc accounts 1869-72

St Thomas School, Lynmouth Road, N16.
Also known as Upper Clapton and
Stamford Hill School. Opened 1828.
(LMA: EO/DIV 4/ST.THO)

St Thomas School [*continued*]
A&D 1912-39 (girls); 1913-26, 1938-39
(infants); 1938-39 (junior mixed); 1940-41
(senior emergency)
LB 1876-1904, 1913-17 (infants);
1930-53 (girls)

St Thomas's Church of England School,
Everilda Street, N1. Opened 1856.

St Thomas's School, Picton Place, Duke Street,
W1. Opened 1862.

St Ursula's Convent School, Crooms Hill,
Greenwich, SE10. Opened 1877.

St Victoire's Convent School, Victoria Park
Road, E9. Closed 1972-74.

St Vincent's Roman Catholic School, Wigmore
Street and Blandford Street, W1. Opened
1888.

St Vincent's Roman Catholic School,
Carlisle Place, Victoria Street, SW1.
(LMA: EO/DIV 2/ST.VIN)
A&D 1914-56 (girls); 1940-43 (mixed)
LB 1914-39, 1945-65 (girls); 1940-45 (mixed)

St William of York Roman Catholic School,
Eltringham Street, SW18. fl.1961.

St William of York Roman Catholic School
Upper School in Gifford Street, N1; Lower
School in Brewery Road, N7. Opened
1957.
A&D 1956-68 (LMA Modern Records Section)

St Winifred's Roman Catholic School,
Effingham Road, SE12. Opened 1903.

Sadler's Wells Ballet School, Colet Gardens,
W14. Founded 1931 at Sadler's Wells
Theatre; moved to Hammersmith, 1947;
renamed Royal Ballet School, 1956.

Salesian College, Surrey Lane, SW11.

Salter's Hill School,
West Norwood, SE27. Opened 1880
(previously Hamilton Road Temporary
Street); renamed Kingswood Primary
School, 1951. (LMA: EO/DIV 8/SAL)
A&D 1875-1934 (boys); 1875-1939 (girls);
1875-1930 (infants)
LB 1875-1933 (boys); 1875-1938 (girls);
1875-1922 (infants); 1934-38 (junior boys)
Misc punishment 1927-29, 1935-36

Saltram Crescent High School, Kilburn, W9.
Opened 1891; closed c1913.

Samuel Pepys School, Wallbutton Road, SE4.
fl.1971; merged into Hatcham Wood
School, 1982.

Samuel Rhodes School, Dowrey Street, N1.
Opened 1972 (special).

Sandford Lane Ragged School,
Stoke Newington High Street, N16.
Opened 1846; closed 1872.

Sandford Row School, Walworth, SE17.
Opened 1891; Nelson School after 1932.
(LMA: EO/DIV 8/SAN)
A&D 1889-1903 (boys); 1903-30 (girls)
LB 1891-1938 (infants); 1900-39
(manual training centre)

Sandhurst Road School, SE6. Opened 1904;
renamed Sandhurst School, 1951; closed
1970s. (LMA: EO/DIV 6/SAN)
A&D 1899-1913 (mixed); 1904-29,
1933-39 (girls); 1905-29 (boys)
LB 1904-24 (girls); 1905-26 (manual training
centre); 1907-25 (boys); 1911-20 (evening);
1925-28 (senior mixed)

Santley Street School, Ferndale Road, SW4.
Opened 1902; renamed Santley Primary
and Secondary School, 1951.
A&D 1898-1939 (infants); 1938-39 (boys)
(LMA: EO/DIV 8/SAN);   1968-97
(Lambeth Archives)
LB 1898-1939 (boys); 1898-1937
(infants);   1951-54   (senior   boys)
(LMA: EO/DIV 8/SAN);   1937-73
(Lambeth Archives)
Misc punishment 1989; minute books 1988-97
(Lambeth Archives)

Sarah Siddons School, North Wharf Road, W2.
Opened 1961.

Sarum Hall, Eton Avenue, NW3. Opened 1929;
closed 1986.

Saunders Road or Saunders Grove School,
Notting Hill, W11. Opened 1874; renamed
Saunders Grove School, 1938; closed 1963.
(LMA: EO/DIV 1/SAU)
A&D 1874-1936 (boys); 1874-1936 (girls);
1883-92 (infants); 1890-1910, 1936-39
(infant boys); 1892-1939 (infant girls)
LB 1885-1910 (evening)

Sawley Road School, Sawley Road, W12.
Opened 1912; renamed Wormholt Park
School, 1922.

Sayer Street School. Opened 1893 (partially
sighted opened 1915).
LB 1913-37 (myopic - mixed)

Scarsdale Road School, Albany Road, SE5.
Opened   1875;   closed   1940s.
(LMA: EO/DIV 7/SCA)
A&D 1895-1913 (infant girls); 1898-1941
(infant boys); 1902-44 (girls); 1929-45
(boys)
LB 1875-1929 (girls); 1913-29 (infants);
1929-39 (boys)

Scawfell Street School, Hackney Road, E2.
Opened 1885; later Scawfell Secondary
School; part of Haggerston Secondary
School, 1959. (LMA: EO/DIV 4/SCA)
A&D 1913-39, 1943-56 (boys); 1918-31
(infants); 1946-59 (mixed); 1956 (girls)
LB 1885-1906 (infants); 1943-56 (senior boys)
Misc punishment 1953-55

School Board for London. Various schools.
(LMA: SBL)
A&D 1874-1921

School for Sons of Missionaries, Blackheath
(Independent). Opened 1852.

Scott Lidgett School, Drummond Road, SE16.
fl.1971.

Scrutton Street School, Shoreditch, EC2.
Opened 1875. (LMA: EO/DIV 4/SCR)
LB 1882-1905 (evening)

Sebbon Street School, Sable Street,
Canonbury Road, N1. Opened 1916;
renamed William Tyndale Primary School,
1951. (LMA: EO/DIV 3/SEB)
A&D 1906-30 (infants); 1906-16 (junior mixed)
LB 1914-31 (junior mixed and infants)

Sebright School, Maidstone Street, E2. fl.1971.

Sedgehill School, Sedgehill Road, SE6.
(LMA: EO/DIV 7/SED)
A&D 1957-59 (mixed)

Sellincourt Road School, Tooting Graveney,
SW17. Opened 1907; renamed Sellincourt
School, 1951. (LMA: EO/DIV 9/SEL)

100

Sellincourt Road School [*continued*]
A&D 1904-12 (girls and infants); 1904-17, 1935-44 (senior mixed); 1907-29 (junior mixed); 1912-33 (infants); 1918-35 (mixed)
LB 1904-13 (girls); 1904-36 (infants)
Misc visitors 1907-36

Senior Street School, Paddington, W2. Opened 1915; renamed Edward Wilson School, 1951. (LMA: EO/DIV 2/SEN)
A&D 1915-30 (infants); 1932-47 (senior boys)

Senrab Street School, Charles Street, Stepney, E1. Opened 1907; renamed Marion Richardson Primary School, 1951. (LMA: EO/DIV 5/SEN)
A&D 1896-1907 (mixed); 1907-37 (boys); 1907-39 (girls); 1928-39 (infants)
LB 1907-37 (boys); 1907-31 (girls)

Servite Roman Catholic School, Winterton Place, SW10. Opened 1872.

Settles Street School, Stepney, E1. Opened 1874; closed 1932 (LMA: EO/DIV 5/SET)
A&D 1874-1914 (infants); 1889-1920 (girls)

Settringham School, Lyndhurst Gardens, NW3. Opened 1938; closed *c*1950.

Seven Mills School, Malabar Street, E14. fl.1971.

Sewardstone Road School, Bethnal Green, E2. Opened 1911. (LMA: EO/DIV 5/SEW)
A&D 1906-21, 1930-39 (junior mixed)

Shackleton Secondary School, SE26. Opened 1876 as Sydenham Hill Road School; renamed Sydenham Central School, 1927; renamed 1951; closed 1958.

Shacklewell School, Shacklewell Row, E8. Opened 1876. (LMA: EO/DIV 4/SHC)
A&D 1934-38, 1946-53 (senior boys); 1943-46 (senior mixed); 1946-53 (senior girls)
LB 1929-40 (girls); 1931-42 (boys)

Shaftesbury Park School, Ashbury Road, SW11. fl.1971.

Shap Street School, Pearson Street, Kingsland Road, E2. Opened 1875; closed 1939. (LMA: EO/DIV 4/SHP)
A&D 1875-1932 (boys); 1875-1939 (girls); 1902-39 (infants); 1932-39 (junior boys)
LB 1875-1932 (boys); 1875-1926 (girls); 1875-1939 (infants)

Shelburne Road School, Hornsey Road, N7. Opened 1910 as St Barnabas School; renamed Shelburne School, 1951; part of Highbury Fields School, *c*1981. (LMA: EO/DIV 3/SHE and ACC/3488)
A&D 1901-31 (girls); 1910-30 (infants); 1923-31 (mixed); 1931-39 (senior mixed); 1941-57 (class registers); 1944-58 (senior boys)
LB 1901-13, 1924-31 (girls); 1901-35 (infants); 1913-24, 1945 (mixed); 1924-44 (boys); 1913-58 (ACC/3488)

Shepperton Road School, New North Road, N1. Opened 1879; renamed Shepperton School, 1951; closed 1957. (LMA: EO/DIV 3/SHP)
A&D 1940 (mixed); 1943-56 (junior boys)
LB 1879-1932 (boys); 1932-57 (primary)

Sherbrooke Road School, Dawes Road, SW6. Opened 1885; renamed Sherbrooke School 1951; closed 1992. (LMA: EO/DIV 1/SHE)
A&D 1885-89 (boys); 1901-33, 1946-47 (junior mixed); 1913-28 (girls); 1933-39 (senior boys). (LMA: EO/DIV 1/SHE)
LB 1885-97, 1908-13 (Hammersmith and Fulham Archives); 1885-1913 (boys); 1901-13 (junior boys); 1903-13 (girls); 1913-34 (infants). (LMA: EO/DIV 1/SHE)
Misc visitors 1901-38 (LMA: EO/DIV 1/SHE)

Sheringdale School, Standen Road, SW18. fl.1971.

Sherington Road School, SE7. Opened 1907; reorganised as Central School, 1911; renamed Sherington Road again, 1922; renamed Sherington Primary School, 1951. (LMA: EO/DIV 6/SHE) (*see also* Charlton Central School)
A&D 1907-11 (boys); 1932-39 (junior girls); 1940-45 (girls and infant girls)
LB 1907-11 (boys)

Shillington Street School, Falcon Road, Battersea, SW11. Opened 1883; renamed Shillington School, 1951. (LMA: EO/DIV 9/SHI)
A&D 1874-83 (girls); 1892-1938, 1948-59 (boys); 1897-1928 (mixed); 1967-79 (senior mixed)
LB 1879-1913 (infants); 1932-35 (evening); 1939-43 (LMA: ACC/3531 - while evacuated to Cranleigh, Surrey); 1961-80 (senior mixed)

Shirley House School, Old Charlton
(Independent) (boys). Opened 1860.

Shooter's Hill Church of England School,
Red Lion Lane, SE18. Opened 1857 as
Christ Church National School; Primary
School became Christ Church Primary
School, 1951. (LMA: EO/DIV 6/SHO and
DIV 7/SHO)
A&D 1920-70 (boys); 1907-45 (junior mixed
and infants)
LB 1913-33 (mixed); 1913-33 (infants)
Misc 1922-45 (fee registers)

Shoreditch Board of Guardians see
Brentwood School District

Shoreditch Central School, Hoxton Road,
Old Street, N1. Opened 1912; renamed
Shoreditch School, after 1937.
(LMA: EO/DIV 4/SHR)
A&D 1941-57 (mixed)
LB 1870-1904 (infants)
Misc 1910-13, 1934-39 (infants)

Shoreditch Handicraft Training College,
Pitfield Street, N1.

Shoreditch Recreational Institute.
Opened *c*1898; closed 1962.
(LMA: EO/DIV 4/SHO)
A&D 1955-56 (boys)

Sidney Road School, Homerton High Street,
E9. Opened 1882; closed after 1938
(LMA: EO/DIV 4/SID)
A&D 1879-1911, 1918-31 (boys); 1895-1903,
1928-33 (junior boys); 1895-1903 (junior
girls); 1900-33 (girls); 1903-38 (infants)
LB 1876-1933 (boys); 1882-1933 (girls);
1882-1938 (infants); 1886-1913 (evening)

Sigdon Road School, Dalston Lane, E8. Opened
1898; renamed Amherst School, 1951.
(LMA: EO/DIV 4/SIG)
A&D 1898-1934 (girls); 1914-32 (boys)
LB 1898-1913 (infants)

Silverthorne School see **Southampton Way
School**

Silwood Street School, Rotherhithe, SE16.
Opened 1881; closed 1940s.
(LMA: EO/DIV 7/SIL)
A&D 1912-36 (boys); 1919-36 (girls); 1931-39
(infants)
LB 1939-40 in EO/WAR/5/14 when evacuated
to Worthing

Simon Marks Jewish Primary School, Cazenove
Road and Kyverdale Road, N16. Opened
1956.

Single Street School, Bow Common Lane,
Burdett Road, E3. Opened 1885.
(LMA: EO/DIV 5/SIN)
A&D 1931-38 (infants)
LB 1909-13, 1928-33 (girls)

Sirdar Road School, Notting Hill, W11. Opened
1880 as St Clements Road School; renamed
1904; renamed Avondale Park School,
1936. (LMA: EO/DIV 1/SIR)
A&D 1907-39 (girls); 1916-39 (boys)
LB 1905-36 (girls); 1912-36 (boys); 1923-29
(mentally defective)
Misc honours 1924-39

Sir Francis Drake School see **Trundley's
Road School**

Sir James Barrie School, Stewarts Road, SW8.
fl.1971.

Sir John Cass Foundation School, St James'
Duke's Place, City, EC3. In Aldgate
1710-62; Church Row 1762-1869; Jewry
Street 1869-1908; in 1944 the Secondary
School merged with the Red Coat School.
(LMA: EO/DIV 5/SIR)
A&D 1896-1935 (mixed); 1896-1905 (girls);
1905-40 (infants); 1913-45 (Upper School)
(Guildhall Library)
LB 1909-13 (infants) (LMA); 1905-13
(Guildhall Library)
Misc Foundation minute books 1726-1960;
apprenticeship indentures 1863-1910, 1975
(Guildhall Library)

Sir John Lillie School, Lillie Road, SW6.
Opened 1893 as Lillie Road School;
renamed 1951. (LMA: EO/DIV 1/SJL)
A&D 1940-46 (mixed); 1946-63 (junior mixed)

Sir Philip Magnus School, Penton Rise, WC1.

Sir Thomas Abney Primary School, Fairholt
Road, N16. Opened 1954.

Sir Walter St.John's School, Battersea High
Street, SW11. (Independent) (boys).
Opened 1700. (LMA: ACC/2181 and
ACC/2321)
A&D 1872-1946
Misc minute books 1827-1975

LONDON SCHOOL RECORDS

Sir William Burrough School, Salmon Lane, E14. fl.1971.

Sir William Collins Secondary School *see* Medburn School

Skinners' Company School for Girls, Stamford Hill, N16. Opened 1890.

Slade School, Plumstead Common Road, SE18. Opened 1878; renamed Timbercroft School, 1929. (LMA: EO/DIV 6/SLA)
A&D 1878-1940 (boys); 1878-1931 (girls); 1898-1922 (infants); 1920-22 (junior boys); 1929-39 (mixed); 1939-84 (LMA Modern Records Section)
LB 1866-77 (mixed); 1878-1922 (boys); 1878-1922 (infants); 1903-13 (manual training centre); 1915-31 (girls); 1929-39 (mentally defective - mixed)
Misc punishment 1946-68
(LMA Modern Records Section)

Sleaford Street School, Battersea Park Road, SW8. Opened 1874; renamed John Milton School, 1951. (LMA: EO/DIV 9/SLE)
A&D 1874-1939 (infants); 1907-39 (girls); 1911-32 (boys); 1932-39 (junior boys)
LB 1874-1929 (girls); 1874-1913, 1931-39 (infants)

Sloane School, Hortensia Road, SW10. Opened 1895; formerly South Western Polytechnic Institute; in 1970 amalgamated with Carlyle School, Buckingham Gate School and Ebury School to form Pimlico Comprenhensive. (LMA: EO/DIV 1/SLO)
A&D 1904-41, 1945-48, 1958-61, 1964-66 (boys)
LB 1967-70 (boys)
Misc staff 1895-1970; punishment 1962-70

Smallwood Road School, Garratt Lane, SW17. Opened 1898.

Smeed Road School, Old Ford, Poplar, E3. Opened 1885; renamed Fordway School, 1951. (LMA: EO/DIV 5/SME)
A&D 1890-1939 (infants); 1892-1932 (girls); 1932-39 (junior girls)
LB 1885-1932 (girls); 1885-1939 (infants); 1931-32 (junior boys); 1932-39 (junior girls)

Smith Street School, Stepney, E1. Opened 1899; closed 1928. (LMA: EO/DIV 5/SMI)
A&D 1899-1928 (infants); 1899-1928 (mixed)

Snowsfields School, Kirby Grove, Bermondsey, SE1. Opened 1881. (LMA: EO/DIV 8/SNO)
A&D 1898-1935 (infants); 1903-31 (girls); 1924-34 (junior girls)
LB 1881-1939 (infants); 1902-34 (girls)

Soho Parochial School. An amalgamation of St Peter and St James Westminster Schools, 1892.

Solomon Wolfson Jewish School, Lancaster Road, W11. fl.1956.

Somerford Street School, Bethnal Green, E1. Opened 1876 as London Street School; renamed 1881; Stewart Headlam School, 1924. (LMA: EO/DIV 5/SOM)
A&D 1889-1929 (boys); 1893-1926 (mixed); 1895-1926 (infants); 1897-1930 (girls)
LB 1881-1926 (infants); 1899-1924 (evening); 1908-30 (girls); 1913-14 (mixed); 1913-29 (boys)

Somerville School, Wavertree Road, SW2.

Southampton Street School, Camberwell, SE5. Opened 1874; renamed Dovedale Manor School; Oliver Goldsmith School, 1931; Southampton Way School, 1938; Dovedale Manor School again, 1951. (LMA: EO/DIV 7/SOU)
A&D 1874-1924 (boys); 1874-1945 (girls); 1889-1937 (infants); 1949-51 (secondary boys)
LB 1889-1961 (infants - in ILEA/DOO8/03); 1902-13 (infants)

Southampton Street School, Pentonville, N1. (LMA: EO/DIV 3/SOU)
LB 1895-98 (mixed - deaf)

Southampton Way School, SE5. Opened 1874 as Southampton Street School; renamed Oliver Goldsmith School 1931; renamed 1938; later Silverthorne School. (LMA: EO/DIV 7/SOW)
LB 1933-45 (girls); 1933-45 (infants)

Southbank International School, Kensington Park Road, W11. Opened 1979.

South East London Secondary Technical School, Upper School in Stanley Street; Lower School in Creek Road both SE8. (LMA: EO/DIV 6/SOU)
A&D 1946-55 (boys); 1946-48 (boys over compulsory leaving age)

Southend Church of England School, Bromley Road, Catford, SE6.

Southern Grove School, Mile End Road, E3. Opened 1874; the Secondary School renamed Elizabeth Barrett Browning School, 1951. (LMA: EO/DIV 5/SOU)
A&D 1883-1931 (boys); 1917-39, 1942-56 (infants); 1919-39 (girls)
LB 1926-37 (girls); 1929-39 (infants)

Southfields School, The, Wimbledon Park Road, SW18. (LMA: EO/DIV 9/SOU)
A&D 1904-25 (junior girls); 1904-25 (infants); 1905-25 (junior boys)

South Hackney Central School, Cassland Road, Well Street, E9. *see* Lauriston Road School; opened 1916; renamed Cassland Secondary School, 1951. (LMA: EO/DIV 4/SOU)
A&D 1910-12 (mixed); also 1928-60 (LMA: ACC/3454/3-7)
LB 1928-37 (mixed).
(LMA: EO/DIV 4/SOU/LB/1); 1958-62 (LMA: ACC/3454/15)
Misc punishment 1910-13 (LMA: EO/DIV 4/SOU/MISC/1); 1941-66 (LMA: ACC/3454/16-17)

South Hackney Parochial School, Percy Road, Hackney, E9. Founded 1810 as St John's Chapel School; renamed 1850; renamed St John of Jerusalem School, Ainsworth Road, E9, 1956. (LMA: P79/JNJ)
Misc minute books 1834-55, 1859-73; staff 1916-34

South Hampstead High School, Winchester Gardens, NW3. Opened 1876; moved to Maresfield Gardens, NW3, 1882.

South Hampstead Preparatory School, Finchley Road, Hampstead (Independent) (boys). Opened 1897.

South Islington and Pentonville British School, Denmark Terrace, N1. Opened 1842; closed by 1893.

South Kensington Preparatory School, Rosary Gardens, Kensington, SW7. (Independent) (boys).

South Lambeth Road School, Kennington, SW8. Opened 1877. (LMA: EO/DIV 8/SLR)
A&D 1914-24 (junior mixed)

South Lambeth Jewish School, Walworth. (LMA: EO/DIV 8/SLJ)
A&D 1896-1939 (infants); 1909-39 (boys); 1909-39 (girls)

Southlands College, Wimbledon Park Side, SW19. Opened 1873. (LMA: EO/DIV 9/SOL)
A&D 1908-32 (girls); 1910-37 (infants)

Southlands Practising Wesleyan School, Battersea. fl.1905/25.

Southlands School, Battersea. (temporary) Opened 1927; fl.1940.

South London Technical Art School, Kennington Park Road, SE11.
A&D 1846-51, 1930-43 (Guildhall Library)

South Macclesfield Street Infants' School, South Macclesfield Street, Finsbury, EC1.
LB 1872-92 (LMA)

Southmead School, Princes Way, SW19. fl.1971.

South Metropolitan School District. Constituted by Bermondsey, Camberwell and Greenwich Boards of Guardians 1849-1902, St Mary Newington Board of Guardians 1854-69, Stepney Board of Guardians 1873-1902 and Woolwich Board of Guardians 1868-1902. (LMA: SMSD)
A&D 1855-1901
Misc minute books 1849-1905; staff 1854-1902

South Rise Infant School *see* Earl Street School

Southwark Central School, West Square, SE11. Opened 1885. (LMA: EO/DIV 8/SOU)
A&D 1923-44 (girls)
LB 1933-39 (girls)

Southwark Chapel Sunday School, Long Lane, SE1.
Misc minute books 1863-1912 (Southwark Local Studies Lib)

Southwark Park School, Rotherhithe, SE16. Opened 1874.

Southwark Park Wesleyan Methodist School, Rotherhithe, SE16.
Misc minute books 1923-34 (Southwark Local Studies Lib)

Southwark Sunday School Society
(Congregational)
Misc minute books 1799-1937; staff 1826-41;
accounts 1864-85; letters c1880 (Southwark
Local Studies Lib)

South Western Polytechnic Day School,
Manresa Road, Chelsea (Independent)
(boys). Opened 1895.

Southwold School, Detmold Road, E5. Opened
1886 as Detmold Road School; renamed ,
1951.

Spanish and Portuguese School.
(LMA: EO/DIV 5/SPA)
A&D 1899-1910 (infants)

Spencer Park School, Trinity Road, SW18.
fl.1971.

Spitalfields Charity School, Quaker Street, E1.
Founded 1782.

Spitalfields School of Design, Crispin Street
later White Lion Street, E1. Opened 1842;
by 1881 City School of Art.

Springfield School, Crimsworth Road, SW8.
Opened 1882; formerly Fountain Street
School. (LMA: EO/DIV 8/SPR)
A&D 1888-1933 (girls); 1894-1939 (infants)
LB 1899-1922, 1929-33 (girls);
1912-44 (infants)

Springwell House Open Air School,
Clapham Common North Side, SW4.
Opened 1919. (LMA: EO/DIV 9/SPR)
A&D 1917-52, 1956-60 (mixed); 1973-82
(junior mixed and infants)
LB 1937-60 (physically defective - mixed)

Stafford College, Forest Hill (Independent)
(boys). Opened 1863.

Stafford Road School, E3.
Opened as Tredegar Wesleyan School,
1869; renamed 1911; closed 1924.
(LMA: EO/DIV 5/STA)
A&D 1876-82 (junior mixed);
1882-1903 (infants)
LB 1913-24 (infants)

**Stafford Street Wesleyan Methodist Sunday
School**, SE15.
A&D 1894-1933 (Southwark Local Studies Lib)

Stamford Hill Collegiate School, Stamford Hill
(Independent) (boys). Opened 1790.

Stanhope Street School, Euston Road, NW1.
(LMA: EO/DIV 2/SHP)
LB 1891-1913, 1919-29 (evening);
1895-1916 (deaf)

Stanley Central School, Camden Street, NW1.
Opened 1910; renamed Lyulph Stanley
School, 1927. (LMA: EO/DIV 2/STC and
EO/DIV 2/STA)
A&D 1913-33 (girls)
LB 1910-13 (mixed); 1917-30 (girls)

Stanley School, The, Mornington Road,
Deptford, SE8. Opened 1879 as Stanley
Street School, renamed 1951. (LMA:
EO/DIV 6/STA and EO/DIV 7/STA)
A&D 1879-1957 (boys); 1890-1930 (girls);
1909-37 (infants); 1913-34 (mixed deaf);
1930-36 (senior girls)
LB 1910-13 (infants)

Starcross School, St Pancras *see*
Exmouth Street School

Star Road School, SW6. Opened 1880 as Star
Lane School, later Star Road; renamed
Queen's Court School, 1955; *see also*
Fulham County Secondary School
LB 1876-97 (boys); 1880-1906 (girls);
1899-1913 (infants) (Hammersmith and
Fulham Archives)

Starch Green British School, Victoria Road,
W12. Transferred to School Board 1873
when renamed Victoria School.

Station Road School, Upper Street, N1. Opened
1885; closed 1927 and used by Laycock
School.

Stebon School, Streatfield Street, E14. fl.1971.

Stephen Street School, Lisson Grove, NW1.
Opened 1874; renamed Cosway Street
School, 1911, Cosway Primary School,
1951. (LMA: EO/DIV 2/STE)
A&D 1895-1907 (boys); 1895-1927 (girls);
1907-25 (infants)
LB 1874-1900 (girls); 1885-1915 (evening)

Stephen the Yeoman Ragged School,
Bermondsey. fl.1905/6.

Stepney Board of Guardians see
South Metropolitan School District

105

Stepney Greencoat School, Salmon Lane, E14. fl.1971.

Stepney Green School, Ben Johnson Road, E1. fl.1971.

Stepney Jewish School, Stepney Green, E1. Opened 1869. (LMA: EO/DIV 5/STE)
A&D 1869-1929 (boys); 1874-1939 (girls); 1874-1902, 1908-39 (infants); 1929-69 (junior mixed and infants)
LB 1913-39 (boys); 1913-39 (girls); 1884-1939 (infants); 1954-70 (mixed)
Misc Cash 1874-80, 1898-1910; punishment 1939-67

Stepping Stone School, Fitzjohn's Avenue, NW3. Opened 1964.

Sternold College, Sternhold Avenue, SW2.

Stewart Headlam School, Somerford Street, E1. Opened 1876 as London Street School; renamed Somerford Street School, 1881; renamed 1924. (LMA: EO/DIV 5/STH)
A&D 1925-39 (boys); 1926-37, 1945-62 (infants); 1927-39 (girls)
LB 1930-39 (junior boys); 1930-39 (junior girls)

Stillness Road School, Brockley Rise, SE23. Opened 1905. (LMA: EO/DIV 7/STI)
A&D 1924-25, 1935-39 (junior mixed)

Stockwell College, Brixton. (LMA: EO/DIV 8/STC)
A&D 1861-67, 1871-1935 (infants); 1894-1935 (senior girls); 1896-1928 (junior girls)

Stockwell Road School, Lambeth, SW9. Opened 1877; renamed Stockwell Primary School, 1951. (LMA: EO/DIV 8/STO)
A&D 1921-39 (girls); 1930-39 (infants)
LB 1913-39 (infants); 1921-38 (girls)

Stockwell School, Lingham Street, Brixton, SW9. Opened 1825.

Stoke Newington Central School, N16. Opened 1927; renamed Clissold Secondary School, 1951; closed 1956. (LMA: EO/DIV 4/STO)
A&D 1931-55 (senior mixed)

Stoke Newington Grammar School, Manor Road, N16. Opened 1886; closed 1925.

Stoke Newington High Street School see **High Street School**, Stoke Newington.

Stoke Newington Parochial School, Lordship Road, N16. Opened 1830.

Stoke Newington Ragged Schools, N16. **Misc** minute books 1855-84; accounts 1855-97 (Hackney Archives)

Stoke Newington School, Clissold Park, N16. Opened 1982.

Stonhouse Street School, Clapham High Street, SW4. Opened 1881; renamed Clapham Manor School, 1951. (LMA: EO/DIV 9/STO)
A&D 1927-39 (infants); 1928-39 (junior boys); 1934-39 (senior mixed)
LB 1931-39 (infants); 1934-39 (mixed)

Stormont House School, Downs Park Road, Clapton, E5. Opened 1919.
LB 1904-11 (boys); 1934-39 (mixed)

Stowey Open Air School, South Side, Clapham, SW4. Opened 1920. (LMA:EO/DIV 9/STW)
A&D 1937-39 (mixed)

Strand School (King's College), Elm Park, Brixton Hill, SW2. Opened 1893. (LMA: EO/DIV 8/STR)
A&D 1902-38 (boys)

Stratheden House School, Blackheath (Independent) (boys). Opened 1869.

Streatham College, Streatham Common (Independent) (boys). Opened 1896.

Streatham County Secondary School, Welham Road, Mitcham Lane, SW17. Opened 1906.

Streatham Grammar School, Mitcham Lane, SW16. (Independent) (boys). Opened 1880.

Streatham Hill and Clapham High School, Abbotswood Road, SW16 or Wavertree Road, SW2. Opened 1887.

Streatham Kindergarten, Pinfold Road, SW16.

Streatham National School. Opened 1837.

Streatham School, Streatham Common (Independent Preparatory School) (boys). Opened 1785.

Streatham Subscribers' School. (LMA: A/SSS) **Misc** minute books and accounts 1830-41

Stuart School, Sussex Road, Coldharbour Lane, SW9. Sussex Road School to 1951. (LMA: EO/DIV 8/STU)
A&D 1954-56 (mixed); 1957-60 (junior mixed)

Sudbourne Road School, Hayter Road, Brixton Hill, SW2. Opened 1927; renamed Sudbourne School, 1951. (LMA: EO/DIV 8/SUD)
A&D 1914-35 (infants); 1914-34 (mixed)
LB 1914-31 (mixed); 1914-35 (junior mixed)

Suffolk Grove School, Rotherhithe New Road, SE16.

Sulivan School, Peterborough Road, SW6. Previously primary part of Hurlingham School; renamed 1951.

Sumner Road School, Peckham, SE15. Opened 1876; closed 1940s. (LMA: EO/DIV 7/SUM)
A&D 1887-1931 (girls); 1906-36 (infants)

Sun Babies Nursery, Hackney.
A&D 1942-50 (Hackney Archives)

Sunnyhill Road School, Streatham High Road, SW16. Opened 1901. (LMA: EO/DIV 9/SUN)
A&D 1901-38 (infants); 1901-39 (blind) (mixed)

Surrey Lane School, Battersea, SW11. Opened 1885; renamed John Burgess Primary School and William Blake Secondary School, 1951. (LMA: EO/DIV 9/SUR)
A&D 1904-14 (girls)
LB 1895-1928 (deaf); 1905-13 (girls)

Surrey Square School, SE17. Opened 1885.

Susan Lawrence School, Cordelia Street, E14. fl.1971.

Sussex House, Cadogan Gardens, SW1. Opened 1952.

Sussex Road School, Coldharbour Lane, SW9. Opened 1894; renamed Stuart School, 1951. (LMA: EO/DIV 8/SUS)

Sussex Road School [*continued*]
A&D 1894-1937 (girls); 1904-17, 1946-48 (junior mixed); 1907-27 (boys); 1921-53 (mixed); 1938-52 (infants); 1952-54 (primary)
LB 1894-1937 (girls); 1907-13, 1946-56 (infants); 1913-28, 1940 (boys); 1938-39 (senior girls); 1946-51 (mixed)

Sutton's Hospital see **Charterhouse**

Swaffield Road School, Wandsworth Road, SW18. Opened 1897; renamed Swaffield Primary School, 1951. (LMA: EO/DIV 9/SWA)
A&D 1895-1933 (girls); 1911-32 (boys)
LB 1895-1913 (boys); 1895-1934 (girls); 1898-1907 (evening); 1940-43 (senior boys during evacuation to Cranleigh, Surrey in Acc.3531/1)

Swan Street School, City. Opened 1893.

Swedish Institute, Cromwell Road, SW7.

Sydenham Central School. Opened 1876 as Sydenham Hill Road School; renamed Shackleton Secondary School, 1951; closed 1958. (LMA: EO/DIV 7/SYD 1)
A&D 1927 (girls)

Sydenham Church of England School, Kirkdale, SE26. Opened 1831.

Sydenham County Secondary School, Dartmouth Road, SE26. Opened 1905 as Dartmouth Road School; renamed c1938. (LMA: EO/DIV 7/SYD 3)
A&D 1938-56 (girls)

Sydenham High School, Westwood Hill, SE26. Opened 1887.

Sydenham Hill Road School, SE26. Opened 1876; renamed Sydenham Central School, 1927; renamed Kelvin Grove School, 1937. (LMA: EO/DIV 7/SYD 2)
A&D 1890-1913 (girls); 1906-39 (boys); 1907-39 (senior girls)
LB 1871-1936 (girls); 1894-1930 (infants); 1911-39 (boys)
Misc honours 1933-37

Sylvia Young Theatre School, Rossmore Road, NW1. Opened 1981.

Tanner Street School, Bermondsey, SE1.

Tavistock Place School, WC1.
(LMA: EO/DIV 2/TAV)
LB 1913-33 (mixed)

Teesdale Street School, Hackney Road,
Bethnal Green, E2. Claremont Street
School 1873-78; Teesdale Street School,
1878; renamed Teesdale Primary School,
1951. (LMA: EO/DIV 5/TEE)
A&D 1894-1933 (infants); 1908-39 (girls)
LB 1873-1939 (girls); 1873-1925 (infants);
1913-29 (boys)

Telferscot Road School, Emanuel Road,
Clapham, SW12. Opened 1903; renamed
Telforscot Primary School, 1951.
(LMA: EO/DIV 9/TEL)
A&D 1902-39, 1943-60 (infants); 1902-26
(mixed); 1917-65 (senior mixed)
LB 1902-71 (infants); 1902-46 (senior mixed);
1924-34 (junior mixed); 1958-59, 1963-65
(secondary)
Misc punishment 1958-65

Templars School, Tollet Street, E1. fl.1971.

Tenison's School, Leicester Square
(Independent) (boys). Opened 1685;
reconstituted 1871.

Tennyson Street School, Battersea, SW8.
Opened 1877. (LMA: EO/DIV 9/TEN)
A&D 1901-25 (junior mixed)

Thanet Street Church of England School,
Cartwright Gardens, Euston Road, WC1.
Opened 1874. (LMA: EO/DIV 2/THA)
A&D 1879-1939 (girls); 1884-1901, 1915-39
(infants); 1894-1939 (boys)
LB 1863-1912 (boys); 1872-1902, 1913-39
(infants); 1938-39 (mixed)

Thomas Calton School, Choumert Road, SE15.
fl.1971.

Thomas Doggett School, Briset Road, SE9.
(LMA: EO/DIV 6/THO)
A&D 1968-70 (boys)
LB 1968-70 (boys)
Misc punishment 1968-70

Thomas Fairchild Junior Mixed School,
Napier Grove, N1.
LB 1950-77 (LMA Modern Records Section)

Thomas Jones School, Latimer Road, W10.
Previously known as Latimer Road School;
renamed 1951.

Thomas's Preparatory School, Battersea High
Street, SW11. Opened 1977.

Thomas Street Central School, Opened 1876.
(LMA: EO/DIV 5/THO 2)
LB 1913-39 (girls)

Thomas Street School, Burdett Road, E14.
Opened 1876; renamed Thomas Road
School, 1938. (LMA: EO/DIV 5/THO 1)
A&D 1885-1923 (girls); 1897-1931 (mixed)
LB 1876-98, 1913-39 (infants);
1913-38 (mixed)

Thornfield Road School, Thornfield Road,
W12. Opened 1916; renamed 1917
Coverdale Road School.

Thornhill School, Barnsbury, N1.
Opened 1881 as Thornhill Road School;
renamed 1951. (LMA: EO/DIV 3/THO)
LB 1929-39 (infants)

Thorntree Road School, Pound Park Road,
SE7. Opened 1927; renamed Thorntree
School, 1951.

Threave House School, Heath Drive, NW3.
Opened 1886; closed 1932.

Tidemill Primary School *see*
Frankham Street School

Tidey Street School, E3. Opened 1906.
(LMA: EO/DIV 5/TID)
A&D 1906 (mixed)
LB 1906 (mixed); 1906 (infants)

Timbercroft School, Flaxton Road, SE18.
Opened 1885 as Slade School; renamed
1929. (LMA: EO/DIV 6/TIM)
A&D 1902-19 (mixed); 1906-20, 1931-39,
1944-62 (infants); 1931-39 (boys); 1931-39
(junior girls)
LB 1902-13, 1931-39 (infants); 1902-31 (senior
mixed); 1906-20 (junior mixed); 1931-38
(junior girls); 1931-39 (mixed)

Tollet Street School, Mile End, E1. (physically
and mentally defective). Opened 1914.
(LMA: EO/DIV 5/TOL)
A&D 1914-36 (deaf) (mixed); 1928-40 (boys)
LB 1914-34 (mentally defective);
1914-39 (deaf)

Tollington Park Central School, Marriott Road, N4. Opened 1910 as Montem Street Central School; renamed Marriott Road Central School, 1914; renamed again 1925. (LMA: EO/DIV 3/TOL)
LB 1928-57 (boys)

Tollington Park College, Tollington Park, N4. (Independent) (boys). Opened 1879.

Tollington Park School *see* **Montem Road School**.

Tooting Graveney School, SW17. Opened 1891. (LMA: EO/DIV 9/TOO)
A&D 1869-96 (boys); 1889-1928 (girls); 1890-1928 (junior boys)

Tooting High School, Upper Tooting (Independent) (boys). Opened 1899.

Tooting Roman Catholic School, Undine Street, SW17. Opened 1903.

Torriano Avenue School, St Pancras, NW5. Opened 1910.

Torridon Road School, Hither Green, SE6. Opened 1906; renamed Torridon School, 1951. (LMA: EO/DIV 7/TOR)
A&D 1904-52 (infants); 1946-47 (girls)
LB 1907-31 (manual training centre); 1945-47 (girls)

Tottenham Road School, Balls Pond Road, N1. Opened 1874 (infants); 1887 (mixed); renamed De Beauvoir School, 1951. (LMA: EO/DIV 4/TOT)
A&D 1887-1939 (junior mixed); 1888-1939 (boys); 1888-1939 (girls); 1891-1939 (infants)
LB 1874-94 (Hackney Archives); 1899-1913, 1932-39 (infants); 1913-32 (boys); 1913-32 (girls); 1913-32 (junior mixed); 1927-39 (evening); 1900-35 (manual training centre)

Tower Bridge Junior School, Fair Street. SE1. Opened 1895. (LMA: EO/DIV 8/TOW)
A&D 1934-39 (junior boys); 1934-39 (junior girls)

Tower Bridge Senior School, SE1. Opened 1874.

Tower Hamlets School, Chamber Street and Richard Street, E1. (LMA: EO/DIV 5/TOW)

Tower Hamlets School [*continued*]
A&D 1915-39 (girls); 1916-39 (infants); 1919-39 (boys)
LB 1886-93 (boys)

Tower Hill Roman Catholic School, Chamber Street, Aldgate High Street, E1. Opened 1903; renamed English Martyrs School, 1971.

Tower Hill School, EC3.
A&D 1724, 1889 (Guildhall Library)
Misc administrative records 1687-1889 (Guildhall Library)

Tower Ward School. Opened in Botolph Lane, 1707. United with Billingsgate Ward School, 1874. (q.v.)
A&D 1848-54 (boys); 1872-82 (girls) (Guildhall Library)
Misc minute books 1836-62; estate records 1846-84 (Guildhall Library)

Townmead Road School, Fulham, SW6. Opened 1900; renamed Townmead School, 1933; closed 1935; building used by Chelsea Central Secondary School from 1946. (LMA: EO/DIV 1/TOW and ACC/2405)
LB 1900-13 (boys); 1900-34 (infants); 1906-31 (manual training centre); 1913-36 (girls)

Townsend School, Old Kent Road, SE17. fl.1971.

Trafalgar Road School *see* Old Woolwich Road

Trafalgar Square School, White Horse Lane, E1. Opened 1885; renamed Trafalgar School, 1938. (LMA: EO/DIV 5/TRA)
A&D 1897-1929 (mixed); 1913-32 (girls); 1929-39 (boys)
LB 1925-28 (hospital class)

Tredegar Road Wesleyan School, Bow, E3. Opened 1865; closed 1924. (LMA: EO/DIV 5/TRE)
A&D 1910-24 (infants)
LB 1867-78, 1896-1906 (mixed); 1869-1905 (infants)

Triangle Roman Catholic School, Mare Street, Hackney, E8. Opened 1903.
LB 1913-33 (mixed); 1913-33 (infants); 1927-39 (boys)

Trinity Church of England School, Upper Tulse Hill School, SW2 see **Holy Trinity Upper Tooting**

Trinity College of Music, Manchester Square, W1. Opened 1872.

Trinity House School, Harper Road, SE1. fl.1971.

Trinity Place School, New North Road, Hoxton, N1. Opened 1878; closed 1927. (LMA: EO/DIV 4/TRP)
A&D 1900-27 (infants); 1906-27 (boys); 1906-27 (girls)
LB 1878-1902 (boys); 1878-1927 (infants); 1902-27 (mixed)

Trinity School, Harrow Road, W2. Opened 1874.

Trotman's School, Bunhill Row, EC1.
A&D 1844-99 (Guildhall Library)
Misc administrative records 1827-1979 (Guildhall Library)

Trundley's Road or Lane School, Deptford, SE8. Opened 1893; later renamed Sir Francis Drake School. (LMA: EO/DIV 7/TRU)
LB 1908-18 (mixed); 1913-20, 1925-39 (infants)

Tudor Secondary School
see **Queen's Head Street School**

Tufnell Park Primary School, Dalmeny Road, N7. Opened 1955.

Tulse Hill School, Upper Tulse Hill, SW2.

Turin Street School, Bethnal Green, E2. Opened 1875; closed 1929. (LMA: EO/DIV 5/TUR)
A&D 1875-1927 (boys); 1897-1928 (infants); 1898-1926 (girls)
LB 1875-87, 1902-27 (boys); 1875-93, 1912-29 (infants); 1913-27 (girls)

Turner's Free School for Poor Boys, Primrose Street, Bishopsgate, EC2. From 1880 Turner Exhibition Fund for the training of female pupil teachers at church training colleges.
A&D 1769-1832; exhbitioners' lists 1881-1966; exhbition applications 1881-1927, 1960-65, 1974-79, 1982-87 (Guildhall Library)

Turner's Free School for Poor Boys [*continued*]
Misc estate records 1775-1835; administrative records 1771-1990 (Guildhall Library)

Turney Road School, Turney Road, SE21. renamed Turney Primary School, 1950. (LMA: EO/DIV 8/TUR)
LB 1929-39 (mixed)

Turnham School, Turnham Road, SE4. Opened 1935.

Twig Folly School, Bethnal Green. Opened 1878; closed 1880. (LMA: EO/DIV 5/TWI)
A&D 1878-80 (boys)

Tyburn Roman Catholic School, Orchardston Street and Fisherton Street, NW8.

Tyssen School, Oldfield Street, N16. Opened 1939.

Union Street School, Beresford Street, SE18. Opened 1872 as Powis Street School; renamed 1884; renamed Powis Street School, 1938. (LMA: EO/DIV 6/UNI)
A&D 1884-1932 (boys); 1892-1929 (infants); 1904-39 (girls)
LB 1884-1932 (boys); 1884-1927 (infants); 1901-13 (mixed); 1932-39 (junior girls)

United Society School, Rotherhithe.
Misc minute books 1837-51, 1860-74 (Southwark Local Studies Lib)

University College School Preparatory Branch, Holly Hill, Hampstead (Independent) (boys). Opened 1891.

University College School, Frognal, Hampstead, NW3. (Independent) (boys). Opened 1832 Gower Street, moved to Hampstead, 1907.
Registers Alphabetical and Chronological Register 1831-1891 (T. Orme, 1892); Register 1860-1931 (anon, 1931); Register 1925-1988 (F. Isaacs, 1988); School Register 1901-1963 (N. Holland, 1964)

University College School Junior Branch, Holly Hill, Hampstead, NW3. Opened 1891.

Upper Clapton and Stamford Hill School, Lynmouth Road, N16. Opened 1884.

Upper Grange Road School, SE1.
(LMA: EO/DIV 7/UPP)
LB 1873-95 (boys)

Upper Hornsey Road School, Seven Sisters
Road, Holloway, N7. Opened 1897;
renamed Isledon School, 1951.
(LMA: EO/DIV 3/UPP)
A&D 1886-97, 1919-30, 1945-57 (infants);
1911-25, 1944-53 (senior boys); 1942-45
(junior mixed); 1944-53 (senior girls)
LB 1894-1924 (infants); 1929-39 (girls);
1944-53 (senior boys)
Misc honours 1932 (senior girls)

Upper Kennington Lane School, SE11.
(LMA: EO/DIV 8/UPP)
A&D 1885-92 (boys)

Upper Marylebone School, W1. Opened 1914;
renamed Clipstone School, 1936.
(LMA: EO/DIV 2/UPP)
LB 1914-33 (infants); 1915-39
(handicrafts centre)

Upper North Street School, East India Dock
Road, Poplar, E14. Opened 1882; renamed
Mayflower Primary School, 1951. (LMA:
EO/DIV 5/UPP)
LB 1885-1912 (evening)

Upper Tooting Church of England School,
Trinity Road, SW17. Opened 1863.

Upton House School, Urswick Road,
Homerton, E9. Opened 1878; closed 1913,
reopened 1928 (also Open Air School);
merged into Homerton House School,
1982. (LMA: EO/DIV 4/UPT)
A&D 1928-39 (mixed)
LB 1928-39 (mixed)

Upton House Truant School, E9.
(LMA: LCC/EO/SS/7)
A&D 1894-1915

Vallance Road School, Whitechapel, E1.
(temporary school). Opened 1899; renamed
Robert Montefiore School, 1916.
(LMA: EO/DIV 5/VAL)
A&D 1902-12 (infants)

Vanburgh Primary School *see·*
Glenister Road School

Varna Hall School, SW6.
Previously known as St Peter's Church
Schools; transferred to School Board 1891;
partially closed 1893 and children
transferred to Munster Road School; closed
1904 and pupils transferred to Sherbrooke
Road School; also known as Varna Road
School. (LMA: EO/DIV 1/VAR)
A&D 1891-93 (junior mixed)
LB 1891-93 (junior mixed)

Vauxhall Central School, Lawn Lane, SW8.
Opened 1908. (LMA: EO/DIV 8/VAU 1)
A&D 1925-43 (senior mixed)
LB 1938-44 (mixed)
Misc honours 1933-38

Vauxhall Street School,
Kennington Lane, SE11. Opened 1874;
renamed Vauxhall Primary School, 1951.
(LMA: EO/DIV 8/VAU 2)
A&D 1882-1929 (infants); 1898-1913 (girls);
1942-53 (boys)
LB 1874-1934 (infants)

Venetian Road School, Caldecot Road, SE5.
Secondary School for physically
handicapped opened 1910.
(LMA: EO/DIV 8/VEN)
A&D 1923-47, 1951-58 (girls); 1938-52 (boys)
LB 1934-60 (boys)
Misc punishment 1906-57

Vernon Square School,
Kings Cross Road, WC1. Opened 1915;
renamed Vernon Secondary School, 1951.
(LMA: EO/DIV 3/VER)
A&D 1929-31 (girls); 1930-39 (junior mixed);
1933-39 (infants)
LB 1929-31 (girls); 1930-39 (senior mixed);
1931-39 (junior mixed); 1933-39 (infants);
1940-41 (mixed) (emergency)

Vicarage Road, SE18. Opened 1881; closed
1928, having been infants only since
1923/4. (LMA: EO/DIV 6/VIC)
A&D 1881-1923 (boys); 1881-1923 (girls);
1893-1928 (infants)
LB 1878-1923 (girls); 1878-81, 1902-28
(infants); 1881-1915 (boys); 1927-28
(junior mixed)

Victoria College of Music, Holland Park
Avenue, W11.

Victoria Road Special School, Peckham High Street, SE15. renamed Highshore Secondary School, 1951. (LMA: EO/DIV 7/VIC)
LB 1932-39 (boys)

Victoria School, The, Becklow Road, Uxbridge Road, W12. Previously Starch Green School (British); reopened 1876. (LMA: EO/DIV 1/VIC)
LB 1876-1910, 1927-31 (boys); 1894-1913 (junior mixed); 1896-1939 (infants); 1900-39 (girls); 1937-40 (senior boys)
Misc punishment 1944-62

Victory Place School, Rodney Road, Walworth, SE17. Opened 1875. (LMA: EO/DIV 8/VIC)
A&D 1946-47 (junior mixed)

Villareal School, Whitechapel, E1. Opened 1895; closed 1923. (LMA: EO/DIV 5/VIL)
A&D 1895-1923 (girls); 1909-23 (infants)

Vintry Ward Charity School, City.
Misc estate records 1842, 1900-01; administrative records 1730 (Guildhall Library)

Virginia Road School, Shoreditch High Street, E2. Opened 1875; formerly New Castle Street School; renamed Virginia Primary School, 1951. (LMA: EO/DIV 5/VIR)
A&D 1875-1928 (boys); 1875-1939 (infants); 1902-30 (girls)
LB 1900-43 (infants); 1913-29 (boys); 1914-30 (girls); 1939-43 (mixed)

Vittoria Place School, Payne Street, Copenhagen Street, N1. Opened 1879; renamed Vittoria School, 1951. (LMA: EO/DIV 3/VIT)
A&D 1887-1900 (girls); 1899-1939 (infants); 1902-39 (boys)

Wadding Street Temporary School, Walworth, SE1. Closed 1900 and transferred to Paragon School. (LMA: EO/DIV 8/WAD)
LB 1895-1900 (infants)

Waldron Road School, Tranmere Road, SW18. Opened 1885.

Waller Road School, Queens Road, SE14. Opened 1888 as Bennetts Grove School; renamed Edmund Waller Primary School, 1951. (LMA: EO/DIV 6/WAL)

Waller Road School [*continued*]
A&D 1888-1971 (infants)
LB 1888-1958 (infants); 1906-32 (boys)
Misc visitors 1888-1958

Walnut Tree Walk School, Kennington Road, SE11. Opened 1875. (LMA: EO/DIV 8/WAL)
A&D 1875-1933 (girls); 1875-1961 (infants); 1882-1933 (boys); 1908-24 (mixed); 1943-61 (junior mixed)
LB 1875-1933 (girls); 1875-1939 (infants); 1882-1933 (boys)

Walsingham School. (LMA: EO/DIV 9/WSG)
A&D 1982-85

Walton Street School, Upper Chelsea, SW3. Opened 1879. (LMA: EO/DIV 1/WAL)
LB 1885-86, 1900-08 (girls); 1885-86, 1900-08 (infants); 1909-37 (mixed - invalids)

Walworth Central School, Mina Road, Old Kent Road, SE17. Opened 1882 (boys); 1905 (girls). (LMA: EO/DIV 8/WAL)
A&D 1924-41 (girls)

Walworth Road Baptist Sunday School, SE17.
Misc minute books 1929-69 (Southwark Local Studies Lib)

Wandle School, Earlsfield, Wandsworth, SW18. Dunts Hill School 1904-06; opened 1906. (LMA: EO/DIV 9/WAL)
A&D 1906-39 (junior mixed); 1910-39 (boys); 1910-39 (girls); 1940-44 (senior mixed)
LB 1906-21 (infants); 1906-13, 1932-39 (junior mixed); 1913-23, 1939 (senior mixed); 1913-32 (girls); 1913-32 (mixed); 1923-28 (boys)

Wandsworth and Clapham Board of Guardians see **North Surrey School District**.

Wandsworth Central School, Allfarthing Lane, Wandsworth, SW18. Opened 1922.

Wandsworth and Battersea Evening Institute formerly Ethelburga Street, SW11. (LMA: EO/DIV 9/WAN 1)
LB 1885-1930

Wandsworth Road School, SW8. Opened 1813. (LMA: EO/DIV 9/WAN 3)
A&D 1867-85 (boys)

Wandsworth Roman Catholic School,
Wandsworth High Street, SW18. Opened
1859. (LMA: EO/DIV 9/WAN 4)
A&D 1911-28 (mixed)

Wandsworth School, Sutherland Grove, SW18.
Opened 1895.

Wandsworth Technical College, High Street,
SW18. (LMA: EO/DIV 9/WAN 5)
A&D 1926-56 (boys)

Wandsworth Technical Institute,
High Street, SW18. Opened 1895.
(LMA: EO/DIV 9/WAN 2)
A&D 1946-58 (girls)
LB 1945-58 (girls)

Wapping Charity School, Wapping, E1.
Misc administrative records 1794-1807
(Guildhall Library)

Wapping District Charity School
Misc minute books 1807-21 (Tower Hamlets
Library)

Warple Way School, Wandsworth, SW18.
Opened 1880. (LMA: EO/DIV 9/WAR)
A&D 1898-1915 (mixed); 1904-39 (girls);
1924-39 (infants)

Warwick House School, King Henry's Road,
NW3. Opened 1883; moved 1939 to
Lymington Road; closed c1969.

Warwick Primary School, Ranelagh Road,
St George Westminster. Opened 1915 as
Ranelagh Road School (q.v.); renamed
1929; renamed Churchill Gardens School,
1951. (LMA: EO/DIV 2/WAR 2)
A&D 1943-58 (infants)

Warwick Senior School, Buckingham Palace
Road, St George Westminster, SW1.
Opened 1898 as St George's Row School;
renamed 1929. (LMA: EO/DIV 2/WAR 1)
A&D 1929-39 (infants); 1945-47 (mixed)
LB 1923-39, 1945-47 (senior mixed);
1931-39 (infants)

Waterloo Road School, SE1. Opened 1881.
(LMA: EO/DIV 8/WAT)
A&D 1892-1938 (infants)
LB 1913-40 (mixed)
Misc minute book 1916-21

Waterloo Street School,
Macbeth Street, W6. Opened 1875;
renamed Waterside School, 1938; closed
1961. (LMA: EO/DIV 1/WAS)
A&D 1874-85 (junior mixed); 1875-1935
(boys); 1885-1931 (girls); 1913-39 (infants)

Waterside School, Macbeth Street, W6.
Opened 1875 as Waterloo Street School;
renamed 1938; closed 1961.
(LMA: EO/DIV 1/WAT)
A&D 1947-61 (junior mixed & infants)
LB 1913-31 (girls); 1931-32 (infants); 1932-61
(junior mixed and infants)

Waverley Secondary School *see*
Ancona Road School

Waverly School, Camberwell see
Adys Road School

Weavers' Fields School, Mape Street, E2.
fl.1971.

Webb Street School, Tower Bridge Road, SE1.
Opened 1880; Webb Street Primary School
became Grange Primary School, 1951.
(LMA: EO/DIV 8/WEB)
A&D 1888-1939 (infants); 1936-41
(junior boys)
LB 1936-39 (boys); 1936-39 (girls)

Webber Street School, SE1.
(LMA: EO/DIV 8/WBR)
A&D 1916-39 (mixed)

Wedgewood School, Bagleys Lane, SW6.
Previously part of Langford Road ESN
School; renamed 1950.

Weigh House Boys' Charity School, City Road,
EC1.
A&D 1788-1804 (Guildhall Library)
Misc administrative records 1788-1813
(Guildhall Library)

Wellington Court Preparatory School,
Hampstead (Independent). Opened 1869.

Wellington Road Blind Centre.
(LMA: EO/DIV 4/WELL 1)
LB 1894-1921 (mixed)

Wellington Road School, Bow Road, E3.
Opened 1928; renamed Wellington Way
School, 1938; renamed Wellington School,
1951. (LMA: EO/DIV 5/WEL)

Wellington Road School [*continued*]
A&D 1931-39 (infants)
LB 1931-39 (infants)

Wellington Road School, N7. Opened 1879; renamed Westbourne Road; 1951 Alfred Pritchard Primary School; closed by 1965.

Wellington Street School, N1. Opened 1877; later Redvers Street School. (LMA: EO/DIV 4/WELL 2)
LB 1877-1902 (girls)

Well Street Chapel School, Hackney, E9. Opened 1811.

Wendell Park School, W12. Opened 1896 as Bassein Park Road School; renamed Cobbold Road School, 1901; renamed 1925; Secondary School closed 1962. (LMA: EO/DIV 1/WEN)
A&D 1876-90, 1911-35 (boys); 1896-1901, 1912-40, 1954-61 (mixed); 1901-07 (infants); 1923-36 (girls)
LB 1948-58 (senior mixed)
Misc punishment 1962

Wenlock Road School, Edward Street, Shepherdess Walk, City Road, N1. Opened 1880; later Horizon School. (LMA: EO/DIV 4/WEN)
LB 1927-39 (boys)

Wesleyan College, Horseferry Road, SW1. (LMA: EO/DIV 2/WEC)
A&D 1912-20 (junior mixed and senior girls); 1915-20 (infants)
LB 1885-1913 (mixed); 1898-1913 (girls); 1913-20 (infants); 1913-20 (junior mixed); 1913-20 (senior girls)

Wesleyan Day School, Lower Norwood. Opened 1860; renamed John Wesley Primary School, 1951.
LB 1863-1912 (Lambeth Archives)
Misc minute books 1870-89 (Southwark Local Studies Lib)

Westbourne Church of England School, Great Western Road, W2. Opened 1851.

Westbourne Road School, St James Road, N7. Opened 1897. (LMA: EO/DIV 3/WES)
A&D 1914-38 (boys); 1917-49 (infants); 1917-38 (girls); 1938-39, 1943-45 (junior mixed)
LB 1931-35 (evening)

West Central District Post Office School, WC1. (LMA: EO/DIV 2/WCP)
LB 1911-20 (boys)

Western Church of England School, York Street, Bryanston Square, W1. Opened 1824.

West Greenwich School, Blackheath Road, SE10 and Albyn Road, SE8.
A&D 1962-80 (LMA Modern Records Section)

West Hackney Parochial School. Opened *c*1830; closed 1906. (LMA: P79/WH)
Misc minute books 1835-71

West Heath School, Ferncroft Avenue, Hampstead, NW3. (Independent) (mixed). Opened 1901.

West Hill School, Broomhill Road and Merton Road, SW18. Opened 1903. (LMA: EO/DIV 9/WES)
A&D 1903-16 (senior mixed)

Westhorne Manor School, Henwick Road, SE9. Opened 1930 as Henwick Road School; renamed 1936; closed 1961. (LMA: EO/DIV 6/WES)
A&D 1936-39 (girls); 1940-62 (mixed)
LB 1936-39 (boys); 1936-39 (senior girls)
Misc punishment 1959-62

West Kensington Central School, Gorleston Street, Hammersmith Road, W14. Opened 1875 as part of William Street School; renamed 1921; closed 1958, pupils to Holland Park Comprehensive; premises to Mary Boon School. (LMA: EO/DIV 1/WES)
A&D 1928-58 (girls); 1930-36, 1941-42 (senior mixed); 1936-58 (boys)
LB 1932-40 (girls); 1936-39 (boys)
Misc honours 1926-38

West London Emergency School for Girls, Fulham Cross, Munster Road, SW6. Held in premises of Fulham County School 1940-45.

West London School District. Constituted by Fulham, Hammersmith and Paddington Boards of Guardians 1868-1930; St George Hanover Square Board of Guardians 1868-70; St George Board of Guardians 1870-1913; Westminster Board of Guardians 1913-30. (LMA: WLSD)

West London School District [*continued*]
A&D 1872-1943
LB 1904-45
Misc minute books 1868-1930; staff 1865-1930

Westlow Hill Temporary School, SE19. Closed
1886 and transferred to Woodland Road
School. (LMA: EO/DIV 8/WEH)
LB 1877-86 (infants)

Westminster Abbey Choir School,
Deans Yard, SW1.

Westminster Board of Guardians see
West London School District

Westminster Bridge Road School,
Southwark, SE1. Opened 1877; renamed
James Pascall Secondary School, 1951.
(LMA: EO/DIV 8/WES)
A&D 1898-1906, 1937-50 (infants);
1945-52 (mixed)
LB 1877-1951. (infants); 1932-39 (girls)
Misc punishment 1901-37

Westminster Cathedral Choir School,
Ambrosden Avenue, SW1. Opened 1901.

Westminster Cathedral Roman Catholic School,
Great Smith Street, SW1.

Westminster City School, Palace Street,
Westminster, SW1. (Independent) (boys).
Opened 1633.

Westminster Day Continuation School.
(LMA: EO/DIV 2/WED)
LB 1921-52 (mixed)

Westminster Jews' Free School. Founded 1811
in Soho; moved 1884 to Hanway Place,
W1; closed 1945. (LMA: EO/DIV 2/WEJ
and ACC/4047)
A&D 1868-1917 (girls); 1870-1939 (boys);
1917-39 (infants)
LB 1871-1913, 1928-39 (mixed); 1871-1913,
1928-39 (infants); 1913-28 (boys and girls)
Misc minute books 1829-1989; punishment
1845-1938

Westminster National Free School.
Misc Committee of Management 1812-21;
Annual reports 1812-27 (Church of
England Records Centre); some records
1810-18 (Westminster Archives)

Westminster School (St Peter's College),
Dean's Yard, SW1. (Independent) (boys).
Opened 1560, but with medieval origins.
Registers A list of the Scholars of St Peter's
College, Westminster, as they were elected
to Christ Church College, Oxford and
Trinity College, Cambridge from 1561 to
the present time (J. Welch, 1788); Alumni
Westmonasterienses [1561-1851] (J.
Welch, 1852); School Register 1764-1883
(G.F.R. Barker and A.H. Stenning, 1892);
The Record of Old Westminsters: vols. 1
and 2 earliest times to 1927 ((G.F.R.
Barker and A.H. Stenning, 1928); vol. 3-4
1883-1989 (J.B. Whitmore et al., 1961-92);
Supplementary volume: Addenda and
Corrigenda and list of 1919-37
(J.B. Whitmore and G.R.Y. Radcliffe,
1938); Supplementary volume: Addenda
and Corrigenda to vol. 3 and list 1961-74
(F.E. Pagan, 1975)

Westminster Under School, Vincent Square,
SW1. Opened 1943.

Westminster United Schools (viz. Palmer, i.e.
Blackcoat, Emery Hill, St Margaret's
Hospital, i.e. Greencoat, Emanuel, i.e.
Browncoat).
Records 1873-1962 (Westminster Archives)

Westminster Technical Institute, Vincent
Square, SW1. (LMA: EO/DIV 2/WET)
LB 1911-24 (manual training centre); also
minutes etc. 1887-1951. (Westminster
Archives)

Westminster Wesleyan Practising School.
Opened 1850. (LMA: EO/DIV 2/WEP)
LB 1907-13 (infants)

Westmoreland Road Roman Catholic School,
Bayswater, W2. Opened 1857.

West Norwood Central School, Carnac Street,
Gipsy Road, SE27. Opened 1928.
(LMA: EO/DIV 8/WEN)
A&D 1928-49 (mixed); 1943-54 (senior mixed)

Weston Street School, Old Kent Road, SE1.
Opened 1874; renamed Tabard School,
1951. (LMA: EO/DIV 8/WET)
A&D 1930-56 (infants)
LB 1930-56 (infants)

West Square Secondary School, St George's
Road, SE11. (LMA: EO/DIV 8/WEQ)
A&D 1953-64 (boys)

Westville Road School, Askew Road, W12.
Opened 1886; destroyed 1944, but rebuilt;
renamed Westville Primary School, 1952.
(LMA: EO/DIV 1/WEV)
LB 1886-1913, 1930-39 (boys);
1890-1939 (evening)

Weymouth Terrace British School, Shoreditch,
E2. (LMA: N/M/19)
LB 1863-91

Whitechapel Board of Guardians see
Forest Gate School District

Whitechapel Foundation School, Lower Burial
Ground, E1. Opened 1813; moved to
Leman Street, E1, 1858; renamed Davenant
Foundation School, 1930 (q.v.).

Whitelands College, West Hill, SW15.

White Lion Street School, Penton Street,
Pentonville Road, N1. Opened 1875 as
Penton Grove School; renamed 1899.
(LMA: EO/DIV 3/WHI)
A&D 1875-1925 (boys); 1875-88, 1900-11,
1929-25 (infants); 1887-1923, 1930-37
(girls)
LB 1875-1935 (girls); 1906-39 (boys);
1906-26 (infants)

Whitfield Street School, W1.
(LMA: EO/DIV 2/WHI)
LB 1887-1905 (evening)

The Whitmore School, Grange Road, Hoxton,
N1. Opened 1897; Gopsall Street School
1897-1951. (LMA: EO/DIV 4/WHI)
A&D 1931-39 (senior boys)
LB 1913-39 (infants)

Whitney School, The, John Ruskin Street, SE5.
Opened 1899 as John Ruskin School;
renamed 1950. (LMA: EO/DIV 8/WHI)
A&D 1942-69 (mixed)
LB 1951-69 (mixed)

Whittington School, Highgate Hill, N19.
Opened 1882; closed 1957.
(LMA: EO/DIV 3/WHT)
LB 1942-56 (infants)

Wickham Lane School, Oakmere Road, SE2.
Opened 1903; renamed Oakmere Secondary
School, 1959. (LMA: EO/DIV 6/WIC)
A&D 1902-28 (mixed); 1903-59 (infants);
1903-10 (junior mixed); 1909-29
(mixed invalids)

Wickham Lane School [*continued*]
LB 1902-30, 1933-59 (infants); 1902-13
(mixed); 1903-15 (junior mixed); 1903-10
(manual training centre)
Misc visitors 1947-55

Wick Road School, E9. (temporary) *see*
Morning Lane School 1879-84.
(LMA: EO/DIV 4/WIC)
A&D 1883-84 (boys)

Wingfield School, Weigall Road, SE12.
fl.1971.

Wilberforce School, Kilburn Lane,
Paddington, W10. Opened 1887.
(LMA: EO/DIV 2/WIL)
A&D 1899-1929 (girls); 1909-29 (junior boys);
1916-39 (infants); 1930-39 (junior mixed)
LB 1887-1903, 1913-31 (girls); 1893-1929
(boys); 1931-39 (junior mixed)

Wild Street School, Holborn, WC2.
Opened 1885.

William Blake School, Bridge Lane, SW11.
fl.1971.

William Ellis Endowed School, Gospel Oak,
NW5. (Independent) (boys). Opened 1865.

William Forster School, Benwell Road, N7.
Opened 1889 as Forster School (q.v.);
renamed 1955; closed 1961.
(LMA: EO/DIV 3/WIL)
A&D 1946-61 (infants)

William Morris Academy, St Dunstan's Road,
W6. Opened 1994 in St Edmund's Roman
Catholic School premises.

William Patten School *see* **Church Street School**

William Penn School, Red Post Hill, SE24.
fl.1971.

William Street School, Earsby Street, W14.
Opened 1875; senior school renamed West
Kensington Central School, 1921; primary
school renamed Avonmore School, 1936.
(LMA: EO/DIV 1/WIL)
A&D 1908-28 (senior girls); 1908-39
(senior mixed)
LB 1873-1930 (girls); 1873-1923 (infants);
1899-1935 (boys); 1908-13 (mixed);
1913-38 (senior mixed); 1913-23 (junior
mixed)

William Tyndale Primary School *see* **Sebbon Street School**

Willington School, Colinette Road, SW15.

Willowfield School *see* **Caldecot Road School**

Wilmot Street School, Bethnal Green, E2. Opened 1873; renamed Wilmot Primary School, 1951. (LMA: EO/DIV 5/WIL)
A&D 1873-79, 1885-1929 (boys); 1899-1939 (infants); 1945-46 (senior girls)
LB 1873-1930 (boys); 1882-1913 (evening); 1890-1913, 1945-51 (girls); 1913-36 (infants); 1963-65 (secondary girls)
Misc punishment 1954-62

Wilson's Grammar School, Peckham Road, Camberwell, SE5. (Independent) (boys). Opened 1615.
see Camberwell Grammar School; a short history of the foundation (D.H. Allport, 1964)

Wilton Road School, Parkholme Road, Dalston, E8. Opened 1886; renamed Wilton Way School, 1951; closed 1963. (LMA: EO/DIV 4/WIL)
A&D 1886-99, 1916-26 (infants)
LB 1912-37 (infants)

Wilton Way Secondary School, Parkholme Road, Dalston, E8. Opened 1886 as Wilton Road School; later Shacklewell School; closed 1963. (LMA: EO/DIV 4/WIW)
A&D 1950-63 (mixed)
LB 1946-63 (senior mixed)
Misc punishment 1960-63

Winchester Street School, Pentonville Road, N1. Opened 1874; renamed Winton School, 1938; also known as Killick Street School. (LMA: EO/DIV 3/WIN)
A&D 1881-1911 (boys); 1891-1904 (girls); 1904-30 (infants)
LB 1874-1901 (boys); 1874-1903 (girls)
Misc punishment 1931-51

Windsor Road School later Berkshire Road School and Lea Marsh School, Hackney, E9. (LMA: EO/DIV 4/WNS)
LB 1899-1906 (boys); 1899-1910 (girls)
Misc 1876-83 (boys prize list)

Windsor Street School, N1. Closed and transferred to Anglers Gardens 1874. (LMA: EO/DIV 3/WND)
LB 1872-75 (boys)

Winstanley Road School, Clapham Junction, SW11. Opened 1874. (LMA: EO/DIV 9/WIN)
LB 1900-13 (infants)

Winton School, Killick Street, N1. Opened 1874 as Winchester Street School; renamed 1938.

Wirtemberg School. (LMA: EO/DIV 9/WIR)
A&D 1918-39 (junior girls)

Wix's Lane School, Clapham Common, North Side, SW4. Opened 1903. (LMA: EO/DIV 9/WIX)
A&D 1903-27 (boys); 1903-31 (girls); 1915-39 (infants)
LB 1903-31 (boys); 1903-31 (girls); 1931-38 (junior mixed)

Wolverley Street School, Bethnal Green, E2. Opened 1877. (LMA: EO/DIV 5/WOL)
A&D 1873-82 (boys); 1904-38 (infants)
LB 1877-1938 (infants); 1913-31 (boys)

Woodberry Down Comprehensive School, N4. Opened 1955; merged into Stoke Newington Comprehensive School, 1982.

Woodberry Down Primary School, N4. Opened 1951.

Wood Close School, Church Row, Bethnal Green, E2. Opened 1901.
A&D 1901-47 (boys); 1901-20 (girls); 1901-18 (infants); 1918-47 (mixed) (LMA: EO/DIV 5/WOD); 1920-47 (Tower Hamlets Library)
LB 1901-36 (bcys); 1901-29 (girls); 1901-39 (infants) (LMA: EO/DIV 5/WOD)

Woodhill School, Woodhill, SE18. Opened 1883 as Wood Street School; renamed 1931. (LMA: EO/DIV 6/WOH)
A&D 1931-39 (girls); 1936-39 (infants); 1941-43 (mixed); 1941-66 (junior mixed and infants)

Woodland Road School, Westow Hill, Upper Norwood, SE19. Opened 1887. (LMA: EO/DIV 8/WOO)
A&D 1873-1921 (boys); 1877-1939 (infants); 1901-21 (girls); 1920-39 (mixed)
LB 1887-1939 (infants); 1904-13 (boys); 1913-21 (girls)

Woodland Street National School, Hackney, E8. see **Holy Trinity**, Mayfield Road.

Wood Lane Open Air School, Wood Lane,
W12. Opened 1929; renamed Wood Lane
School, 1950.

Woodmansterne School,
Streatham Vale, SW16. Opened 1930.
(LMA: EO/DIV 9/WOO)
A&D 1951-56 (junior mixed)

Woods Road School, Harders Road,
Queens Road, SE15. Opened 1881;
renamed John Donne Primary School,
1951. (LMA: EO/DIV 7/WOO)
A&D 1879-1938 (girls)
LB 1942-50 (mixed)

Woodstock School *see* **Ruby Street School**

Wood Street School, Woolwich, SE18.
Opened 1883; renamed Woodhill Primary
School, 1931. (LMA: EO/DIV 6/WOD)
A&D 1895-1931 (boys); 1897-1932 (girls);
1932-56 (senior boys); 1932-39 (junior
mixed)
LB 1895-1909 (evening)

Wood Vale School, Elder Road, SE27. (LMA:
EO/DIV 8/WOV and EO/DIV 9/WOV)
A&D 1950-67 (mixed)
LB 1950-67 (mixed)
Misc punishment 1950-63

Woolmore Street School, Cotton Street,
Poplar, E14. Opened 1876; renamed
Woolmore Primary School, 1951.
(LMA: EO/DIV 5/WOO)
A&D 1882-1939 (infants)
LB 1876-1904 (mixed); 1913-39 (infants)

Woolwich Board of Guardians see
South Metropolitan School District

Woolwich Central School, Plumstead
Common Road, SE18. Opened 1877;
closed 1958. (LMA: EO/DIV 6/WOO 2)
A&D 1942-58 (boys); 1942-45 (mixed)
LB 1928-58 (boys)

Woolwich Polytechnic, Wellington Street,
SE18.

Woolwich Pupil Teachers,
Maxey Road, Plumstead, SE18. Opened
1894. (LMA: EO/DIV 6/WOO 1)
LB 1887-1910 (mixed)

Woolwich St Mary Church of England School,
Kingsman Street, Church Street, SE18.
Opened 1840; renamed St Mary's School,
1951. (LMA: EO/DIV 6/WOO 3)
A&D 1894-1934 (girls); 1908-43 (infants)
LB 1913-34 (boys); 1913-34 (girls);
1913-33 (infants)

Wordsworth School, Stoke Newington, N16.
Opened 1878; assumed by local authority
1900; closed 1969.

Wormholt Park School, Bryony Road, W12.
Opened 1912 as Sawley Road School;
renamed 1922.

Wornington Road School, Golborne Road,
W10. Opened 1874; renamed Wornington
Road Infants School 1947; Florence
Gladstone Secondary School, 1951.
(LMA: EO/DIV 1/WOR)
A&D 1874-1958 (girls); 1918-39 (boys);
1939-77 (infants); 1941-52 (girls, class
registers); 1942-43 (senior mixed, class
registers)
LB 1874-1931 (boys); 1874-1921 (girls);
1874-1915, 1947-77 (infants); 1894-1913
(mixed - blind); 1924-39, 1946-51 (senior
girls); 1930-39 (junior boys)
Misc school photographs 1930-39;
punishment 1942-43

Wrights Road School, E3. Opened 1877;
renamed Roman Road School, 1891.
(LMA: EO/DIV 5/WRI)
LB 1880-1907 (evening); 1877-91 (girls)

Wyborne School, Ivor Grove, SE9. fl.1971.

Wycliffe Special School, Wycliffe Road,
Battersea, SW11. Opened 1905. (LMA:
EO/DIV 8/WYC and EO/DIV 9/WYC)
A&D 1905-36 (senior mixed)
LB 1935-36 (junior mixed)

Wykeham House School, Hampstead. Opened
1895; moved to Abbey Road, Kilburn,
*c*1908; closed 1933.

Wyvil Primary School, Wyvil Road, SW8.

Yerbury Road School, Upper Holloway, N19.
Temporary school opened 1878; moved to
Shepperton Road, 1879; moved to Yerbury
Road, 1884; renamed Yerbury Primary
School, 1951. (LMA: EO/DIV 3/YER)

Yerbury Road School [*continued*]
A&D 1884-1926 (boys); 1884-1939 (infants); 1922-61 (junior boys); 1928-45 (junior girls); 1937-51 (class registers)
LB 1897-1939 (girls); 1932-39 (boys); 1975-79 (junior mixed)
Misc punishment 1956-71

Yesodey Hatorah Schools, Amhurst Park, N16. (Jewish).

Yesodey Hatorah Schools, Stamford Hill, N16. (Jewish).

York Road School, Kings Cross, N1. Opened 1874; renamed York Way School, 1937. (LMA: EO/DIV 3/YOR 1)
A&D 1928-39 (infants)
LB 1911-14, 1930-39 (infants); 1929-39 (girls); 1931-36 (junior boys)

Yorkshire Society School, Westminster Bridge Road, SE1. (Independent) (boys). Opened 1812.

York Way School, Kings Cross, N1. Opened 1874 as York Road School; renamed 1937; closed c1969. (LMA: EO/DIV 3/YOR 2)
A&D 1946-65 (infants)
LB 1948-69 (infants)
Misc punishment 1950-63

Zoar Street Charity School, SE1.
Misc 1687-1744 (Southwark Local Studies Lib)

LONDON SCHOOLS BY POSTAL DISTRICT

Schools listed by postal district. In addition, at end are those schools in Downham Estate and Bromley, Kent which are within the LCC area, but outside the London Postal District.

E1 Mile End; St George in the East; Shadwell; Spitalfields; Stepney; Wapping; Whitechapel

All Saints School, Buxton Street, Mile End New Town 12
Baker Street School 15
Bancroft's School, Mile End 16
Ben Jonson School, Harford Street, Stepney 17
Berner Street School, St George in the East 18
Betts Street School, Cable Street, Stepney 18
Bishop Challoner Secondary School 18
Blakesley Street School, Sutton Street, St George in the East 19
Brewhouse Lane School, Wapping High Street 21
Broad Street School 21
Buckle Street Jews' School, Leman Street, Whitechapel 22
Buxton Street School 23
Cable Street School 23
Canon Barnett School, Gunthorpe Street 24
Central Foundation School for Girls, Spital Square 25
Cephas Street Secondary School, Mile End 25
Chapman School, Bigland Street 25
Chicksand Street School 26
Christ Church School, Brick Lane, Spitalfields 27
Christian Street School, Commercial Road 28
Commercial Street School, Whitechapel High Street 31
Davenant School, St Mary Street, Whitechapel Road 34
Deal Street School, Mile End 34
Dempsey Street School, Jubilee Street, Mile End 34
English Martyrs Roman Catholic School, St Mark Street 39
Fairclough Street School, Back Church Lane, Commercial Road 39
Fieldgate Street School 40
Finch Street Special School, Stepney 40
Foundation School, Whitechapel 41
Garden Street School, Stepney 43
Geere House Open Air School, Mile End 43
George Yard School, Whitechapel 44
Good Shepherd Roman Catholic School, Stepney Square 45
Gravel Lane School, Houndsditch 46
Hamlet of Ratcliff Church of England School, White Horse Street later Road 48
Hanbury Street School, Whitechapel 48
Harry Gosling School, Henriques Street 49
Harry Roberts Nursery School, Harford Street 49
Heckford Street School, Brook Street, Ratcliff 50
Hermitage School 51
Highway School, The, St George Street 51
Jews' Free School, Bell Lane, Spitalfields 56
Jews' Infants School, Commercial School, Spitalfields 56
John Scurr School, Cephas Street 56
Johnson Street Roman Catholic School 57
London Street School 62
Lower Chapman Street School, Bigland Street, St George in the East 62
Lowood School, Shadwell 62
Middlesex Society Charity School, St George in the East 65
Mile End Central School, Myrdle Street, Commercial Road East 65
Myrdle Street School, Commercial Road East 67
Nathaniel Heckford School, Cable Street 67
Nicholas Gibson School, The Highway 68

E1 [*continued*]

Ocean Street School 70
Old Castle Street School, Old Castle Street 70
Old Montague Street School 71
Pell Street School, St George in the East 73
Pennoyer's Free School, Whitechapel 73
Portsoken Street School, Minories 75
Raleigh Street School, Ocean Street 77
Redcoat Church of England Secondary School. Stepney Green 78
Redman's Row School, Jubilee Street, Mile End 78
Robert Montefiore School, Vallance Road 79
Rutland Street School, Bedford Street 81
St Ann's Roman Catholic Boys' School, Spitalfields 82
St Anne's Roman Catholic School, Buxton Street and Underwood Road, Mile End New Town 82
St Bartholomew School, Coventry Street, Bethnal Green 83
St Bernard's Roman Catholic Central Schools, Baker Street, Stepney 83
St Boniface Roman Catholic School, Adler Street 83
St George in the East Central School, Cable Street 85
St George in the East National School 85
St Joseph's Roman Catholic School, Gun Street, Spitalfields 89
St Joseph's School, Crispin Street, Whitechapel 89
St Mark's Church of England School, Royal Mint Street 90
St Mary and St Michael Roman Catholic School, Lucas Street and Sutton Street 91
St Mary's School, Spital Square, Whitechapel 93
St Patrick's Roman Catholic School, Green Bank, Wapping 95
St Paul's Church of England School, Wellclose Square 95
St Paul's National School, Shadwell High Street 96
St Peter's School, Cephas Street 97
St Peter's School, London Docks 97
St Peter's School, Red Lion Street 97
St Stephen's National School, Spitalfields 98
St Thomas Colet Church of England School, Arbour Square 99
Senrab Street School, Charles Street, Stepney 101
Settles Street School, Stepney 101
Smith Street School, Stepney 103
Somerford Street School, Bethnal Green 103
Spitalfields Charity School, Quaker Street 105
Spitalfields School of Design, Crispin Street later White Lion Street 105
Stepney Green School, Ben Johnson Road 106
Stepney Jewish School, Stepney Green 106
Stewart Headlam School, Somerford Street 106
Templars School, Tollet Street 108
Thomas Street Central School 108
Tollet Street School, Mile End 108
Tower Hamlets School, Chamber Street and Richard Street 109
Tower Hill Roman Catholic School, Chamber Street, Aldgate High Street 109
Trafalgar Square School, White Horse Lane 109
Vallance Road School, Whitechapel 111
Villareal School, Whitechapel 112
Wapping Charity School, Wapping 113
Wapping District Charity School 113
Whitechapel Foundation School, Lower Burial Ground 116

E2 Bethnal Green; Shoreditch (part)

Approach Road School, Bethnal Green 13
Bonner Street School, Bethnal Green 19

E2 [*continued*]

Bowbrook School, Cranbrook Terrace 20
Brunswick Street Special School, Shoreditch 22
Columbia Road School, Hackney Road 30
Cranbrook Road School, Green Street 32
Cranbrook Terrace School, Bethnal Green 32
Daneford School, Gosset Street 34
Daniel Street School, Gossett Street, Bethnal Green Road 34
Essex Street School, Globe Road 39
Globe Terrace School, Bethnal Green 44
Hague Street School, Bethnal Green Road 47
Laburnum Street School, Kingsland Road 59
Lawrence School, The, Mansford Street, Old Bethnal Green Road 60
Maidstone Street School, Goldsmiths Row, Hackney Road 63
Mansford Street Secondary School, Bethnal Green Road 63
Morpeth Street Central School, Bethnal Green 67
Mowlem Street School, Bishop's Road, Cambridge Heath 67
New Castle Street School, Bethnal Green 68
Nicholl Street School, Bethnal Green 68
Our Lady of Assumption Roman Catholic School, Bonner Road, Old Ford Road 71
Parliament Street Roman Catholic School, Cambridge Road 72
Parmiter's School, Victoria Park 73
Portman Place School, Globe Road, Bethnal Green 75
Pritchard's Road School, Hackney Road, Bethnal Green 76
Raine's School, Cannon Street Road, St George in the East 77
Randal Cremer School, Shoreditch 77
Rochelle Street School, Mount Street 79
St Barnabas' School, Bethnal Green 83
St Bernard's Roman Catholic Central Schools, Old Bethnal Green Road and Mansford Street 83
St Columba's School, Kingsland Road, Shoreditch 84
St Gregory the Great Secondary School, Bethnal Green 86
St John the Baptist Roman Catholic School, Bonner Road 89
St John's School, Peel Grove, Bethnal Green 88
St Jude's Church of England School, Old Bethnal Green Road 89
St Matthias' School, Granby Street, Bethnal Green 94
St Peter's School, Hackney Road 97
St Phillip's Church of England School, Mount Street 98
Scawfell Street School, Hackney Road 100
Sebright School, Maidstone Street 100
Sewardstone Road School, Bethnal Green 101
Shap Street School, Pearson Street, Kingsland Road 101
Teesdale Street School, Hackney Road, Bethnal Green 108
Turin Street School, Bethnal Green 110
Twig Folly School, Bethnal Green 110
Virginia Road School, Shoreditch High Street 112
Weavers' Fields School, Mape Street 113
Weymouth Terrace British School, Shoreditch 116
Wilmot Street School, Bethnal Green 117
Wolverley Street School, Bethnal Green 117
Wood Close School, Church Row, Bethnal Green 117

E3 Bromley by Bow; Mile End (part); Stratford le Bow

All Saints National School, Bow Lane, Poplar 12
Atley Road School, Old Ford Road 15
Barnado's School, Doctor 16
Botolph Road School 20

E3 [*continued*]

Bow Road Open Air School 20
Bow Secondary School for Girls, Fairfield Road 20
Bromley National School, Bromley St Leonard 21
Bruce Road School 22
Burdett Road School 22
Carpenters' Company Technical School, Stratford le Bow 24
Chisenhale Road School, Bethnal Green 27
Coborn School for Girls, Bow Road 30
Coopers' Company's School, Tredegar Square, Bow 31
Copperfield Road School 31
Devons Road School, Campbell Road 35
Fairfield Road School, Bow Road 39
Fordway School, Monier Road 41
George Lansbury School, Atley Road 44
Grove Road School 46
Guardian Angels Roman Catholic School, Whitman Road 47
High Street School, Bow 51
Holy Name Roman Catholic School, Bow Common Lane 53
Holy Trinity School, Bridge Street, Mile End 53
Imperial Street School 55
Knapp Road School, Bow 59
Malmesbury Road School, Coburn Road, Bow Road 63
Marner Street School, St Leonards Street, Bow 64
Montieth Road School, Old Ford Road 66
Old Ford School 70
Old Palace Road School, St Leonard's Street 71
Olga Street School, Medway Road, Roman Road 71
Phoenix School, Bow Road 74
Roman Road School, Old Ford 80
St Agnes Roman Catholic School, Arrow Road or Botolph Road, Bow 81
St Luke's Church of England School, Canal Road, Mile End 90
St Paul's Road School, Burdett Road, Mile End 96
Single Street School, Bow Common Lane, Burdett Road 102
Smeed Road School, Old Ford, Poplar 103
Southern Grove School, Mile End Road 104
Stafford Road School 105
Tidey Street School 108
Tredegar Road Wesleyan School, Bow 109
Wellington Road School, Bow Road 113
Wrights Road School 118

E5 Clapton; Hackney (part)

Baden-Powell School, Ferron Road 15
Brooke House Secondary School, Kenninghall Road 21
Chatsworth Road Temporary School 26
Clapton Park Secondary School, Laura Place, Lower Clapton Road 29
Clapton Roman Catholic School, Kenninghall Road, Upper Clapton 29
Daubeney Road School, Ashenden Road, Clapton 34
Detmold Road School, Hackney 35
Downs Side School, Rendlesham Road 36
Hackney Day Nursery 47
Hackney Downs School, Downs Park Road 47
Hackney Pupil Teachers Training Centre, Tottenham Road 47
Harrington Hill Primary School 49
Laura Place School 60

E5 [*continued*]

Lubavitch House School, Clapton Common 62
Mandeville Street School, Millfields Road 63
Millfields Road Central School 66
Millfields Road School, Lower Clapton Road 66
Mount Pleasant County Secondary School, Upper Clapton, Hackney 67
North Hackney Central School, Hilsea Street and Elmcroft Street 69
Northwold Road School, Upper Clapton Road 70
Ottaway Street School, Lower Clapton 71
Priory House School, The Common, Upper Clapton 76
Rushmore Road School, Chatsworth Road, Lower Clapton 81
St James's School, Powell Road, Lower Clapton 87
St Scholastica's Roman Catholic School, Kenninghall Road 98
Southwold School, Detmold Road 105
Stormont House School, Downs Park Road, Clapton 106

E8 Dalston; Hackney (part); Homerton (part)

Ada Street School, Hackney 11
Amherst School, Dalston Lane 13
Bay Street School, Dalston 17
Colverstone School, Colverstone Crescent 31
Dalston Central School, Lansdowne Drive 33
Dalston County Secondary School, Shacklewell Lane 34
Dalston Wesleyan School, Mayfield Terrace 34
Eleanor Road School, Richmond Road, Mare Street 37
Gayhurst Road School, London Fields 43
Holy Trinity School, Beechfield Road and Mayfield Road, Dalston 53
Kingsland Birkbeck School, Colverstone Crescent 58
Lamb Lane School, London Fields, Hackney 59
London Fields School, Westgate Street, The Triangle 62
Queen's Road School, Dalston 77
Queensbridge Road School, Dalston 76
St John the Baptist Roman Catholic School, Mare Street 89
St Michael and All Angels School, Lamb Lane, London Fields 94
St Paul School, Broke Road, Dalston 95
St Paul's School later St Paul with St Michael School, Pownall Road, Haggerston 96
Shacklewell School, Shacklewell Row 101
Sigdon Road School, Dalston Lane 102
Sun Babies Nursery, Hackney 107
Triangle Roman Catholic School, Mare Street, Hackney 109
West Hackney Parochial School 114
Wilton Road School, Parkholme Road, Dalston 117
Wilton Way Secondary School, Parkholme Road, Dalston 117
Woodland Street National School, Hackney 117

E9 Hackney (part); Homerton (part)

Berger Road School, Wick Road, Homerton 18
Berkshire Road School, Wallis Road, Hackney 18
Cadogan Terrace Temporary School, Hackney 23
Cardinal Pole Roman Catholic Secondary School, Kenworthy Road 24
Cassland Road School, Well Street, Mare Street 24
Chatham Place School, Hackney 26
Chelmer Road School, Homerton 26
Derby Road School 35
Furrow Lane School, Homerton 43

E9 [*continued*]

Gainsborough Road School, Eastway, Hackney Wick 43
Glyn Road School, Homerton High Street 45
Hackney Free and Parochial School, Isabella Road and Paragon Road, Homerton 47
Hackney Unitarian School, Paradise Fields later Chatham Place 47
Homerton House Comprehensive School 54
Homerton Parochial School, High Street 54
Homerton Row School, Homerton High Street 54
Homerton Wesleyan School, Church Road 54
Hoxton House School, Shoreditch 54
Joseph Priestley Secondary School, Morning Lane 57
Kenworthy Road School, Homerton 58
Kingsmead School, Kings Mead Way 58
Lauriston County Secondary School, Derby Road 60
Lauriston Road Central School 60
Lea Marsh School 61
Morning Lane School, Mare Street 67
Orchard Primary School, Well Street, Hackney 71
Ram's Episcopal Chapel School, Urswick Road, Lower Clapton 77
St Barnabas School, Queens Road (later Berger Road), Homerton 83
St Dominic's Roman Catholic Primary School, Ballance Road 84
St John of Jerusalem School, Kingshold Road 88
St John the Baptist Roman Catholic School, King Edward's Road 89
St Mary and St Dominic's Roman Catholic Boys School, Ballance Road, Homerton 91
St Victoire's Convent School, Victoria Park Road 99
Sidney Road School, Homerton High Street 102
South Hackney Central School, Cassland Road, Well Street 104
South Hackney Parochial School, Percy Road, Hackney 104
Upton House School, Urswick Road, Homerton 111
Upton House Truant School 111
Well Street Chapel School, Hackney 114
Wick Road School 116
Windsor Road School later Berkshire Road School and Lea Marsh School, Hackney 117

E14 Isle of Dogs; Limehouse; Poplar

All Saints School, Newby Place 13
Alton Street School, Guildford Road, Poplar 13
Bow Creek School 20
Bromley Hall Road School, Poplar 21
Cardinal Griffin Roman Catholic School, Canton Street 24
Cayley Street School 25
Chrisp Street School 27
Christ Church National School, Poplar 27
Cotton Street School 32
Cubitt Town School, Poplar 33
Culloden Street School, Brunswick Road, Poplar 33
Cyril Jackson School, Northey Street, Three Colt Street 33
Dalgleish Street School, Salmon Lane 33
Dingle Lane School, Poplar 35
Farrance Street School, Burdett Road 40
Garford Street School 43
George Green School, East India Rock Road 44
Gill Street School, West India Dock Road 44
Glengall Road School, Manchester Road, Cubitt Town 44
Glengall Secondary School 44
Halley Street School 48

E14 [*continued*]

Harbinger School, Cahir Street 49
Hay Currie School, Poplar 50
Holy Child Roman Catholic School, Grundy Street or Upper North Street 52
Hutton Poplars Residential School, Poplar 55
Isle of Dogs School, Glengall Road, Poplar 55
Janet Street School 56
Langford Park School, Byron Street and Farrance Street 59
Manorfield School, Wyvis Street 63
Martin Frobisher Secondary School 64
Mayflower School, Upper North Street 64
Millwall Central School, Poplar 66
Millwall School, Glengall Road, Poplar 66
Northey Street School, Limehouse 69
Oban Street School, Bromley 70
Our Lady of Assumpton Roman Catholic School, Copenhagen Place 71
Pigot Street School 74
Poplar and Blackwall National School, Bow Lane now Bazely Street, later Poplar High Street 75
Poplar Technical College, Poplar High Street 75
Ricardo Street School, Kerbey Street, East India Dock Road 78
St Anne's School, Dixon Street 82
St Edmund's Roman Catholic School, Westferry Road 84
St Gabriels School, Morris Road, Bow 85
St John's School, Roserton Road, Poplar 88
St Leonard's Road School, Poplar 90
St Luke's School, Westferry Road, Milwall 90
St Mary and St Joseph Roman Catholic School, Wade's Place 91
St Matthias Church of England School, Grundy Street and Bullivant Street, Poplar 94
St Saviour's School, Northumberland Street and Hobday Street, Poplar 98
Sacred Heart Roman Catholic School, Willow Row, Three Colt Street 81
Seven Mills School, Malabar Street 101
Sir William Burrough School, Salmon Lane 103
Stebon School, Streatfield Street 105
Stepney Greencoat School, Salmon Lane 106
Susan Lawrence School, Cordelia Street 107
Thomas Street School, Burdett Road 108
Upper North Street School, East India Dock Road, Poplar 111
Woolmore Street School, Cotton Street, Poplar 118

E16 North Woolwich

Elizabeth Street School, High Street, North Woolwich 38
North Woolwich Secondary School, Woodman Street 70

EC1 City (North West); Clerkenwell; Holborn

Aldersgate Ward and Packington School, Aldersgate Street 12
Baldwin's Gardens National School, St Andrew Holborn 15
Baltic Street School 15
Bath Street School, City Road 16
Central Street School, Old Street 25
Charterhouse School also known as Sutton's Hospital, Smithfield 26
Chequer Street School, Bunhill Row, Old Street 26
Christchurch School, Herbrand Street, Holborn 27
Christopher Hatton School 28
Clerkenwell Parochial School, Amwell Street 29
Compton Primary School, Compton Street, Clerkenwell 31

EC1 [*continued*]

Cripplegate Within Ward School 33
Dame Anne Packington School, St Botolph Aldersgate 34
Dissenters' Charity School, Bartholomew Close 35
Farringdon Within Ward Schools, City 40
Field Lane Foundation, Vine Street, Clerkenwell 40
Frank Barnes School, Central Street 42
Hall Street Wesleyan School 48
Hatton Garden Charity School, St Andrew Holborn 50
Holy Family Roman Catholic School, Saffron Hill, Holborn 53
Hugh Myddleton Central School, Corporation Row 54
Hugh Myddleton Junior School, Bowling Green Lane 54
Hugh Myddleton School, Corporation Row 54
Italia Conti Academy of Theatre Arts, Goswell Road 55
Laystall Street School, Grays Inn Road 61
Mercers' School, Barnard's Inn, Holborn 65
Merchant Taylors' School, Charterhouse Square 65
Moorfields School, Radnor Street 66
Moreland Street School, Goswell Road 67
Northampton Polytechnic, St John Street 69
Northampton Secondary School, Chequer Street 69
Owen's School, Owen's Row, Islington 72
Prior Weston School, Whitecross Street 75
Radnor Street School 77
Rosebery Avenue School 80
St Andrew's Parochial School, Hatton Garden 82
St Bartholomew the Great School, West Smithfield 83
St Catherine Laboure School, Herbal Hill 84
St Etheldreda's Roman Catholic School, Saffron Hill 85
St Giles Cripplegate Boys' School, Red Cross Street 86
St Giles Cripplegate Girls' School (Lady Holles School) 86
St John's Lane School 88
St Joseph Roman Catholic School, Lambs Passage, Bunhill Row 89
St Luke's Parochial School, Old Street 90
St Mark's School, Brewer Street and Old Street, North Goswell Street 91
St Peter's and St Paul's Roman Catholic School, Amwell Street 97
St Peter's Italian Roman Catholic School, Little Saffron Hill 97
St Peter's Saffron Hill National School, Onslow Street, Saffron Hill 97
St Sepulchre's School, Giltspur Street, Newgate Street 98
St Thomas School, Charterhouse 99
South Macclesfield Street Infants' School, South Macclesfield Street, Finsbury 104
Trotman's School, Bunhill Row 110
Weigh House Boys' Charity School, City Road 113

EC2 City (North East)

Bishopsgate Ward School, Peter Street 18
Broad Street Ward School, Leg and Ball Alley, London Wall 21
Central Foundation School for Boys, Cowper Street 25
City of London School for Girls, Barbican 29
Coleman Street Ward School, London Wall, City 30
Cordwainer and Bread Street Wards Charity School, City 31
Cornhill, Lime Street and Langbourn Wards School 32
Curtain Road School, Old Street 33
Finsbury Technical College 40
Gresham College, Basinghall Street and Gresham Street 46
Guildhall School of Music and Drama, Barbican 47

EC2 [*continued*]

Langbourn Ward School 59
Peter Joye's Charity School, St Ann Blackfriars 74
St Alban's School, Baldwin's Gardens 81
St Botolph Bishopsgate Parochial Charity School 83
St Leonard Shoreditch Infants' School 90
Scrutton Street School, Shoreditch 100
Turner's Free School for Poor Boys, Primrose Street, Bishopsgate 110

EC3 City (South East)

Aldgate Ward School, Aldgate 12
Billingsgate and Tower Wards School 18
Christ's Hospital, Great Tower Street 28
City of London School of Instruction and Industry, St James Duke's Place 29
National Society's Central School, Baldwins Garden's, Holborn 67
St Andrew Undershaft School 82
St Botolph Aldgate Parochial School 83
St George Botolph Lane School, City 85
St Katharine's School, St Katharine by the Tower 90
St Margaret Pattens School, City 90
Sir John Cass Foundation School, St James' Duke's Place, City 102
Tower Hill School 109
Tower Ward School 109
Vintry Ward Charity School, City 112

EC4 City (South West)

Castle Baynard Ward School 24
City of London School, Victoria Embankment 29
Neale's Mathematical School, St Dunstan in the West 67
Queenhithe Ward School 76
St Brides School 83
St Dunstan in the West Parochial Charity School 84
St Paul's Cathedral Choir School, New Change 95

N1 Islington (part); Shoreditch (part)

All Saints School, Muriel Street, Wynford Road 12
Allen Street School, Islington 12
Angel Court Ragged School, Rufford's Buildings, Islington 13
Anglers Gardens School, Essex Road 13
Ball's Pond Road Mission School, Ball's Pond Road 15
Barnsbury Park School 16
Barnsbury Secondary School, Barnsbury Park, Liverpool Road 16
Bishop Gifford Roman Catholic Secondary School 18
Blessed Sacrament Roman Catholic Primary School, Boadicea Street 19
Britannia Row School, Essex Road 21
Buckingham Street School, Boadicea Street, Edward Square 22
Burbage Primary School 22
Caledonian Road School 23
Canal Road School, Hoxton 23
Canonbury Road School 24
Catherine Street School, Hoxton 24
Charles Lamb Primary School, Popham Road 25
Chatham Gardens School, Provost Street, City Road 26
Cloudesley School, Dowrey Street 30

LONDON SCHOOLS BY POSTAL DISTRICT

N1 [*continued*]

Colebrooke School, Colebrooke Row 30
Copenhagen School, Boadicea Street 31
Copenhagen Street Ragged School 31
Crondall Street School, Hoxton Street 33
Dame Alice Owen School, Goswell Road, Islington 34
De Beauvoir School, Tottenham Road 34
Ecclesbourne Road School, New North Road 37
Edith Cavell School, Enfield Road 37
Edmund Halley School, Shoreditch 37
Enfield Road School, Kingsland Road 39
Fellows Street School, Haggerston 40
Geffrye School, Sarah Street 43
Gifford Street School, Caledonian Road 44
Gopsall Street School, Haggerston 45
Haggerston Road School 47
Hammond Square School, Hoxton Street 48
Hanover Street School, St Peter Street 49
Highbury and Islington High School, Canonbury Place 51
Holy Trinity School, Cloudesley Square 53
Hoxton Academy Chapel Sunday School 54
Islington and North London Shoe-Black Brigade School, York Road 55
Islington Chapel School, Church (later Gaskin)Street 55
Kingsland Roman Catholic School, Tottenham Road, Kingsland 58
Laycock Junior School, Laycock Street 60
Laycock Secondary School, Upper Street 60
Laysterne School, Shoreditch 61
Napier Street School, Shepherdess Walk, Hoxton 67
Offord Road Special School 70
Penton Grove School 73
Pentonville Charity School, Finsbury 73
Pitfield School, Shoreditch 74
Popham Road School, New North Road 75
Queen's Head Street School, Essex Road 76
Redvers Street School, Kingsland Road 78
Richard Street School, Liverpool Road 78
Risinghill Comprehensive School 78
Risinghill Street School 78
Ritchie School, Liverpool Road, Islington 79
Rosemary School, Prebend Street 80
Rotherfield Street School, Essex Road 80
St Andrew's School, Matilda Street, Barnsbury 82
St Barnabas School, Sherburne Road 83
St Bartholomew Church of England School, Shepperton Road 83
St John the Evangelist Roman Catholic School, Duncan Street, Islington 89
St John's Church of England School later St John the Baptist School, New North Road, Hoxton 88
St John's Road School, Hoxton 88
St Jude's District Church of England School, Ball's Pond Road 89
St Jude's School also known as St Jude and St Paul School, Mildmay Park 90
St Mary Haggerston School 91
St Mary Islington Church of England Primary School, Halton Road 91
St Matthew's Church of England School, New Norfolk (later Rotherfield) Street 93
St Matthew's School, Nelson Place, City Road 93
St Michael's Church of England School, Bingfield Street 94
St Monica's Roman Catholic School, Hoxton Square 95
St Paul's School, Dorset Street, Essex Road 96
St Philip the Evangelist National School, Hale (later Rees) Street 98

N1 [*continued*]

St Stephen's National School, Essex Road 98
St Thomas's Church of England School, Everilda Street 99
Samuel Rhodes School, Dowrey Street 100
Sebbon Street School, Sable Street, Canonbury Road 100
Shepperton Road School, New North Road 101
Shoreditch Central School, Hoxton Road, Old Street 102
Shoreditch Handicraft Training College, Pitfield Street 102
Shoreditch Recreational Institute 102
Southampton Street School, Pentonville 103
South Islington and Pentonville British School, Denmark Terrace 104
Station Road School, Upper Street 105
The Whitmore School, Grange Road, Hoxton 116
Thomas Fairchild Junior Mixed School, Napier Grove 108
Thornhill School, Barnsbury 108
Tottenham Road School, Balls Pond Road 109
Trinity Place School, New North Road, Hoxton 110
Vittoria Place School, Payne Street, Copenhagen Street 112
Wellington Street School 114
Wenlock Road 24
Wenlock Road School, Edward Street, Shepherdess Walk, City Road 114
White Lion Street School, Penton Street, Pentonville Road 116
Winchester Street School, Pentonville Road 117
Windsor Street School 117
Winton School, Killick Street 117
York Road School, Kings Cross 119
York Way School, Kings Cross 119

N4 Highbury (part); Tollington Park

Ambler Road School 13
Blackstock Road School, Highbury 19
Christ the King Roman Catholic Primary School, Tollington Park 28
Edward Seguin School, Prah Road 37
Finsbury Park Junior School 40
Finsbury Park Secondary School, Blackstock Road 40
George Orwell School, Turle Road 44
Hanley School, Islington 49
Jack Ashley School, Blackstock Road, Finsbury Park 55
Montem Street School, Marriott Road, Tollington Park 66
Pooles Park School, Lennox Road, Seven Sisters Road 74
Romilly Road School 80
St Anne's Tollington Park School, Pooles Park. 82
Tollington Park Central School, Marriott Road 109
Tollington Park College, Tollington Park 109
Woodberry Down Comprehensive School 117
Woodberry Down Primary School 117

N5 Highbury (part); Highgate (part)

Arundell House School, Highbury New Park 14
Drayton Park School, Holloway Road 36
Gillespie Road School, Blackstock Road, Highbury 44
High School for Boys, Highbury Grange, Highbury 51
Highbury County School, Highbury Grove 51
Highbury Hill High School, Highbury Hill 51
Highbury Industrial School 51

N5 [*continued*]

Highbury Park School, Highbury Park 51
Highbury Quadrant School, Highbury New Park 51
Highbury Vale School, Conewood Street 51
Highbury Wesleyan School 51
London College of Divinity, Aubert Park 62
St Joan of Arc Roman Catholic Primary School, Northolme Road 87
St John's School, Park Place later Conewood Street, Highbury Vale 88
St Michael's School, North Road, Highgate 95

N6 Highgate (part)

Channing School, Highgate 25
Highgate School, North Road, Highgate 51
Holly Court Open Air School, Merton Lane, West Hill, Highgate 52
St Aloysius College, Hornsey Lane 81

N7 Holloway (part); Islington (part)

Albany Day School, Albany Place 11
Alfred Pritchard School, Islington 12
Barnsbury Central School, Hope Street, Islington 16
Blundell Street School, Caledonian Road 19
Grafton Road School, Seven Sisters Road 45
Harvist Road School 49
Holloway Literary Institute, Hilldrop Road 52
Holloway School, Hilldrop Road 52
Hornsey Road Wesleyan Day School 54
Hungerford Road School, York Road, Camden Road 54
Isledon Secondary School 55
Mount Carmel Roman Catholic School, Eden Grove 67
Northern Polytechnic Day School, Holloway Road 69
Our Lady of Sion School, Eden Grove 71
Our Lady of the Sacred Heart Roman Catholic School, Eden Grove, Holloway 72
Pakeman Street School, Holloway 72
Ring Cross School, Eden Grove, Holloway 78
Robert Blair School 79
St Clements School, Cumberland Street, Barnsbury 84
St James School, George's Road, Holloway 86
St Mark's School, Grove Road, Holloway Road 91
St Mary Magdalene's School, Liverpool Road 92
St William of York Roman Catholic School (Lower School), Brewery Road, N1 99
St William of York Roman Catholic School (Upper School), Gifford Street, N1 99
Shelburne Road School, Hornsey Road 101
Tufnell Park Primary School, Dalmeny Road 110
Upper Hornsey Road School, Seven Sisters Road, Holloway 111
Wellington Road School 114
Westbourne Road School, St James Road 114
William Forster School, Benwell Road 116

N16 Stamford Hill (part); Stoke Newington

Avigdor High School, Lordship Road 15
Avigdor Primary School, Lordship Road 15
Benthal Road School 17
Church Street School, Stoke Newington 28
Clissold Park School, Clissold Road 30

N16 [*continued*]

Clissold Secondary School 30
Craven Park School, Castlewood Road, Stamford Hill 32
Crusoe House School, Clissold Road 33
Daniel Defoe School, Ayrsome Road 34
Finsbury Park College, Green Lanes, Stoke Newington 40
Fleetwood School, Stoke Newington High Street 41
Fountayne School, Cazenove Road 41
Grasmere Primary School, Albion Road 45
Grazebrook Primary School, Lordship Road 46
High Street School, Stoke Newington 51
Holmleigh Primary School, Dunsmure Road 52
Jewish Secondary School, Amhurst Park 56
Jubilee School, Filey Avenue 57
Kingsland British School, Stoke Newington Road 58
Lubavitch House School, Stamford Hill 62
Matthias Road Deaf School, Stoke Newington 64
Modern School, Paradise House, Stoke Newington 66
New River School, Clissold Road 68
Newington Green School 68
Oldfield Road School, Kynaston Road, Stoke Newington High Street 70
Paradise House School, Paradise Row 72
Parkwood Primary School, Queen's Drive 72
Princess May Road School, Stoke Newington 75
Raleigh Memorial School, Albion Road 77
St Ignatius' College, Stamford Hill 86
St John's College, Green Lanes, Stoke Newington 88
St Mary Church of England Primary School, Barn Street 91
St Matthias' School, Wordsworth Road, Stoke Newington 94
St Thomas School, Lynmouth Road 99
Sandford Lane Ragged School, Stoke Newington High Street 100
Simon Marks Jewish Primary School, Cazenove Road and Kyverdale Road 102
Sir Thomas Abney Primary School, Fairholt Road 102
Skinners' Company School for Girls, Stamford Hill 103
Stamford Hill Collegiate School, Stamford Hill 105
Stoke Newington Central School 106
Stoke Newington Grammar School, Manor Road 106
Stoke Newington Parochial School, Lordship Road 106
Stoke Newington Ragged Schools 106
Stoke Newington School, Clissold Park 106
Tyssen School, Oldfield Street 110
Upper Clapton and Stamford Hill School, Lynmouth Road 110
Wordsworth School, Stoke Newington 118
Yesodey Hatorah Schools, Amhurst Park 119
Yesodey Hatorah Schools, Stamford Hill 119

N17 Stamford Hill (part)

The Forster School, Hornsey Road 41

N19 Holloway (part); Islington (part)

Archway Secondary School, Duncombe Road 14
Ashmount School, Ashmount Road 14
Cottenham Road School, Marlborough Road 32
Denmark Terrace School, Blenheim Road, Islington 35
Duncombe Road School, Hornsey Rise 36

N19 [*continued*]

Elthorne Road School 38
Harborough School, Elthorne Road 49
Hargrave Park School, Junction Road, Upper Holloway 49
Oxford House School, Junction Road, Upper Holloway 72
St Anne's School, Brookfield, Chester Road, Dartmouth Park Hill 82
St John's Church of England School, Pemberton Gardens, Upper Holloway 88
St Joseph Roman Catholic School, Highgate Hill 89
St Mark's School, Sussex Way, Tollington Park 91
St Paul's School, Blenheim Road 96
Whittington School, Highgate Hill 116
Yerbury Road School, Upper Holloway 118

NW1 Camden Town; St Marylebone (part); St Pancras

Aldenham Street School, Pancras Road 11
Bell Street School 17
Bellfields Secondary School 17
Blandford Square Roman Catholic School (later St Edward), Marylebone Road 19
Brecknock School, York Road, Camden Town 20
Camden Street School, Camden Town 23
Camden Town All Saints' Parish Church of England School, Camden Street 23
Cantlowe Secondary School 24
Cavendish School, Arlington Road 25
Chester Road School 26
Christ Church Albany Street School, St Pancras 27
Christ Church Cosway Street School, Marylebone 27
Christ Church School, Somers Town 28
Cosway Street School, St Marylebone 32
Elizabeth Garrett Anderson School 38
Exmouth Street School, Starcross Street 39
Fleet Central School, St Pancras 41
Francis Holland School, Clarence Gate 42
Great College Street School, Kentish Town Road 46
Harmood Street Special School, Chalk Farm Road 49
Haverstock School, Crogsland Road 50
Hawley Crescent School, Buck Street and Kentish Town Road 50
Jews Free School, Camden Road 56
Kentish Town Wesleyan School 58
King Street School, Camden Street 58
Lancing Street School 59
Lyulph Stanley Central School, Camden Street, St Pancras 62
Manchester Street School, Kings Cross 63
Mary Ward School, St Pancras 64
Medburn School, Charrington Street, Crowndale Road, St Pancras 64
Middlesex Street Presbyterian School, Somers Town 65
Netley Street School, Hampstead Road 68
New Jerusalem School, St Pancras 68
Princess Road School, Regents Park Road 75
Richard Cobden School, St Pancras 78
Robert Louis Stevenson School 79
Royal Academy of Music, Marylebone Road 80
Royal College Street School 80
Rutherford School, Penfold Street 81
St Aloysius Roman Catholic School, Aldenham Street, Somers Town 81
St Edwards Roman Catholic School 85
St Edwards Roman Catholic School, Broad Street, Westminster later Lisson Grove 84

LONDON SCHOOLS BY POSTAL DISTRICT

NW1 [*continued*]

St Francis Xavier Roman Catholic School, Upper William Street, Marylebone 85
St Mark's School, Marylebone Road 91
St Mary and St Pancras Church of England School, Polygon Road 91
St Mary Magdalene's School, Munster Square 92
St Mary's School, Clarendon Square, Somers Town 93
St Marylebone Central School 92
St Marylebone Grammar School, Marylebone Road 92
St Matthew's School, Arlington Road, Camden 94
St Michael's School, Arlington Road, Camden Town 94
St Pancras Church of England School, Lancing Street 95
St Paul's Bentinck School, Rossmore Road, Marylebone Road 95
Stanhope Street School, Euston Road 105
Stanley Central School, Camden Street 105
Stephen Street School, Lisson Grove 105
Sylvia Young Theatre School, Rossmore Road 107

NW2 Cricklewood

Blenheim House School, Oxgate Gardens 19
Haberdashers' Aske's School, Westbere Road, Cricklewood 47
Hampstead School, Westbere Road 48
North West London Jewish School, Minster Road, Cricklewood 70

NW3 Hampstead (part); Haverstock Hill

Alexandra Orphanage School, Maitland Park, Haverstock Hill 12
Bartram's Roman Catholic School, Haverstock Hill 16
Belsize School, Buckland Crescent 17
Burgess Hill School, Hampstead 22
Christ Church School, Hampstead Square 27
Devonshire House Preparatory School, Arkwright Road 35
Fitzjohn's Primary School, Fitzjohn's Avenue 41
Fleet Road School, Hampstead 41
Frognal School, Fitzjohn's Avenue 42
Hall School, Crossfield Road, Hampstead 48
Hampstead Parochial School, Holly Bush Vale 48
Hampstead Preparatory School, Shepherd's Walk, Hampstead 48
Haverstock Hill School and Haverstock Central School 50
Heath Mount Preparatory School, Hampstead, 50
Heath Street British School, Heath Street 50
Herewward House School, Strathray Gardens 51
Holy Trinity School, College Crescent, Kilburn 53
John Keats School, Adelaide Road 56
Lyndhurst House Preparatory School, Lyndhurst Gardens, Hampstead 62
Mansfield Road Special School, St Pancas 63
New End School, Heath Street 68
North Bridge House School, Netherhall Gardens 69
North End School, Sandy Road 69
Peterborough Lodge School, Finchley Road, Hampstead 73
Purcell School, Lyndhurst Terrace 76
Queen's House School, Fitzjohn's Avenue 76
Rosary Roman Catholic School, Haverstock Hill 80
Rosslyn Hill British School, Willoughby Road 80
Royal Sailors' Orphan Girls' School, Fitzjohn's Avenue 81
Royal Soldiers' Daughters' Home, Rosslyn Hill 81
Russian Soviet Embassy School, Heath Drive 81

LONDON SCHOOLS BY POSTAL DISTRICT

NW3 [*continued*]

St Andrew's National School, Haverstock Hill 82
St Anthony's, Fitzjohns Avenue 82
St Christopher's School, Belsize Lane, Hampstead 84
St Margaret's School, Kidderpore Gardens, 90
St Mary's Convent School, England's Lane 92
St Mary's Roman Catholic School, Holly Place 93
St Mary's Town and Country School, Eton Avenue 93
St Paul's Church of England Primary School, Winchester Road, Hampstead 95
Sarum Hall, Eton Avenue 100
Settringham School, Lyndhurst Gardens 101
South Hampstead High School, Winchester Gardens 104
South Hampstead Preparatory School, Finchley Road, Hampstead 104
Stepping Stone School, Fitzjohn's Avenue 106
Threave House School, Heath Drive 108
University College School, Frognal, Hampstead 110
University College School Junior Branch, Holly Hill, Hampstead 110
University College School Preparatory Branch, Holly Hill, Hampstead 110
Warwick House School, King Henry's Road 113
Wellington Court Preparatory School, Hampstead 113
West Heath School, Ferncroft Avenue, Hampstead 114
Wykeham House School, Hampstead 118

NW5 Kentish Town; St Pancras (part)

Acland Road School, Lupton Street, St Pancras 11
Brookfield Secondary School 21
Burghley Road and Burghley Central Schools, Highgate Road, St Pancras 22
Camden School for Girls, Sandall Road 23
Eleanor Palmer School, Raveley Street 37
Falkland Road Wesleyan School, St Pancras 40
Hillmartin College, Busby Place, Camden Road 52
Kentish Town Church of England School, Islip Street, Kentish Town Road 58
La Sainte Union Convent School, Croftdown Road 60
North London College, Sandall Road 69
North-Western Polytechnic, Kentish Town Road and Prince of Wales Road 69
Parliament Hill School, Highgate Road 72
Queen's Crescent School, St Pancras 76
Rhyl Street School, Malden Road, Kentish Town 78
Ryland Secondary School, Prince of Wales Road 81
St Dominic's Roman Catholic School, Southampton Road, Haverstock Hill 84
St Patrick's Roman Catholic School, Raglan Street 95
St Richard of Chichester Roman Catholic School, Reed's Place, and Prince of Wales Road 98
Torriano Avenue School, St Pancras 109
William Ellis Endowed School, Gospel Oak 116

NW6 Gospel Oak; Hampstead (part); Kilburn

All Souls School, Fairhazel Gardens, Finchley Road, Hampstead 13
Beckford School, Dornfell Street, Hampstead 17
Brondesbury and Kilburn High School for Girls, Salusbury Road 21
Emmanuel School, Lyncroft Gardens, Mill Lane, West Hampstead 38
Harben Secondary School, Kelson Street, Netherwood Street, Hampstead 49
Henley House School, Mortimer Road (later Crescent) 50
Iverson Road School, Kilburn 55
Jewish Preparatory School, Andover Place 56
Kilburn Grammar School, Salusbury Road 58

NW6 [*continued*]

Kilburn Polytechnic, Priory Park Road 58
Kingsgate Road School, Messina Avenue, Kilburn High Road 58
Mazenod Roman Catholic School, Mazenod Avenue, Kilburn 64
St Augustine Church of England School, Kilburn Park Road 83
St John Church of England Primary School, Kilburn 87
St Mary's Church of England School, West Hampstead 92
St Mary's Kilburn School, West End Lane 92

NW8 St John's Wood; St Marylebone (part)

Allen-Olney School, St John's Wood 12
Arnold House School, Loudoun Road, St John's Wood 14
Barrow Hill Road School, St Marylebone 16
Capland Street Primary School, Lisson Grove 24
Capland Street Secondary School, Grove Road 24
Emmanuel School, Northwick Terrace, St John's Wood 38
Gateforth Street School, Church Street, St Marylebone 43
Gateway School, Church Street 43
George Eliot School, Marlborough Hill 43
Loudoun House School, Loudoun Road 62
Netherwood Street School, Kilburn 68
Nightingale Street School, St Johns Wood 68
Quintin Kynaston School, Marlborough Hill 77
Regent's Park School, Grove Road 78
Richmond Street Roman Catholic School. Now St John's Wood Roman Catholic School 78
Robinsfield School, Ordnance Hill 79
St John's Wood Roman Catholic School, Orchardson Street 88
St Mark's School, Hamilton Terrace 91
St Stephen's School, Avenue Road, St John's Wood 98
Tyburn Roman Catholic School, Orchardston Street and Fisherton Street 110

NW10 Kensal Green

College Park Secondary School, Valliere Road 30
Kenmont Gardens School, Harrow Road 57

NW11 Golders Green; Hampstead (part)

Henrietta Barnett School 50
King Alfred School Society, Ellerdale Road, Hampstead 58

SE1 Bermondsey (part); Lambeth (part); Southwark

Addington Street School, York Road 11
All Saints Roman Catholic School, Tooley Street 12
All Saints School, Waterloo Road 13
Archbishop Tait's School, Lambeth Road 13
Archbishop Temple Central School, Lambeth Road 14
Bacon's Free School, Grange Road 15
Bankside School 16
Benevolent Society of St Patrick School, Stamford Street 17
Bermondsey Central School, Monnow Road, Southwark Park Road 18
Bermondsey County Secondary School 18
Bermondsey United Charity Schools 18
Blackfriars School, Gray Street, Southwark 18
Borough Paragon Secondary School, Searles Road 20

SE1 [*continued*]

Borough Polytechnic Technical Day School, Borough Road 20
Borough Road School, Southwark 20
Boutcher School, Grange Road, Bermondsey 20
Charles Dickens School, Lant Street, Borough High Street 25
Christchurch School, Bear Lane, Southwark 27
Elizabeth Newcomen School, Southwark 38
Eveline Lowe School, Marlborough Grove 39
Fair Street School, Horsleydown 40
Friar Street School, Blackfriars Road 42
Harper Street School, New Kent Road 49
Hatfield Street School, Stamford Street 49
Henry Street School 50
Holy Trinity School, Carlisle Street, Westminster Bridge Road 53
James Pascall Secondary School 55
Johanna Street School, Lower Marsh, Lambeth 56
John Harvard School, Copperfield Street, Gravel Lane 56
John Rennie School 56
John Street, Kent Road, Sunday School 57
Joseph Lancaster School, Harper Road 57
Joseph Lancaster School, Rockingham Street 57
King Street Sunday School 58
Lambeth Boys' Parochial School 59
Lambeth Orphans' Asylum, Westminster Bridge Road 59
Lansdowne Place Half Time School 59
Lant Street School 60
Laxon Street School, Long Lane 60
Leathersellers' College, Tower Bridge 61
London School of Printing, Stamford Street 62
Magdalen Street School, Rotherhithe 63
Marlborough Grove School 63
Mawbey Road School, Old Kent Road 64
Melior Street Roman Catholic School 65
Monnow Road School, Southwark 66
Neckinger School, Bermondsey 67
Newcomen's Domestic Trade School for Girls, Borough 68
Notre Dame Secondary School, St George's Road 70
Old Kent Road Ragged and Industrial Schools, Park Road 70
Old Kent Road Special School, Southwark 70
Orange Street School 71
Page's Walk School, Old Kent Road 72
Paragon School, New Kent Road 72
Pocock Street School, Blackfriars Road 74
Riley Street School, Bermondsey 78
Rolls Road School, Bermondsey 80
Rushworth School, Webber Street 81
St Andrew's School, Roupell Street, Exton Street, Waterloo Road 82
St George the Martyr School, Borough Road 86
St George's School, Westminster Bridge Road 86
St John and All Saints School, Waterloo Road 87
St Joseph's Roman Catholic School, Borough High Street 89
St Joseph's Roman Catholic School, George Road, Dockhead 89
St Jude's School, Colnbrook Street 90
St Mary Magdalen School, Grange Walk, Tower Bridge Road 92
St Mary Overie School 92
St Mary's Roman Catholic School, Arnold's Place, Dockhead 93
St Michael's Roman Catholic School, Arnold's Place, Dockhead 94

SE1 [*continued*]

St Olave's School, Tower Bridge 95
St Patrick (Benevolent Society of) School, Cornwall Road, Lambeth 95
St Paul's School, Vauxhall 96
St Saviour and St Olave School, New Kent Road 98
St Saviour Southwark School, Redcross Street 98
Snowsfields School, Kirby Grove, Bermondsey 103
Southwark Chapel Sunday School, Long Lane 104
Southwark Sunday School Society 105
Stephen the Yeoman Ragged School, Bermondsey 105
Tanner Street School, Bermondsey 107
Tower Bridge Junior School, Fair Street. 109
Tower Bridge Senior School 109
Trinity House School, Harper Road 110
Upper Grange Road School 111
Wadding Street Temporary School, Walworth 112
Waterloo Road School 113
Webb Street School, Tower Bridge Road 113
Webber Street School 113
Westminster Bridge Road School, Southwark 115
Weston Street School, Old Kent Road 115
Yorkshire Society School, Westminster Bridge Road 119
Zoar Street Charity School 119

SE2 Abbey Wood

Abbey Wood Secondary School, Eynsham Bridge 11
Bostall Lane, Abbey Wood 20
Boxgrove School, Boxgrove Road, Abbey Wood 20
Church Manor Way School 28
De Lucy School, Cookhill Road 34
Goldie Leigh Hospital School, Abbey Wood 45
Greening Road School 46
Manorway Primary School 63
Oakmere Secondary School, Wickham Lane 70
St Thomas à Becket Roman Catholic School, Mottisfont Road 99
Wickham Lane School, Oakmere Road 116

SE3 Blackheath

All Saints' School, The Vale, Blackheath 12
Blackheath and Kidbrooke Bluecoat Church of England School, Old Dover Road 19
Blackheath High School, Vanbrugh Park 19
Blackheath Proprietory School, Blackheath 19
Brooklands School, Medebourne Close, Casterbridge Road 22
Invicta Road, Westcombe Hill 55
John Ball School, Southvale, Tranquil Vale 56
Kidbrooke Park School, Hargood Road 58
Lindisfarne School, Blackheath 61
Morden Terrace School, Orchard Hill 67
Roan School, Maze Hill 79
Royal Air Force Memorial School, Vanbrugh Castle, Maze Hill 80
School for Sons of Missionaries, Blackheath 100
St Joseph's Academy, Lee Terrace 89
Stratheden House School, Blackheath 106

LONDON SCHOOLS BY POSTAL DISTRICT

SE4 Brockley

Brockley Central School, Wallbutton Road, Vesta Road 21
Brockley County School, Hillyfields 21
Brockley Road School, Brockley 21
Brockley Roman Catholic School (later St Mary Magdalen School), Howson Road 21
Crofton Park Central School 33
Gordonbrook Road School, Brockley 45
John Stainer School, St Asaph Road 57
Mantle Road School, Brockley 63
Samuel Pepys School, Wallbutton Road 100
St Peter's College, Manor Road, Wickham Park, Brockley 97
Turnham School, Turnham Road 110

SE5 Camberwell

Acorn Street School, Camberwell 11
Avenue Secondary School, Bethwin Road, Walworth 15
Bantry Road School 16
Bessemer Grange Primary School, Dylways 18
Brunswick Park School, Camberwell 22
Caldecot Road School, Bessemer Road, Denmark Hill 23
Camberwell Parochial School (Sir John Kirk Mission), Toulon Street 23
Charles Edward Brooke School for Girls, Halsmere Road, Camberwell 25
Cobourg Road School, Old Kent Road 30
Comber Grove School, Camberwell New Road 31
Cork Street School 31
Cormont Road School, Myatts Fields, Flodden Road 31
Crawford Street School, Camberwell 32
Denmark Hill School, Grove Lane 35
D'Eynsford Road School 35
Dog Kennel Hill School, Grovehill Road 35
Dovedale Manor School 35
George Street School, Camberwell Road 44
Gloucester Road School, Camberwell 45
Green Coat Church of England School, Camberwell Green 46
John Ruskin School, John Ruskin Street, Walworth Road 56
Mary Datchelor School, Grove Lane, Camberwell 64
Miss Pace's School, Camberwell 66
Oliver Goldsmith School, Cork Street, Waterloo Street 71
Pitman Street Roman Catholic School, Wyndham Road, Camberwell 74
Ruby Street School, Old Kent Road 81
St Alban's Roman Catholic School, Herring Street, Camberwell 81
St Gabriel's College, Cormont Road 85
St George's School, New Church Road, Camberwell 85
St Giles' Greencoat and National Schools, Camberwell 86
St John the Divine School, Warham Street, Camberwell New Road 89
St Joseph's Roman Catholic School, Pitman Street 89
St Matthew's Church of England School, Denmark Hill 93
St Matthew's School, Camberwell New Road 93
St Michael and All Angels School, Farmers Road, Camberwell 94
St Michael and All Angels Secondary Modern School, Toulon Street and Wyndham Road 94
Scarsdale Road School, Albany Road 100
Southampton Street School, Camberwell 103
Southampton Way School 103
Venetian Road School, Caldecot Road 111
Whitney School, The, John Ruskin Street 116
Wilson's Grammar School, Peckham Road, Camberwell 117

LONDON SCHOOLS BY POSTAL DISTRICT

SE6 Catford; Rushey Green

Abbotshall Road School 11
Athelney Street School, Bellingham Estate, Catford 14
Brownhill Road School, Rushey Green 22
Catford Central School, Brownhill Road and Hither Green 24
Elfrida Primary School, Elfrida Crescent 37
Forster Park School, Boundfield Road 41
Hazelbank Road School 50
Holbeach Road School, Rushey Green 52
Holy Trinity School, Dartmouth Road, Forest Hill, Sydenham 53
King Alfred Girls' School, Holbeach Road 58
Lewisham Grammar School, Catford 61
Lewisham Park School, Lewisham 61
Lewisham Prendergast School, Rushey Green 61
Plassy Road School, Rushey Green 74
Prendergast School, Hawstead Road 75
Rathfern Road School, Stanstead Road, Catford 77
St Augustine's Roman Catholic School, Beckenham Hill Road 83
St Dunstan's College, Catford 84
Sandhurst Road School 100
Sedgehill School, Sedgehill Road 100
Southend Church of England School, Bromley Road, Catford 104
Torridon Road School, Hither Green 109

SE7 Charlton

Charlton Central School, Sherington Road 25
Charlton Manor School, Hornfair Road 26
Charlton National School, Woolwich Road 26
Charlton Park Open Air School, Charlton Park Road 26
Charlton School, Woolwich Road 26
Cherry Orchard School, Rectory Field Crescent 26
Fossdene Secondary School, Victoria Road 41
Lombard Wall School, Woolwich Road 61
Maryon Park School, Woolwich Road, Old Charlton 64
Our Lady of Grace Roman Catholic School, Charlton Road 71
Sherington Road School 101
Shirley House School, Old Charlton 102
Thorntree Road School, Pound Park Road 108

SE8 Deptford (part)

Alverton Street School 13
Clyde Street School, Wotton Road, Deptford 30
Creek Road School 32
Deptford Park School, Evelyn Street 35
Deptford Pupil Teachers Institute 35
Deptford Roman Catholic School. Deptford High Street 35
Edward Street School 37
Frankham Street School, Deptford High Street 42
Grove Street School, Evelyn Street 46
High Street Deptford Temporary School 51
Holland Street School. 52
Hughes Fields School, Creek Road or Benbow Street, Deptford 54
John Evelyn School, Alverton Street 56
Lucas Street School, Lewisham High Road 62
Midway Place School, Bush Road, Rotherhithe New Road 65

SE8 [*continued*]

Ravensbourne School, Alleyn Road 77
Rotherhithe Nautical School, Bush Road, Rotherhithe New Road 65
St John's School, St John's Row, Deptford 88
St Joseph's Roman Catholic School, Deptford High Street 89
St Stephen's School, Albyn Road, Lewisham 98
South East London Secondary Technical School (Lower School), Creek Road 103
South East London Secondary Technical School (Upper School), Stanley Street 103
Stanley School, The, Mornington Road, Deptford 105
Trundley's Road or Lane School, Deptford 110
West Greenwich School, Albyn Road 114

SE9 Eltham

Alderwood School, Rainham Close, Avery Hill 12
Avery Hill Training College, Eltham 15
Babington House School, North Park 15
Crown Woods School, Riefield Road 33
Deansfield Road School, Rochester Way 34
Ealdham Square School, Ealdham Square, Eltham Green 36
Eltham Central School 38
Eltham Church of England School, Roper Street 38
Eltham College (The Royal Naval School) 38
Eltham Green Comprehensive School, Queenscroft Road 38
Eltham Hill School, Eltham Hill 38
Gordon School, Grange Hill Road 45
Greenacres School, Witherston Way 46
Haimo Road School, Westhorne Avenue 47
Henwick Road School, Well Hall Road 51
Middle Park School, Gregory Crescent 65
Moatbridge School, Eltham Palace Road 66
Montbelle School, Montbelle Road 66
Pope Street School, Foots Cray Road, New Eltham 74
Reay Central School, Hackford Road, Kennington 77
Roper Street School later Grange Hill Road 80
Ruxley Manor School, Milverton Way 81
St Mary's Roman Catholic School, Eltham High Street 93
St Thomas More Roman Catholic School, Appleton Road 99
Thomas Doggett School, Briset Road 108
Westhorne Manor School, Henwick Road 114
Wyborne School, Ivor Grove 118

SE10 Blackheath (part); Greenwich (part)

Blackheath Road School 19
Blackheath St John's School, Blackheath Road 19
Calvert Road School, Woolwich Road 23
Catherine House School, Greenwich 24
Christ Church School, Christchurch Street 27
Christ's College, Blackheath 28
Dreadnought ESN School, Tunnel Avenue 36
Glenister Road School, Blackwall Lane 44
Greenwich Central School, Catherine Grove 46
Greenwich Park Central School, King George Street 46
Greenwich Road Temporary School 46
Halstow Road School, Woolwich Road, Westcombe Park 48
Holy Trinity School, Blackheath Hill 53

SE10 [*continued*]

Marsh Lane School 64
Maze Hill School, Woodland Place, Trafalgar Road, Greenwich 64
Meridian School, Old Woolwich Road 65
Old Woolwich Road or Trafalgar Road School 71
Randall Place School, Roan Street 77
Riverway Secondary School, Blackwall Lane 79
Roan School, Devonshire Drive, Greenwich 79
Royal Hill School 81
St Alfege with St Peter, Creek Road 81
St Ann's Roman Catholic School, Croom's Hill 82
St Joseph's Roman Catholic School, Pelton Road, Greenwich 89
St Peter's School, Bridge Street 97
St Ursula's Convent School, Crooms Hill, Greenwich 99
West Greenwich School, Blackheath Road 114

SE11 Kennington; Lambeth (part)

Archbishop Sumner's School, Reedworth Street, Kennington Road 13
Archbishop Tenison's Grammar School, Kennington Oval 14
Borough Beaufoy School, Black Prince Road 19
Charlotte Sharman School, West Square 25
Henry Fawcett School, Clayton Street, Kennington 50
Kennington Oval School, Harleyford Road 57
Kennington Road School, Kennington Park 57
Licensed Victuallers' School, Upper Kennington Lane, Lambeth 61
Lollard Street School, Lambeth 61
St Agnes Church of England School, Farmers Road, Kennington Park 81
St Ann's Roman Catholic School, Kennington Lane 82
St Barnabas' School, Kennington 83
St James School, Regency Place, Kennington 87
St Mark's School, Harleyford Road, Kennington 91
St Mary Newington School, Newington Butts 92
St Mary's School, Princes Road 93
St Mary the Less School, Sancroft Street, Kennington 93
St Peter's School, Gye Street, Vauxhall 97
St Peter's School, St Oswald's Place, Kennington Lane 97
St Phillip's School, Reedworth Street, Kennington 98
St Saviour Salamanca School, Rendall Row, Vauxhall Walk 98
South London Technical Art School, Kennington Park Road 104
Southwark Central School, West Square 104
Upper Kennington Lane School 111
Vauxhall Street School, Kennington Lane 111
Walnut Tree Walk School, Kennington Road 112
West Square Secondary School, St George's Road 115

SE12 Lewisham (part)

Baring Road School, Lewisham 16
Burnt Ash Hill School 22
Colfe's Grammar School, Horn Park Lane, Lewisham 30
Cooper's Lane School, Grove Park 31
Grove Park Secondary School, Coopers Lane, Lewisham 46
Horn Park School, Alnwick Road 54
Marvels Lane School, Grove Park 64
Northbrook Church of England School, Hedgley Street 69
Riverston School, Eltham Road, Lee 79

SE12 [*continued*]

St Winifred's Roman Catholic School, Effingham Road 99
Wingfield School, Weigall Road 116

SE13 Hither Green; Lee; Lewisham (part)

Boone Street British School, Lewisham 19
Colfe's Grammar School, Granville Park 30
Ennersdale School, The, Leahurst Road, Lewisham 39
Hither Green School, Beacon Road 52
Kent Road School, Lewisham 58
Lee Church of England School, Lee Church Street 61
Lee Manor School, Leahurst Road 61
Lewisham Bridge School, Elmira Road 61
Manor Lane School, Leahurst Road 63
St Mary's Church of England School, High Street 92
St Saviour's Roman Catholic School, High Street 98
St Stephen's Church of England School, Jerrard Street 98
St Theresa's Roman Catholic School, Belmont Hill 99

SE14 Deptford; Hatcham; New Cross

Addey and Stanhope School, New Cross Road 11
Childeric Road School, Clifton Rise, New Cross 27
Christopher Marlowe School, Angus Street and Monson Road 28
Clifton Hill School, New Cross 30
Cold Blow Lane School, New Cross 30
Haberdashers' Aske's Boys' School 47
Haberdashers' Aske's Hatcham College, Pepys Road, New Cross 47
Haberdashers' Aske's Girls' School, Jerningham Road 47
Kender Street School, New Cross Road, Deptford 57
Monson Road School, New Cross Road 66
New Cross Sunday School 68
Nynhead Street School 70
St James School, New Cross Road, Hatcham 87
Waller Road School, Queens Road 112

SE15 Nunhead; Peckham

Adys Road School, Peckham 11
Arthur Street School, Old Kent Road 14
Asylum Road School, Peckham 14
Bellenden Road School, Camberwell 17
Bird in Bush Road School, Peckham 18
Camden Church of England School, Sumner Road 23
Camelot Street School, Peckham 23
Canterbury Road School, Old Kent Road 24
Cator Street School, Peckham 24
Choumert Road School, Peckham 27
Colls Road School, Peckham 30
Deptford Men's Institute, Queens Road 35
Hatcham School, Old Kent Road 49
Hollydale Road School, Nunhead 52
Ivydale Road School, Nunhead 55
John Donne School, Woods Road 56
Leo Street School, Asylum Road, Peckham 61
Lomond Grove School, Camberwell Road 62

SE15 [*continued*]

Lyndhurst Grove School 62
Meeting House Lane School (ESN), Peckham High Street 65
Nunhead Passage School 70
Peckham Central School, Choumert Road 73
Peckham Central School, Peckham Road 73
Peckham Park School, Friary Road, Peckham 73
Peckham Rye School, Whorlton Road 73
Peckham Secondary School 73
Peckham Wesleyan School. 73
Queens Road Wesleyan Methodist Sunday School 77
Reddins Road School, Glengall Road 78
St Francis' Roman Catholic School, Friary Road, Peckham 85
St John and St Clement's School, East Dulwich 87
St Luke and Camden School, Sumner Road 90
St Mary Magdalene School, Godman Road, Peckham 92
Stafford Street Wesleyan Methodist Sunday School 105
Sumner Road School, Peckham 107
Thomas Calton School, Choumert Road 108
Victoria Road Special School, Peckham High Street 112
Woods Road School, Harders Road, Queens Road 118

SE16 Bermondsey (part); Rotherhithe

Albion Street School, Lower Road, Rotherhithe 11
Alma Junior School, Alexis Street 13
Alma Senior School, Southwark Park Road 13
Aylwin School, The, Southwark Park Road, Bermondsey 15
Christ Church School, Jamaica Road, Rotherhithe 28
Clarence Street School, Rotherhithe 29
Credon Road School, Rotherhithe New Road 32
East Lane School, Bermondsey 37
Farncombe Street School 40
Galley Wall Road School, Rotherhithe New Road 43
Green School, Canon Beck Road, Brunel Road, Rotherhithe 46
Ilderton Road School, Rotherhithe New Road 55
Keeton's Road School, Rotherhithe 57
Peter Hills School, St Marychurch Street, Rotherhithe 73
Redriff School, Rotherhithe Street 78
Riverside School, Farncombe Street, Rotherhithe 79
Rotherhithe Charity School 80
Rotherhithe New Road School 80
St Barnabas Gomm School, Plough Road 83
St James Church of England School, Thurland Road, Rotherhithe 86
St Joseph's Roman Catholic School, Paradise Street, Jamaica Road, Rotherhithe 89
St Mary's Church of England School, Lower Road, Rotherhithe 92
St Paul's School, Rotherhithe Street 96
Scott Lidgett School, Drummond Road 100
Silwood Street School, Rotherhithe 102
Southwark Park School, Rotherhithe 104
Southwark Park Wesleyan Methodist School, Rotherhithe 104
Suffolk Grove School, Rotherhithe New Road 107
United Society School, Rotherhithe 110

LONDON SCHOOLS BY POSTAL DISTRICT

SE17 Camberwell (part); Walworth (part)

Albany Road School, Camberwell 11
All Saints School, East Street, Walworth 12
Boundary Lane School, Camberwell 20
Crampton Street School, Newington Butts 32
English Martyrs Roman Catholic School, Northampton Place 39
Faunce Street School, Harmsworth Street 40
Flint Street School, East Street, Walworth 41
Hemp Row Temporary School 50
Heygate Street (South London Jewish) School, Walworth Road 51
Horsley Street School 54
Keyworth School, Faunce Street 58
King and Queen Street School, Walworth 58
Michael Faraday School, Faraday Street, Portland Street 65
Mina Road School 66
Nelson Street School, Trafalgar Street, Walworth 68
Penrose School 73
Robert Browning School, King and Queen Street 79
St Alban's Church of England School, Manor Place, Walworth 81
St John's School, Larcom Street, Walworth 88
St Paul's School, Surrey Gardens, Walworth 96
St Paul's School, Sutherland Square 96
St Peter's School, Liverpool Grove, Walworth 97
Sandford Row School, Walworth 100
Sayer Street School 100
South Lambeth Jewish School, Walworth 104
Surrey Square School 107
Townsend School, Old Kent Road 109
Victory Place School, Rodney Road, Walworth 112
Walworth Central School, Mina Road, Old Kent Road 112
Walworth Road Baptist Sunday School 112

SE18 Plumstead; Woolwich (part)

All Saints' Church of England School, Herbert Road, Plumstead 12
Ancona Road School, Brewery Road 13
Beresford Street School, Walworth 17
Bloomfield Road School, Sandy Hill Road 19
Burrage Grove School 23
Christ Church School, Shooter's Hill 27
Conway Road School, Lakedale Road 31
Earl Rise School, Earl Rise 36
Earl Street School, Brewery Road 36
Eglington Road School, Herbert Road 37
Fox Hill School, Plumstead Common Road 41
Gallions Mount School, Plumstead High Street 43
Griffin Manor School, Plumstead High Street 46
Hawthorn Cottage School, Welton Road 50
High Street School, Plumstead High Street 51
King's Warren School, The, Old Mill Road, Plumstead Common 59
Mulgrave Place Myopic School, Wellington Street 67
Notre Dame Convent Commercial School for Girls, Eglinton Road, Plumstead 70
Plum Lane School, Plumstead Common 74
Plumstead Central School, Plumstead High Street 74
Plumstead Road School, High Street 74
Powis Street School 75
Purrett Road School, Plumstead High Street 76

LONDON SCHOOLS BY POSTAL DISTRICT

SE18 [*continued*]

Robert Street School, Upper Earl Street, Plumstead 79
Rockliffe Manor School, Bassant Road 79
Rose Cottage School, Welton Road 80
St Margaret's Church of England School, St Margaret's Grove, Plumstead 90
St Mary's School, Kingsmead Street 93
St Michael's and All Angels' Church of England School, Borgard Road 94
St Patrick's Roman Catholic School, Griffin Road 95
St Peter's Roman Catholic School, New Road 97
St Thomas Church of England School, Sand Street 99
Shooter's Hill Church of England School, Red Lion Lane 102
Slade School, Plumstead Common Road 103
Timbercroft School, Flaxton Road 108
Union Street School, Beresford Street 110
Vicarage Road 111
Wood Street School, Woolwich 118
Woodhill School, Woodhill 117
Woolwich Central School, Plumstead Common Road 118
Woolwich Polytechnic, Wellington Street 118
Woolwich Pupil Teachers, Maxey Road, Plumstead 118
Woolwich St Mary Church of England School, Kingsman Street, Church Street 118

SE19 Upper Norwood

Paxton School, Woodland Road 73
Westlow Hill Temporary School 115
Woodland Road School, Westow Hill, Upper Norwood 117

SE21 Dulwich

Brightlands Preparatory School, Dulwich Common 21
Dulwich Church of England Infants School, Turney Road, Dulwich Village 36
Dulwich College, College Road 36
Dulwich College Preparatory School, Alleyn Park 36
Dulwich Hamlet School 36
Dulwich Road Methodist Sunday School 36
Langbourne School, Lyall Avenue 59
Oakfield Preparatory School, Thurlow Park Road, Dulwich 70
Rosemead Preparatory School, Thurlow Park Road 80
Rosendale Road School, Turney Road 80
Turney Road School, Turney Road 110

SE22 East Dulwich; Peckham Rye

Alleyn's School, Townley Road, East Dulwich 12
Dulwich Central School, Peckham Rye 36
Friern School, The, Peckham Rye 42
Goodrich Road School, Lordship Lane 45
Grove Vale School, East Dulwich 47
Heber Road School, Lordship Lane 50
Honor Oak School, Homestall Road 54
James Allen's Girls' School, East Dulwich Grove 55
St Anthony's Roman Catholic School, Lordship Lane, East Dulwich 83
St John's National School, East Dulwich 88

LONDON SCHOOLS BY POSTAL DISTRICT

SE23 Brockley; Forest Hill

Brent Knoll School, Mayow Road 20
Christ Church School, Forest Hill 27
Dalmain Road School, Brockley Rise, Forest Hill 33
Fairlawn School, Honor Oak Road 40
Forest Hill Central School, Brockley Rise 41
Kilmorie Road School, Forest Hill 58
Roger Manwood School, Brockley Rise and Kilmorie Road 79
St Francesca Cabrini Roman Catholic School, Honor Oak Park 85
Stafford College, Forest Hill 105
Stillness Road School, Brockley Rise 106

SE24 Herne Hill

Jessop Road School, Milkwood Road, Herne Hill 56
St Jude's Church of England School, Railton Road, Herne Hill 89
St Saviour Church of England School, Herne Hill Road 98
William Penn School, Red Post Hill 116

SE26 Sydenham

Adamsrill Road School 11
Bell Green Church of England School, Champion Road 17
Dartmouth Road School 34
Eliot Bank School, Thorpewood Avenue 37
Hall School, The, Sydenham 48
Haseltine Road School, Bell Green, Lower Sydenham 49
Kelvin Grove School, Kirkdale, Sydenham 57
Our Lady and St Philip Neri School, Sydenham Road 71
St Bartholomew School, The Peak, Sydenham 83
St Michael's School, Champion Road, Sydenham 94
St Philip's Roman Catholic School, Sydenham Road 97
St Philip's School, Wells Park Road, Upper Sydenham 97
Shackleton Secondary School 101
Sydenham Central School 107
Sydenham Church of England School, Kirkdale 107
Sydenham County Secondary School, Dartmouth Road 107
Sydenham High School, Westwood Hill 107
Sydenham Hill Road School 107

SE27 West Norwood

Eden Road Methodist School, Chapel Road, West Norwood 37
Elm Court School 38
Elm Wood Primary School, Carnac Street 38
Gipsy Road School, West Norwood 44
Grove House School, Elmcourt Road 46
Jewish Orphanage, Knight's Hill 56
John Wesley School 57
Kingswood Primary School, Gypsy Road 59
Norwood School or Norwood Park School, Gypsy Road 70
Salter's Hill School, West Norwood 99
St Luke's School, Elder Road, West Norwood 90
Wesleyan Day School, Lower Norwood 114
West Norwood Central School, Carnac Street, Gipsy Road 115
Wood Vale School, Elder Road 118

LONDON SCHOOLS BY POSTAL DISTRICT

SW1 Westminster (part)

Buckingham Gate Central School, Wilfred Street 22
Christ Church School, Palmer Street 27
Churchill Gardens School, Ranelagh Road 28
Commercial School, Regent Street 31
Ebury Secondary School 37
Francis Holland School, Graham Terrace 42
Garden House School, Sloane Gardens 43
Greencoat Hospital School, Westminster 46
Grey Coat Hospital Girls' Day School, Grey Coat Place, Westminster 46
Hellenic College of London, Pont Street 50
Holy Trinity School, Russell Place, Westminster 53
Holy Trinity School, Sedding Street 53
Horseferry Road School 54
Marlborough Road School 64
Millbank School, Erasmus Street, Millbank Estate 66
More House School, Pont Street 67
Pimlico School, Lupus Street 74
Preparatory School, Sloane Street 75
Ranelagh Road School, Pimlico 77
St Barnabas School, Ebury Street, Pimlico 83
St Gabriel's School, Glasgow Terrace, Pimlico 85
St George's Row School 85
St James the Less Church of England Primary School, Thorndike Street, Westminster 87
St Margaret's Church of England School, Dean Farrar Street 90
St Mary's School, Hide Place, Vincent Square 93
St Matthew's School, Old Pye Street or Victoria Street 94
St Michael's School, Ebury Square, Pimlico 95
St Paul's School, Westbourne Street, Pimlico 97
St Paul's School, Wilton Place 96
St Peter's Church of England School, Lower Belgrave Street 97
St Vincent's Roman Catholic School, Carlisle Place, Victoria Street 99
Sussex House, Cadogan Gardens 107
Warwick Primary School, Ranelagh Road, St George Westminster 113
Warwick Senior School, Buckingham Palace Road, St George Westminster 113
Wesleyan College, Horseferry Road 114
Westminster Abbey Choir School, Deans Yard 115
Westminster Cathedral Choir School, Ambrosden Avenue 115
Westminster Cathedral Roman Catholic School, Great Smith Street 115
Westminster City School, Palace Street, Westminster 115
Westminster Day Continuation School 115
Westminster National Free School 115
Westminster School (St Peter's College), Dean's Yard 115
Westminster Technical Institute, Vincent Square 115
Westminster Under School, Vincent Square 115
Westminster United Schools 115
Westminster Wesleyan Practising School 115

SW2 Brixton; Tulse Hill

Ashby Mill School, Prague Place, Brixton 14
Aspen House School, Christchurch Road 14
Brixton Parish Church School, Water Lane 21
Brockwell School, Tulse Hill 21
Christ Church School, Christchurch Road, Streatham Hill 27
Corpus Christi Roman Catholic School, Trent Road, Brixton Hill 32
Dick Sheppard School, Tulse Hill 35

149

LONDON SCHOOLS BY POSTAL DISTRICT

SW2 [*continued*]

Effra Parade School, Barnwell Road, Brixton 37
Fenstanton School, Abbot's Park, Tulse Hill 40
Holmewood School, Upper Tulse Hill 52
Holy Trinity School, Upper Tooting 53
Holy Trinity School, Upper Tulse Hill 53
Lyham Road School, Lambeth 62
Montrose College, Streatham Hill 66
New Park Road School, Brixton Hill 68
Parkside School, Bartley Road, Lambeth. 72
Richard Atkins School, Kingswood Road 78
St Martin in the Fields High School, Tulse Hill 91
Somerville School, Wavertree Road 103
Sternold College, Sternhold Avenue 106
Strand School (King's College), Elm Park, Brixton Hill 106
Streatham Hill and Clapham High School, Abbotswood Road, SW16 or Wavertree Road 106
Sudbourne Road School, Hayter Road, Brixton Hill 107
Trinity Church of England School, Upper Tulse Hill School 110
Tulse Hill School, Upper Tulse Hill 110

SW3 Chelsea

Cameron House, The Vale, Chelsea 23
Chelsea Central Secondary School, Glebe Place 26
Chelsea Polytechnic, Manresa Road 26
Christ Church School, Royal Hospital Road, Chelsea 28
Cook's Ground School, Glebe Place, Kings Road 31
Draycott Avenue School 36
Holy Trinity School, Cadogan Gardens 53
Kingsley Secondary School 58
Marlborough School, Draycott Avenue 64
Oratory Roman Catholic Central Schools, Stewart's Grove 71
Oratory Roman Catholic School, Bury Street 71
Oratory Roman Catholic School, Ixworth Place 71
St Joseph's Roman Catholic School, Cadogan Street 89
St Luke's School, St Luke's Street, Chelsea 90
St Mark's College School, Chelsea 90
South Western Polytechnic Day School, Manresa Road, Chelsea 105
Walton Street School, Upper Chelsea 112

SW4 Clapham

Allen Edwards School, Studley Road 12
Aristotle Road Secondary School, Clapham High Street 14
Bonneville Road School, Cavendish Road, Clapham 19
City of London Freemen's School, Ferndale Road, Brixton 29
Clapham Central School, Aristotle Road 29
Clapham Church Girls School, Rectory Grove 29
Clapham Manor School, Stonhouse Street 29
Clapham Park School, King's Avenue 29
Clapham Parochial School, Macaulay Road 29
Clapham School 29
Clapham School of Art, Edgley Road 29
Glenbrook School, Clarence Avenue 44
Haselrigge Road School, Clapham 49
Henry Thornton School, South Side, Clapham Common 50
King's Acre School, King's Avenue 58

SW4 [*continued*]

Larkhall Lane School, Union Street, Clapham 60
Macaulay School, Victoria Rise 62
Manor House School, Clapham 63
Marianne Thornton School, Clapham Common West Side 63
St Gerard's Roman Catholic School, Clapham Common 86
St John's Church of England (Bowyer) School, Gaskell Street, Larkhall Lane 88
St Mary's Roman Catholic Girls and Infants School, Crescent Lane 93
St Mary's Roman Catholic Junior Boys School, St Alphonsus Road, Clapham 93
St Mary's Roman Catholic Secondary School, South Side 93
St Paul's School, Clapham 96
Santley Street School, Ferndale Road 100
Springwell House Open Air School, Clapham Common North Side 105
Stonhouse Street School, Clapham High Street 106
Stowey Open Air School, South Side, Clapham 106
Wix's Lane School, Clapham Common, North Side 117

SW5 Kensington (part)

Holy Family School, West Cromwell Road 53
Holy Trinity School, West Cromwell Road 53
St Cuthbert with St Matthias, Warwick Road 84
St Matthias' Church of England School, Warwick Road 94

SW6 Fulham

Ackmar Road School 11
All Saints' School, Fulham High Street 12
Ashington Road Roman Catholic School, Ashington Road, New Kings Road 14
Barclay Hall School, Effie Road 16
Beaufort House School, Lillie Road 17
Biscay Road School, Biscay Road 18
Bishop's Park Secondary School, Finlay Street 18
Burne-Jones ESN Secondary School, Hugon Road 22
Chelsea Central Secondary School, Townmead Road School 26
Chelsea Secondary School, Bagleys Lane, New Kings Road 26
Childerley Street School, Childerley Street 27
Elizabethan Free School, Daisy Lane, Broomhouse Lane 37
Everington Street School 39
Finlay Street Reformatory School, Fulham 40
Finlay Street School, Fulham Palace Road 40
Fulham Central School, Childerley Street 42
Fulham County Secondary School, Munster Road 42
Fulham Day Sanatorium, New Kings Road 42
Gilliatt School, Finlay Street 44
Granville Sharp School, Fulham High Street 45
Halford Road School, North End Road 48
Harwood Road School, Brittania Road 49
Henry Compton School, Kingswood Road 50
Holman Hunt School, New Kings Road 52
Holy Cross Roman Catholic School, Ashington Road 52
Hugon Road School, Hugon Road 54
Hurlingham School, Peterborough Road 55
Kingwood Road School, Fulham Palace Road 59
Lady Margaret School, Parsons Green 59
Lancaster Road School, Wandsworth Bridge Road 59
Langford Road School, Wandsworth Bridge Road 59

SW6 [*continued*]

Lillie Road School 61
London Oratory Roman Catholic School, Seagrave Road 62
Macmurdo Road School, Lysia Street 62
Marist Convent School, Fulham Road 63
Munster Road School, Fulham Road 67
New Kings Road School 68
New Kings School, New Kings Road 68
North End Road School, Lillie Road 69
Parsons Green School, Ackmar Road 73
Peterborough School, Clancarty Road 73
Queen's Manor School, Lysia Street 76
Queensmill Road School, Fulham Palace Road 77
Rosaline Road School, Fulham 80
Rosemount School, New Kings Road 80
St John's Church of England School, Dawes Road 88
St Mark's Church of England School, Bishops Avenue 90
St Thomas' Roman Catholic School, Dawes Road 99
Sherbrooke Road School, Dawes Road 101
Sir John Lillie School, Lillie Road 102
Star Road School 105
Sulivan School, Peterborough Road 107
Townmead Road School, Fulham 109
Varna Hall School 111
Wedgewood School, Bagleys Lane 113
West London Emergency School for Girls, Fulham Cross, Munster Road 114

SW7 Kensington (part)

Brompton National School, Churchyard and Montpelier Street 21
Central School of Speech Training and Dramatic Art, Kensington Gore 25
City and Guilds of London Institute, Exhibition Road 28
Colville School, Kensington 31
Falkner House, Brechin Place 40
Glendower Preparatory School, Queen's Gate 44
Gloucester Grove School, Clareville Street 45
Hampshire School, The, Ennismore Gardens 48
Mander Portman Woodward, Elvaston Place 63
Preparatory School, Queen's Gate, Kensington 75
Queen's Gardens School 76
Royal College of Art, Exhibition Road 80
Royal College of Music, Prince Consort Road 80
Royal School of Needlework, Exhibition Road 81
St James Independent Junior School for Boys, Queen's Gate 86
South Kensington Preparatory School, Rosary Gardens, Kensington 104
Swedish Institute, Cromwell Road 107

SW8 Battersea; Kennington (part); Lambeth (part)

Ashmole School, Kennington 14
Bradmede School, Wandsworth Road 20
Christ Church School, Union Grove, Clapham 28
Church Street School, Clapham Road 28
Claylands Road School 29
Eldon School, Wandsworth Road 37
Fountain Street School, Wandsworth Road, Lambeth 41
Heathbrook School, St Rule Street, Clapham 50

SW8 [*continued*]

Lansdowne School 59
Linden Lodge School, Battersea 61
New Road School, Thessaly Road, Wandsworth Road 68
Newton Preparatory School, Battersea Park Road 68
Notre Dame School, Battersea Park Road 70
Our Lady of The Angels Roman Catholic School, Nine Elms Lane 71
Ponton Road School, Battersea 74
Priory Grove School, Wandsworth 75
Raywood Street School, Battersea 77
St George's School, Thessaly Road 85
St Joseph's Roman Catholic School, Battersea Park Road 89
St Stephen's School, Dorset Road, Kennington 98
Sir James Barrie School, Stewarts Road 102
Sleaford Street School, Battersea Park Road 103
South Lambeth Road School, Kennington 104
Southlands Practising Wesleyan School, Battersea 104
Southlands School, Battersea 104
Springfield School, Crimsworth Road 105
Tennyson Street School, Battersea 108
Vauxhall Central School, Lawn Lane 111
Wandsworth Road School 112
Wyvil Primary School, Wyvil Road 118

SW9 Brixton (part); Kennington (part)

Akerman Road School, Brixton 11
Brixton Central School, Durand Gardens, Kennington 21
Caldwell Primary School, Caldwell Street 23
Charles Edward Brooke School for Girls, Langton Road 25
Christ Church School, Cancell Road, Brixton 27
Clapham Trade School, Clapham Road 29
Cowley School, Cowley Road, Kennington 32
Durand Primary School, Hackford Road 36
Hackford Road School, Russell Street 47
Hill Mead School, Sussex Road 52
Lingham Street Church of England School, Lambeth 61
Loughborough Central School, Minet Road, Loughborough Road 62
St Andrew's Stockwell Church of England School, Lingham Street 82
St John's College, Angell Road, Brixton 88
St John's School, Canterbury Road, Brixton 88
St Michael's Church of England School, Halstead Street, Stockwell 94
Stockwell College, Brixton 106
Stockwell Road School, Lambeth 106
Stockwell School, Lingham Street, Brixton 106
Stuart School, Sussex Road, Coldharbour Lane 107
Sussex Road School, Coldharbour Lane 107

SW10 Chelsea (part)

Ashburnham School, Upcerne Road, Kings Road 14
Carlyle Girls School, Hortensia Road 24
Chelsea Central Secondary School, Upcerne Road 26
Hortensia Road School 54
John Griffiths Roman Catholic School, Prince's Way 56
Parayhouse School, King's Road 72
Park Chapel School, Chelsea 72

SW10 [*continued*]

Park Walk Primary School, Kings Road 72
Redcliffe School, Redcliffe Gardens 78
St Mark's Practising School, Fulham Road 90
St Mary Boltons' Church of England School, Gilston Road 91
Servite Roman Catholic School, Winterton Place 101
Sloane School, Hortensia Road 103

SW11 Battersea (part); Clapham (part)

Basnett Road School, Lavender Hill 16
Battersea Central School, Bridge Lane 16
Battersea Grammar School, St John's Hill, or Abbotswood Road 16
Battersea Park Road School 16
Battersea St Mary's Parochial School, Vicarage Crescent 16
Belleville Road School, Clapham 17
Bolingbroke Road School, Battersea 19
Burns Road School, Battersea 22
Chesterton Primary School, Battersea 26
Christ Church School, Este Road, Battersea 27
Clapham College, Nightingale Lane 29
Clapham County School, Broomwood Road 29
County Secondary School, The, Brownswood Road, Clapham 32
Emanuel School, Battersea Rise, Wandsworth Common 38
Ethelburga Street School, Battersea Bridge Road 39
Falconbrook School 40
Gideon Road School, Battersea 44
High View School, Plough Road 51
Holden Street School, Greyshott Street, Lavender Hill 52
Honeywell Road School, Wandsworth Common 54
John Burgess School, Surrey Lane, Battersea 56
John Burns School, Hanbury Road 56
Joseph Tritton School, Wynter Street 57
Latchmere School, Battersea Park Road 60
Lavender Hill School, Amies Street 60
Mantua Street School, York Road, Clapham Junction 63
Northcote Lodge School, Bolingbroke Grove 69
Old Battersea Roman Catholic School, Trott Street 70
Overhill School 72
Plough Road School, St John's Hill, Clapham Junction 74
St John's School, Usk Road 88
St Mark's School, Battersea Rise 91
St Mary's Parochial School, Vicarage Crescent, Battersea 92
St Mary's Roman Catholic School, Prince of Wales Drive, Battersea Park 93
St Peter's Church of England School, Plough Road, Battersea 97
Salesian College, Surrey Lane 99
Shaftesbury Park School, Ashbury Road 101
Shillington Street School, Falcon Road, Battersea 101
Sir Walter St.John's School, Battersea High Street 102
Surrey Lane School, Battersea 107
Thomas's Preparatory School, Battersea High Street 108
Wandsworth and Battersea Evening Institute formerly Ethelburga Street 112
William Blake School, Bridge Lane 116
Winstanley Road School, Clapham Junction 117
Wycliffe Special School, Wycliffe Road, Battersea 118

LONDON SCHOOLS BY POSTAL DISTRICT

SW12 Balham

Balham Central School later Balham School, Hearnville Road 15
Balham High School, Bedford Hill 15
Balham St Mary's Church of England Primary School, Balham High Road 15
Broomwood Hall School, Nightingale Lane 22
Cavendish Road School, Hydethorpe Road, Clapham 25
Elmfield School, Tooting 38
Hearnville Road School, Chestnut Grove, Balham 50
Henry Cavendish Primary School, Hydethorpe Road, Balham 50
Holy Ghost School, Endlesham Road, Balham 68
Hyde Farm School, Telferscot Road 55
La Retraite High School, Atkins Road 60
Nightingale Square Roman Catholic School, Endlesham Road, Balham 68
Oak Lodge, Nightingale Lane 70
Oldridge Road School, Balham 71
Ravenstone School, Balham High Road 77
St Bede's Roman Catholic Infants' School, Thornton Road 83
St Bernardette Roman Catholic School, Cavendish Road 83
St Mary's Church of England School, Balham High Road 92
Telferscot Road School, Emanuel Road, Clapham 108

SW15 Putney; Roehampton; Wandsworth (part)

All Saints' School, Lower Common, Wandsworth 12
Baptist Women's Training College, Carlton Drive 16
Beavers' Holt School, Stag Lane 17
Brandlehow School, Putney Bridge Road 20
Chartfield School, St Margaret's Crescent 26
Clark's College, Upper Richmond Road 29
Cromwell High School, Putney Bridge Road, Putney 33
Danebury School, Danebury Avenue 34
Deodar Road Temporary School, Putney 35
Ebley House School, Manfred Road 37
Glengyle School, Carlton Drive 44
Granard School, Granard Avenue 45
Heathmere School, Alton Road 50
Hotham Road School, Charlwood Road, Putney 54
Huntingfield Road School, Roehampton 54
Ibstock Place - The Froebel School, Clarence Lane, Roehampton 55
Meyfield School, West Hill 64
Our Lady of Victories Roman Catholic School, Clarendon Drive 72
Prospect House School, Putney Hill 76
Putney Church of England School, Lower Common and Felsham Road 76
Putney County Secondary School, Mayfield, West Hill 76
Putney High School, Putney Hill 76
Putney Park School, Woodborough Road 76
Putney Roman Catholic School, Clarendon Road 76
Putney School of Art, Oxford Road 76
Roehampton Gate School, Danebury Avenue 79
Roehampton Parochial School, Putney Heath West 79
Sacred Heart Roman Catholic School, Roehampton Lane 81
St Mary School, Felsham Road, Putney 92
Whitelands College, West Hill 116
Willington School, Colinette Road 117

LONDON SCHOOLS BY POSTAL DISTRICT

SW16 Streatham

Bishop Thomas Grant Roman Catholic School, Belltrees Grove 18
Crown Lane School, Crown Lane 33
Dunraven School, Adare Walk, Streatham 36
Eardley Road School, Blegborough Road, Streatham 36
Estreham School, Streatham 39
Granton Road School, Streatham Vale 45
Hitherfield Road School, Streatham 52
Immanuel Church of England Primary School, Factory Square, Streatham Common 55
Julians School, Leigham Court Road 57
Lexden House School, Heybridge Avenue, Streatham 61
Mitcham Lane School, Penwortham Road, Streatham 66
Modern School, Streatham High Road 66
Penwortham School, Penwortham Road 73
St Andrew's Roman Catholic School, Polworth Road, Hopton Road, Streatham 82
St Andrew's School, Colmer Road, Wandsworth 82
St Helen's School, North Side, Streatham Common 86
St Leonard's Church of England School, Mitcham Lane 90
Streatham Grammar School, Mitcham Lane 106
Streatham Kindergarten, Pinfold Road 106
Streatham National School 106
Streatham School, Streatham Common 107
Streatham Subscribers' School 107
Sunnyhill Road School, Streatham High Road 107
Woodmansterne School, Streatham Vale 118

SW17 Tooting

Balham and Tooting College of Commerce, Tooting Broadway 15
Balham Grammar School, Balham High Road 15
Bec School, Beachcroft Road, Tooting 17
Broadwater School, Gatton Road, Upper Tooting Road 21
Cotswold School, Franciscan Road 32
Defoe School, Broadwater Road 34
Derinton Road School, Tooting 35
Ensham Central School, Franciscan Road, Tooting 39
Finton House School, Trinity Road 41
Fircroft Road School, Glenburnie Road, Tooting 41
Franciscan Road School, Tooting 42
Furzedown College and School, Welham Road, Mitcham 43
Garratt Green School, Burntwood Lane 43
Graveney Secondary School, Gatton Road, Tooting 46
Hillbrook Secondary School, Upper Tooting 52
Hillcroft School, Beechcroft Road 52
Holy Family Convent High School, Tooting High Street 52
Miss Edge's School, Tooting Bec Gardens 66
Rosa Bassett School, Welham Road 80
St Anselm's Convent School, Tooting Bec Road 82
St Boniface Roman Catholic School, Undine Street 83
Sellincourt Road School, Tooting Graveney 100
Smallwood Road School, Garratt Lane 103
Streatham College, Streatham Common 106
Streatham County Secondary School, Welham Road, Mitcham Lane 106
Tooting Graveney School 109
Tooting High School, Upper Tooting 109
Tooting Roman Catholic School, Undine Street 109
Upper Tooting Church of England School, Trinity Road 111

LONDON SCHOOLS BY POSTAL DISTRICT

SW18 Putney (part); Wandsworth (part)

All Saints School, Putney Bridge Road 13
Allfarthing Lane School, St Anne's Crescent 12
Dunts Hill School, Earlsfield 36
Earlsfield School, Burntwood Lane 36
Elliott Central School, Merton Road, Putney 38
Eltringham Street School, York Road 38
Fountain Road School, Garratt Lane, Wandsworth 41
Frogmore School, Putney Bridge Road 42
Garratt Lane School, near Swaffield Road, Wandsworth 43
Gertrude Sanson Primary School 44
Greenmead Primary School, Littleton Street 46
Highfield School, Trinity Road 51
Lawn Lane School, South Lambeth Road 60
Littleton Street School, Littleton Street 61
Magdalen Road School, Wandsworth 63
Meadway School, Waldron Road 64
Merton Road School, Putney 65
Riversdale School, Merton Road, Southfields 79
Royal Victoria Patriotic School, Trinity Road 81
St Anne's National School, East Hill 82
St Faith's Church of England School, Alma Road, East Hill, Wandsworth 85
St Joseph's Roman Catholic School, Putney Bridge Road 89
St Michael's School, Granville Road, Southfields, Putney 95
St William of York Roman Catholic School, Eltringham Street 99
Sheringdale School, Standen Road 101
Southfields School, The, Wimbledon Park Road 104
Spencer Park School, Trinity Road 105
Swaffield Road School, Wandsworth Road 107
Waldron Road School, Tranmere Road 112
Wandle School, Earlsfield, Wandsworth 112
Wandsworth Central School, Allfarthing Lane, Wandsworth 112
Wandsworth Roman Catholic School, Wandsworth High Street 113
Wandsworth School, Sutherland Grove 113
Wandsworth Technical College, High Street 113
Wandsworth Technical Institute, High Street 113
Warple Way School, Wandsworth 113
West Hill School, Broomhill Road and Merton Road 114

SW19 Wimbledon Park

Albemarle School, Prince's Way 11
Allenswood School, Albert Drive 12
Burdett Coutts and Townsend Foundation, Rochester Street 22
Our Lady Queen of Heaven Roman Catholic School, Victoria Drive 72
Ronald Ross School, Beaumont Road 80
Southlands College, Wimbledon Park Side 104
Southmead School, Princes Way 104

W1 St Marylebone (part); St Pancras (part); Westminster (part)

All Saints' Church of England School, Margaret Street 12
All Souls School, Foley Street, Westminster 13
Barrett Street School, Duke Street, Oxford Street 16
Central Church of England School, High Street, Marylebone 25
Clipstone School, St Marylebone 30
College of Physical Education, Paddington Street 30

LONDON SCHOOLS BY POSTAL DISTRICT

W1 [*continued*]

Curzon Street School 33
Grays Yard School 46
Hampden Gurney with St Luke's Church of England School, Nutford Place 48
Homer Row Roman Catholic School, Crawford Street, St Marylebone 53
London College of Music, Great Marlborough Street 62
Marylebone Commercial Institute, New Cavendish Street 64
Pembridge Hall School, Pembridge Square 73
Poland Street School 74
Polytechnic School of Architecture, Regent Street 74
Polytechnic School of Art, Regent Street 74
Polytechnic School of Engineering, Regent Street 74
Polytechnic School of Photography, Regent Street 74
Polytechnic Secondary Boys School, Regent Street 74
Portland Town Church of England School, St Marylebone 75
Portland Town Roman Catholic School, Upper William Street, St Marylebone 75
Portman Chapel School 75
Pulteney Street School, Peter Street, Wardour Street 76
Queen's College, Harley Street 76
Regent Street School, St Marylebone 78
St Andrew's School, Wells Street 82
St Anne's School, Dean Street, Soho 82
St Anselm's School, Gilbert Street, St George Hanover Square 82
St Charles Roman Catholic School, Ogle Street, St Marylebone 84
St Edwards Roman Catholic School, Dufour's Place, Strand 85
St George Hanover Square School, South Street 85
St George's German Lutheran Church School, Cleveland Street, Fitzroy Square 85
St James and St Peter School, Great Windmill Street 86
St James Roman Catholic School, Marylebone Lane 86
St John Evangelist School, Tottenham Court Road, St Pancras 87
St Luke's School, Nutford Place 90
St Mary Bryanstone Square School, Enford Street 91
St Mary's College, Lancaster Gate 92
St Mary's School, Soho 93
St Mary's School, York Street 93
St Patrick's Roman Catholic School, Great Chapel Street, Soho 95
St Thomas's School, Picton Place, Duke Street 99
St Vincent's Roman Catholic School, Wigmore Street and Blandford Street 99
Soho Parochial School 103
Tenison's School, Leicester Square 108
Trinity College of Music, Manchester Square 110
Upper Marylebone School 111
Western Church of England School, York Street, Bryanston Square 114
Westminster Jews' Free School, Hanway Place 115
Whitfield Street School 116

W2 Bayswater; Paddington (part)

All Saints' Church of England School, Francis Street, Paddington 12
Bayswater Ragged School, Poplar Place, Moscow Road 17
Campbell Street School, Cuthbert Street, Maida Vale, Paddington 23
Cirencester Street Roman Catholic School 28
College Park Secondary School, Monmouth Road 30
Edward Wilson Primary School, Senior Street, Harrow Road 37
Hallfield Primary School, Porchester Gardens 48
High School for Boys, Westbourne Park Villas 51
Holy Trinity School, Bishops Bridge Road 53

W2 [*continued*]

Holy Trinity with St Paul School, Harrow Road 53
Our Lady of Dolours Roman Catholic School, Desborough Street, Paddington 71
Paddington Green School, Park Place Villas 72
Paddington Wharf School, Church Place 72
St James School, Craven Terrace, Hyde Park 86
St John School, Titchborne Row, Edgware Road 88
St Mary Magdalene's School, Harrow Road, Paddington 92
St Mary of the Angels Roman Catholic School, Westmoreland (later Moorhouse) Road 92
St Mary's School, Paddington Gardens, Paddington Green 93
St Matthew's School, Queensway, Bayswater 94
St Michael's Roman Catholic School, Westbourne Park 94
St Michael's School, Star Street, Edgware Road 95
St Paul's Unit, Waverley Terrace, Paddington 97
St Stephen's School, Westbourne Park Road 99
Sarah Siddons School, North Wharf Road 100
Senior Street School, Paddington 101
Trinity School, Harrow Road 110
Westbourne Church of England School, Great Western Road 114
Westmoreland Road Roman Catholic School, Bayswater 115

W4 Hammersmith (part)

Bedford Park High School, Priory Road 17
Chelsea Pupil Teachers, William Street, Hammersmith Road 26
Compton House School for Boys, Sutton Court Road 31

W6 Hammersmith (part)

Albion Road East School, Dalling Road 11
Brackenbury Road School, Goldhawk Road 20
Brook Green School 21
Bute House Preparatory School for Girls, Luxemburg Gardens 23
Captain Marryat Infant School, St Dunstan's Road 24
Colet Court, Hammersmith Road 30
Colet Girls' School, Brook Green 30
Dalling Road School, Dalling Road 33
Elizabeth Burgwin School, Cambridge Grove 38
Elwell's Academy, Hammersmith 38
Field Road School, Field Road 40
Flora Gardens School, Ravenscourt Park 41
Fulham Palace Road School 42
Fulham Primary School 43
Godolphin and Latymer Girls' School, Iffley Road 45
Godolphin Boys' School, Iffley Road 45
Godolphin School, Hammersmith 45
Haarlem Road Pupil Teachers School, Brook Green 47
Hammersmith Literary Institute, Brook Green 48
Hammersmith Road School, Hammersmith Road 48
Hammersmith Roman Catholic School for Girls, Hammersmith Road 48
John Betts School, Paddenswick Road 56
Larmenier Roman Catholic Infants' School, Great Church Lane 60
Latymer Upper School, King Street 60
Latymer's Endowed Foundation, Hammersmith Road 60
Lena Gardens School 61
Melcombe School, Fulham Palace Road 65
North Croft School, Shepherds Bush Road 69

LONDON SCHOOLS BY POSTAL DISTRICT

W6 [*continued*]

Paddenswick Road School, Goldhawk Road 72
Sacred Heart Roman Catholic School, Hammersmith Road 81
St Augustine's Roman Catholic School, Disbrowe Road 83
St Dunstan's Road School 84
St Edmund's Roman Catholic Secondary School, St Dunstan's Road 84
St Helen's Roman Catholic School, Brook Green, Hammersmith 86
St John Church of England School, Glenthorne Road, later Macbeth Street 87
St Joseph's Roman Catholic School, Brook Green 89
St Mark's Church of England School for Girls and Infants, St James Street 90
St Mary's Practising Roman Catholic School, Brook Green 93
St Paul's Church of England School, Queen Caroline Street 95
St Paul's Girls' Preparatory School and School for Girls, Brook Green 96, 97
St Paul's School, Hammersmith 96
St Peter's Church of England School, King Street 97
St Peter's Free Schools, Paddenswick Road 97
St Thomas' Roman Catholic Secondary School, St Dunstan's Road 99
Waterloo Street School, Macbeth Street 113
Waterside School, Macbeth Street 113
William Morris Academy, St Dunstan's Road 116

W8 Kensington (part)

Allen Street School, Kensington High Street 12
Campden Hill School, St George's, Edge Street 23
Cardinal Manning Roman Catholic School, Kensington 24
Elementary School of the Assumption, South End 37
Fox School, The, Edge Street, Church Street, Notting Hill Gate 41
Holland Park School, Campden Hill Road 52
Kensington High School, Upper Phillimore Gardens 57
Kensington Preparatory School, Holland Road, Kensington 57
Kensington Square Roman Catholic School, Ansdell Street 58
Lady Eden's School, Victoria Road 59
St Barnabas' and St Philip's Church of England School, Addison Road, Earls Court Road 83
St George's School, Edge Street 85
St Mary Abbot's School, Kensington High Street 91

W9 Paddington (part)

Amberley Road School, Harrow Road, Maida Hill 13
Bravington Road Special School, Paddington 20
Essendine Road School, Paddington 39
Franklin Delano Roosevelt School, Essendine Road 42
Harrow Road School 49
Kemble School, Amberley Road 57
London County Council Technical Institute Day Secondary School, Saltram Crescent, Paddington 62
Maryfields Primary School 64
Moberley School, Harrow Road 66
Paddington and Maida Vale High School, Elgin Avenue 72
Paddington School, Oakington Road 72
Paddington Technical Institute, Saltram Crescent 72
St George Roman Catholic School, Lanark Road 85
St Joseph Roman Catholic School, Lanark Road 89
St Luke Church of England School, Fernhead Road, West Kilburn 90
St Peter's Church of England School, Chippenham Road or Goldney Road, Paddington 97
St Saviour's Junior Mixed School, Shirland Road 98
Saltram Crescent High School, Kilburn 100

LONDON SCHOOLS BY POSTAL DISTRICT

W10 Kensal Green; Kensington (part); Ladbroke Grove; Paddington

Barlby Road School, Ladbroke Grove 16
Beethoven Street School, Queens Park, Paddington 17
Bevington Road School, Kensington 18
Branston Street School 20
Brunel Secondary School, Kensal Road 22
Convent of Mercy School, Hazlewood Crescent 31
Droop Street School 36
Kensal House School, Paddington 57
Kilburn Lane School, Kensal Green 58
Ladbroke School, Upper School in Lancaster Road, W11; Lower School in St Marks Road 59
Latimer Road School, Notting Hill, North Kensington 60
Middle Row School, Kensal New Town 65
North Kensington Central School, St Marks Road, St Charles Square 69
North Paddington Central School, Kilburn Lane, Kensal Green 69
Oxford Gardens School, Ladbroke Grove 72
Queen's Park Primary School, Droop Street 77
St Andrew's and St Philip's School, Bosworth Road and Appleford Road 82
St Charles Roman Catholic School, St Charles Square 84
St Francis Roman Catholic School, Silchester Road, Kensington 85
St Helen's Church of England School, Latimer Road 86
St John Kensal Green School 87
St Mary's Roman Catholic School, East Row 93
St Quintin Park School 98
St Thomas School, Bosworth Road and Appleford Road 99
Thomas Jones School, Latimer Road 108
Wilberforce School, Kilburn Lane, Paddington 116
Wornington Road School, Golborne Road 118

W11 Kensington (part); Notting Hill

Avondale Park School, Sirdar Road, Notting Hill 15
Bayswater Jewish School, Lancaster Road 17
Buckingham Terrace School, Lonsdale Road, Portobello Road 22
Campden Institute of Home Training, Lancaster Road 23
Isaac Newton School (Secondary School), Lancaster Road, W10 55
Isaac Newton School (Upper School), Wornington Road, W10 55
Kensington School of Music, High Street, Notting Hill Gate 58
Linton House School, Holland Park Avenue, Notting Hill Gate 61
Norland Place School, Holland Park Avenue 69
Our Lady of Sion School, Denbigh Road 71
Portobello Road, Notting Hill 75
St Clement and St James School, Penzance Place 84
St Clements Road School, Notting Hill 84
St Francis Roman Catholic School, Pottery Lane, Kensington 85
St James Independent School for Girls, Pembridge Villas 86
St James's Norland Church of England School, Penzance Place 87
St John Clarendon Road Church of England Secondary School 87
St John's Church of England School, Heathfield Street 88
St Mark's School, St Mark's Road, Notting Hill 91
Saunders Road or Saunders Grove School, Notting Hill 100
Sirdar Road School, Notting Hill 102
Solomon Wolfson Jewish School, Lancaster Road 103
Southbank International School, Kensington Park Road 103
Victoria College of Music, Holland Park Avenue 111

LONDON SCHOOLS BY POSTAL DISTRICT

W12 Hammersmith (part)

Bassein Park Road School, Starch Green 16
Bentworth Road School 17
Burlington Danes School, Wood Lane 22
Canberra School, Australia Road 24
Christopher Wren School, Bloemfontein Road 28
Cobbold Road School, Askew Road 30
Coverdale Road School, Uxbridge Road, Shepherds Bush 32
Ellerslie Road School, Ellerslie Road 38
Erconwald Street School, Erconwald Street 39
Hammersmith County School, The Curve 48
Hammersmith Secondary Technical School for Girls, Lime Grove 48
John Aird School, Cobbold Road 56
Livingstone Primary School, Australia Road 61
Mellitus Street School, Mellitus Street 65
Miles Coverdale School, Coverdale Road 65
North Hammersmith Central School, Bryony Road 69
North Hammersmith Secondary Boys School, Mellitus Street 69
North Hammersmith Secondary School for Girls, Bryony Road 69
Old Oak School, Mellitus Road 71
Pope John Roman Catholic School, Commonwealth Avenue 74
St Clement Danes Boys Grammar School, Du Cane Road 84
St Hubert's School, Mellitus Street 86
St Stephen's Roman Catholic School, Rylett Road 98
St Stephens School, Uxbridge Road 99
Sawley Road School, Sawley Road 100
Starch Green British School, Victoria Road 105
Thornfield Road School, Thornfield Road 108
Victoria School, The, Becklow Road, Uxbridge Road 112
Wendell Park School 114
Westville Road School, Askew Road 116
Wood Lane Open Air School, Wood Lane 118
Wormholt Park School, Bryony Road 118

W14 Kensington (part)

Addison Gardens School, West Kensington 11
Avonmore School, Avonmore Road 15
Cardinal Vaughan Memorial School, Addison Road, Kensington 24
Faroe Road School, Faroe Road 40
Froebel Educational Institute Preparatory School, Colet Gardens 42
Holland Road Roman Catholic School 52
Mary Boon School, Earsby Street 64
Milson Road School, Milson Road 66
Normand Park School, Lillie Road 69
Our Lady of Victories Roman Catholic School, Warwick Road, West Kensington 72
Queen's Court School, Greyhound Road 76
Royal Ballet School, Colet Gardens 80
Sadler's Wells Ballet School, Colet Gardens 99
St Mary's School, Earsby (previously Wllliam) Street 93
St Matthew's School, Milson Road/Ceylon Road, Kensington 93
St Paul's Preparatory School, Colet Court 96
West Kensington Central School, Gorleston Street, Hammersmith Road 114
William Street School, Earsby Street 116

LONDON SCHOOLS BY POSTAL DISTRICT

WC1 Holborn (part); St Pancras (part)

All Saints Gordon Square School, St Pancras 12
Argyle School, Whichbourne Street, St Pancras 14
Bloomsbury School 19
Central School of Arts and Crafts, Southampton Row 25
Coram Fields School, Guilford Street 31
Cromer Street School, Gray Inn Road 33
Foundling Hospital, Guilford Street 41
Herbrand Street School 51
Jew's College, Woburn House, Tavistock Square 56
Princeton Street School, Bedford Row 75
Prospect Terrace School, Sidmouth Street, Grays Inn Road, St Pancras 76
Royal Academy of Dramatic Art, Gower Street 80
St George the Martyr Parochial School, Queen Square, Holborn 86
St John the Evangelist School, Red Lion Square, Holborn 89
St Jude's School, Grays Inn Road 90
Sir Philip Magnus School, Penton Rise 102
Tavistock Place School 108
Thanet Street Church of England School, Cartwright Gardens, Euston Road 108
Vernon Square School, Kings Cross Road 111
West Central District Post Office School 114

WC2 Holborn (part)

Bluecoat School 19
Charing Cross Road School 25
James Street School 56
Macklin Street Roman Catholic School, Drury Lane 62
St Clement Danes Grammar School, Aldwych 84
St Clement Danes School, Drury Lane 84
St Giles in the Fields School, Endell Street 86
St Joseph's Roman Catholic School, Macklin Street 89
St Martin in the Fields School, Adelaide Place 91
St Martin in the Fields School, Shelton Street 91
St Mary's School, Gate Street, Holborn 93
Wild Street School, Holborn 116

Bromley, Kent

Ballamore Road School, Downham Estate 15
Downderry Road School, Downham Estate, Bromley 35
Downham Central School, Goudhurst Road, Bromley 35
Durham Hill School, Downham Estate 36
Launcelot Road School, Downham, Bromley, 60
Malory School, Launcelot Road, Bromley 63
Meeting House School, Downham, Bromley 65
Moorside Road Roman Catholic School, Downham Estate, Lewisham 67
Nansen School, Pendragon Road, Bromley 67
Pastor Bonus Roman Catholic School, Bromley 73
Pendragon Road School, Downham Estate, Bromley 73
Rangefield School, Downham Estate, Bromley 77
St John the Baptist School, Beachborough Road, Downham, Bromley 89

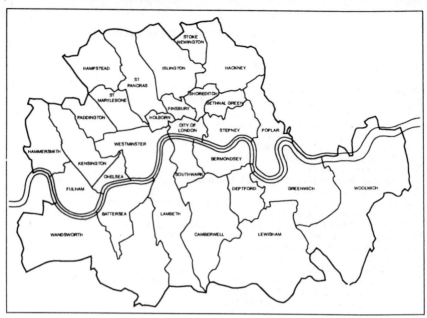

CITY OF LONDON AND METROPOLITAN BOROUGHS 1900-1965

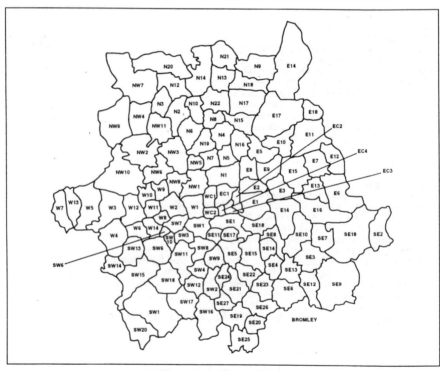

LONDON POSTAL DISTRICTS